The New York Ti

MW00789277

arts
AND
culture

Don McLeese
and the Writers of
The New York Times

CQ PRESS

A Division of SAGE
Washington, D.C.

CQ Press
2300 N Street, NW, Suite 800
Washington, DC 20037

Phone: 202-729-1900; toll-free, 1-866-4CQ-PRESS (1-866-427-7737)

Web: www.cqpress.com

Cover design: Matthew Simmons, www.myselfincluded.com
Cover photo: iStock.com
Composition: C&M Digitals (P) Ltd.

⊗ The paper used in this publication exceeds the requirements of the American National Standard for Information Sciences—Permanence of Paper for Printed Library Materials, ANSI Z39.48-1992.

Printed and bound in the United States of America

14   13   12   11   10   1   2   3   4   5

Library of Congress Cataloging-in-Publication Data

The New York times reader : arts and culture / Don McLeese and the writers of The New York times.
     p. cm. — (TimesCollege from CQ Press)
ISBN 978-1-60426-480-7 (pbk. : alk. paper)
   1. Arts—Press coverage. 2. Arts—Reviews. 3. Journalism—Authorship. I. McLeese, Don. II. New York times. III. Title. IV. Series.

PN4784.A77.N49 2010
070.4'497—dc22

                                                        2010003025

*To the three beyond
criticism—
Maria, Kelly and Molly*

about Don McLeese

Don McLeese has been an award-winning critic of the popular arts at the Chicago Sun-Times and the Austin American-Statesman, and has written for dozens of national publications, including The New York Times Book Review, Rolling Stone (where he was a frequent contributor and columnist), the Oxford American, Entertainment Weekly, salon.com, and many others. He is the author of "Kick Out the Jams" and has contributed to "The Rolling Stone Illustrated History of Rock & Roll," "Rolling Stone's The Decades of Rock & Roll," "The Encyclopedia of Chicago History," "The Best of No Depression: Writing About American Music," the Country Music Foundation's Country on Compact Disc and its "Encyclopedia of Country Music." He is associate professor of journalism at the University of Iowa, where his courses include arts and culture journalism.

contents

foreword

SCOTT VEALE
editor, arts and leisure

© The New York Times

THERE IS A TRADITION AT The New York Times, as there surely is at other newspapers that win Pulitzer Prizes, that the staff gathers in the newsroom following the announcement of an award, both to honor the winner and—less visibly but equally important—to reaffirm the collective mission of the hundreds of reporters, critics, editors, copy editors, photographers and other journalists who dream up and produce the paper day in and day out.

Last year the Pulitzer committee awarded the art critic Holland Cotter of The Times its prize for criticism, singling out "his wide-ranging reviews of art, from Manhattan to China, marked by acute observation, luminous writing and dramatic storytelling."

"In the 17 years I've worked for the paper," Cotter told the assembled staff thronging the newsroom, "no one has ever said that a subject was too esoteric or weird. So I've been able to write about all kinds of fabulous things, which keeps the process fresh. For me, esoteric just means something I haven't explored yet. Weird is what makes me want to get up in the morning."

That seems like an excellent place to start a conversation about the role of critics and arts reporters at The Times. Embedded in those two sets of remarks are the bedrock virtues of top-notch culture writing: Curiosity. Vision. Authority. Independence. Stylistic excellence. Restlessness. Wit.

There are basically two categories of writers in the culture department— reporters and critics—though the boundary that separates them is often porous. While there is a greater commitment than ever to "hard-news" reporting in the culture pages, reporters are also encouraged to pursue analytical features and profiles that allow them greater freedom of thought and style than they might have in their news coverage. And the critics often bring their voice and sensibility to bear on topics—whether in essays or profiles or trend pieces—that require traditional reporting. Some striking examples of both types of writing appear in the pages that follow.

The critics in particular have long held a central place in the paper's arts coverage and in the cultural life of New York City and points beyond. In recent decades, the paper has tried hard to broaden and enliven its criticism, both by seeking out new corners of popular culture (flip ahead, for example, to Roberta Smith's inspired review of the new "Simpsons" postage stamps) and by nurturing stylish, spirited writing (turn to Charles McGrath's delightful profile of the director Mike Nichols for a taste).

Describing one campaign to freshen up culture journalism in the 1990s, according to Edwin Diamond in his 1995 book "Behind the Times: Inside The New York Times," Rebecca Sinkler, the editor of the Book Review, made a simple but sadly necessary observation: "A book is entirely useless if it is dry or dense, or doesn't communicate. The same is true for the reviewer. We often try out authorities in their fields, and often they are not good writers. No matter how much the reviewer knows, if the judgment isn't expressed in a lively way, readers will not read the review." That made sense then, and it makes sense now.

Many years ago, according to New York Times lore, the renowned drama critic Brooks Atkinson followed a legendary opening-night routine in which he would hurry back to his desk at the paper's 43rd Street headquarters after the final curtain, light up his pipe and begin writing in longhand, in pencil, on sheets of lined yellow paper. He would hand his sheets, one paragraph at a time, to a copyboy, who would take them directly to the copy desk (where his words were rarely changed) and then to the composing room, where they were set into type by Linotype operators and where Atkinson would visit after finishing to check his proofs for typographical errors. And that was that: The Times had spoken, and Atkinson's verdict would show up in the late editions of the next morning's paper.

Obviously, the world has changed since then, and so have the newspaper and its relationship with readers, thanks to new technology and especially the Internet. Needless to say, today's reviewer would have quite a different routine from Atkinson's: a pop critic, for example, might show up early at a Bruce Springsteen concert and e-mail the set list to his editors, who would post it on the culture department's blog before the concert began. The reviewer might then post his impressions live on the blog during the show, and later that night post a full review on The Times' Web site, so that concertgoers might log on to get an assessment of the show they just saw. (The print version of the review, by the way, would reach readers a day and a half after the concert.)

Other forms of social media and multimedia storytelling are still evolving, from podcasts of album reviews and interviews with artists and authors, to slideshows and short videos that accompany online versions of reviews and articles. Readers, meanwhile, are invited to respond by e-mail to reviews and articles, and to the paper's daily culture blog, and their collected input creates a conversation of sorts that deepens the paper's coverage even further.

Throughout it all, the core mission of the critic—to seek out the culture world's offerings, and to take measure of them boldly and fearlessly—has remained the same. You'll be hearing a lot in the coming pages about the power of strong arguments, and if there's one thing The Times' editors seek out most in the critics they work with, and push for in their editing, it's a well-built, well-supported, passionately informed position. In fact, the actual works under review, whether television shows or rock concerts or operas, tend to take a backseat in the most compelling critical writing. What stands out in the end is the argument itself—provocative, vibrant, often surprising, expressed with clarity and conviction—and the quality of the mind behind it.

And therein lies the final mystery. While The Times has done a remarkable job over the years bringing memorable critical writing to its pages, there are no hard and fast rules about how to coax it forth—there is, alas, no magic formula. For those of us working at the paper, not to mention aspiring arts journalists, it will always be a journey of discovery. Yet to paraphrase Supreme Court Justice Potter Stewart's famous dictum about defining pornography, you'll know it when you see it.

preface

● LET'S START WITH WHAT THIS BOOK IS NOT. It is not the critical equivalent of "The New York Times' Greatest Hits" or a cultural "Best of The New York Times." Such a volume would surely be worth owning, but it might not serve the educational needs of the modern student. So let's stipulate from the outset that your favorite review from The Times might not be here. Perhaps not mine, either.

So what do we have? A collection of first-rate reviews, critical essays and pieces of reportage that have already withstood the ultimate test: the classroom. Through the courses in arts and culture journalism that I have developed at the University of Iowa, I use plenty of examples of professional criticism to generate discussion, spark debate and serve as exemplars. Well before I became involved with this series, I found that I was turning to The Times more often than to all other sources of art journalism combined.

This volume features examples of criticism and arts reporting guaranteed to generate response, reinforced by interviews with critics from The Times who provide insight into how they approach and practice their craft. It also attempts to codify the key principles underlying effective criticism, showing how to transform opinions ("thumbs up, thumbs down") into compelling arguments that carry the weight of authority.

On a week-to-week basis, it is simply impossible to beat the breadth, depth and range of the critical coverage in The Times. It has long been informally acknowledged as America's "newspaper of record," and in no area is that distinction more deserved than in the field of arts and culture. Now that readers are more likely to read The Times on the Web than in newsprint, the journalism has become far more interactive and multimedia, with blogs, comments, videos, slide shows and other features that enhance the coverage. Other cities may approach New York's significance in various arts (we'll give the movies to Hollywood), but no publication rivals The Times as the epicenter of arts and culture criticism, most broadly defined.

In conferring with colleagues on other campuses who teach journalism courses about covering the arts in general (rather than courses devoted to specific arts, perhaps in other departments, such as literary, film or visual arts criticism), we've agreed that no current textbooks on the market serve the needs of our courses. The available books are either restricted to one art or are so basic that our students (many of whom might have considerable experience with their college newspaper or other publications) have already outgrown them. A book that might have helpful tips for a general assignment reporter who finds herself covering a play doesn't necessarily serve the needs of a university newspaper's arts editor or music critic who aspires to write for Rolling Stone. And no book written until recently can encompass the transformation of arts criticism from a spectator sport to a participatory democracy.

The aspiring critic needs no prior experience to get educational value from this anthology. It can just as easily serve as a crash course in criticism—how to develop an opinion into an argument and how to establish authority with a readership. Most of the students enrolled in these courses are already forming opinions on music, movies, even videogames, engaging in discussion, debating merits. In short, they are already critics, or at least exercising their critical faculties. This book attempts to help instructors, students, even experienced journalists sharpen those critical instincts as they shape engaging, compelling reviews, essays and articles.

My experience in working with students has allowed me to formulate key principles of arts and cultural criticism to which this book adheres, ones that can be illustrated through examples from The Times (or quality criticism anywhere). My decades of writing about various arts, from popular music to literary fiction, inform both my teaching and this book as well.

Before shifting to academe, I served as the pop music critic for the Chicago Sun-Times and the Austin American-Statesman, as well as a columnist, feature writer and frequent reviewer for Rolling Stone. I have written hundreds of book reviews, for the newspapers where I worked, and also for Kirkus Reviews, (the late, lamented) Book Magazine and (yes, as explained in the epilogue) The New York Times Book Review. I have been published in dozens of national magazines—from the Oxford American to Entertainment Weekly— have contributed to a few books and written one.

I have interviewed Bob Dylan, U2, Madonna and the Rolling Stones (on multiple occasions), but also photographer Richard Avedon, actress Susan Sarandon and Nobel Prize–winning novelist Saul Bellow (who sent me a fan letter in response, my proudest possession). I mention all this not to brag— okay, maybe just a little—but to illustrate a central tenet of this volume: that a critic who develops the proper instincts can apply them across the board in arts and culture.

The Times provides a perfect example of this. Janet Maslin, interviewed for this volume as one of the staff book critics, was previously a film critic at The Times and was formerly an alternative-weekly rock critic. Frank Rich, featured prominently in this book's theater section, jumped from his role as The Times' chief theater critic to his spotlight perch as Sunday political columnist (in recognition, perhaps, that politics is simply theater on a larger stage). Before A. O. Scott joined The Times as a film critic, he had established himself mainly as a literary critic (and has a piece in this volume's book section as well as an interview and criticism in the film section).

One of the purposes of a volume such as this, and of courses that might use it, is to teach aspiring critics to be generalists, to learn the principles and sharpen the instincts that they can then apply across the spectrum. Even a critic who concentrates solely on books finds her work enriched by an appreciation of the prevailing currents within the culture at large. All of these arts are engaged in ongoing dialogues not only with themselves but also with the other art forms. Film talks to literature. Theater converses with rock. Hip-hop informs visual art. Culture shapes art, and art enriches culture.

The introductory chapters to this volume deal primarily with criticism in general, the principles applied across the artistic whole. Introductions to the chapters on each of the arts then deal with those considerations more specific to individual forms, how coming to terms with a painting, a spatial art, might differ from coming to terms with a piece of music, a temporal art. Or why film is generally considered a "director's medium" and theater an "actor's medium." The second part of the book then focuses on reportage, which (as we shall see) frequently functions as another form of criticism. Additional Times resources of value for arts and culture writing are on a Web site established specifically for this series, including links to interactive graphics and multi-media presentations that accompanied the stories in this reader. Go to college.cqpress.com/nytimes.

From my experience, students respond best to contemporaneous art and criticism, so this volume is more heavily weighted toward recent work than spread evenly across the decades. (And I'd encourage any instructor of a course using this text to supplement it with each week's reviews from The Times— the movies your students are watching, the music they are downloading.) Yet the past and the present are also engaged in an ongoing dialogue, so students benefit from an understanding of how cultural touchstones such as "Lolita" and "Bonnie and Clyde" were reviled upon release, how "Thelma and Louise" sparked such a feminist furor and how "The Godfather" was recognized as a masterpiece from the outset.

I always stress in my courses that criticism is never the last word—an authoritative thunderbolt hurled by Zeus from the heights of Mount Olympus—but the initial volley in an ongoing dialogue with a readership. In employing this volume, let the dialogue begin; let the arguments rage.

ACKNOWLEDGMENTS

So many to acknowledge, so little space. At CQ Press, I'd like to thank editorial director Charisse Kiino, who brainstormed the series and gave it the green light; editorial assistant Christina Mueller, who greased the wheels; production editor Belinda Josey, who handled page proofs; and original editor Aron Keesbury, who signed me and helped shape the contents before leaving the fold.

Most of all, however, I need to thank Jane Harrigan, my editor throughout the actual writing, who made sharp, incisive and encouraging comments daily, and whose collaboration made this book much better and more fun than it could have been without her. I almost (*almost*) hated to see the process come to an end, and I'd be happy to have Jane edit anything else I write. (Any remaining mistakes or errors of judgment are, of course, my own.)

At The New York Times, the intercession of Alex Ward, Editorial Director of Book Development, proved crucial in getting very busy journalists to help with a worthwhile project. Thanks to Scott Veale, editor of the Arts & Leisure section, for agreeing to write the foreword. I learned a lot from my interviews with Ben Brantley, Janet Maslin, Jon Pareles, A. O. Scott and Roberta Smith, and I trust students and professors will as well. In addition to thanking them, I need to thank Brent Staples of The Times' editorial board, for reasons that the epilogue will make plain.

At the University of Iowa, I'm always grateful for the support of my colleagues in the School of Journalism and Mass Communication, and I'm particularly grateful to the College of Liberal Arts and Sciences for granting me a semester's career development leave to complete this manuscript. I would also like to thank my research assistants, Ann Colwell and Anna Wiegenstein—both stellar student journalists—and the rest of the students who have taken my Arts and Culture courses—my partners and occasional guinea pigs in discovering what works and what doesn't.

introduction

ALL OF US ARE NATURAL CRITICS. Perhaps before we can remember, we found certain flavors of baby food appealing and others appalling, certain television programs captivating and others boring. We were exercising our critical faculties before we knew what those words meant, before we could even say them.

The challenge for aspiring arts writers is to develop the voice, the command, the authority that give their critical opinions weight, that make those assessments more than individual preferences or snap judgments. What distinguishes arts critics—good ones, at least—is their ability to present their opinions as arguments, ones to which readers respond. There is no arguing with an opinion—chocolate or vanilla, thumbs up or thumbs down. You like it because you like it, or you don't because you don't. But an argument can engage, enlighten or infuriate. It can make the reader hear or see or think in a fresh way.

In addition to making arguments, critics must also make deadlines. And since deadlines often force critics to think on the fly, they often discover new dimensions of their response to a work of art through the process of writing about it. Even readers who disagree with a critic's evaluation can appreciate the way in which she comes to terms with the work.

The New York Times gives critics more space and it takes their work more seriously than any other general-interest news organization in the country (if not the world). Reading and analyzing the work of critics at The Times with a critic's eye—learning what works and why—will help the fledgling arts journalist discover his own voice, develop his own authority.

At The Times, "arts" once meant "fine arts," and the standards upheld were generally those of a cultural elite. Today, its coverage encompasses everything from conservatory recitals to hip-hop, and from visual art galleries to video games.

As you analyze the pieces that follow, you'll learn not only to recognize strong arguments, but to craft your own. Ultimately, a critic's evaluation isn't nearly as important as the process through which it is derived. When you read compelling criticism, you can feel the wheels of the critic's brain spinning. You can see the flashbulbs of discovery as he or she comes to terms with the essence of a work through writing about it.

What readers want to see in a piece of criticism is an interesting mind at work. Or, better, an interesting mind at play, for a certain playfulness in coming to terms with arts, themes, ideas and expression informs the most engaging criticism. Critics should feel privileged to be paid to respond to what others pay to experience.

REVIEWER OR CRITIC?

Most journalists involved in covering the arts function as both reviewer and critic, sometimes even within the same piece. Many journalists and readers use the terms interchangeably. But there's a distinction between the two terms, one that indicates different functions, even with the inevitable overlap.

The reviewer serves as a consumer guide, addressing a single piece of work (or perhaps a number of them serially, in capsule reviews) and letting the reader know whether this particular work is worth the money and/or time it requires. People read reviews to find out whether to buy this book, see this movie, commit to this TV series.

Criticism has a wider scope, a broader purpose. It extends beyond the consumer-guide merits of a single work to show where that work fits within the art form as a whole or within the culture at large. Some critical essays address many different works rather than limiting themselves to one. While reviews have a narrower focus, critical essays explore the bigger picture.

Yet both forms advance an opinion, bolstered by argument—one that opens a dialogue in which the reader can agree or challenge. They encourage an active rather than a passive response, as the reader compares the critic's evaluative yardstick with her own. You already have an evaluative yardstick, whether you consciously employ it or not. This book will help you to articulate it, in order to develop your opinions into arguments.

REPORTED PIECES

The critic never stops being a critic, as you'll see in the reported pieces in the second part of this book. A critic's insight informs profiles and trend pieces as well, showing the reader why this artist merits attention, why this trend is significant. When analyzing those pieces, look for the sections that could pass as unadulterated criticism.

Of course, not all arts journalism is written by critics. Some writers specialize in profiles, capturing the person rather than concentrating on the art, and you'll see examples of how some of those profiles differ from those written by critics. And some arts stories are straightforward news or business stories, written by reporters who aren't supposed to express an opinion.

Reporting those kinds of arts stories doesn't differ appreciably from reporting any other news story. They employ the same techniques and should be judged by the same standards. This volume, by contrast, concerns itself with the ways in which arts journalism is different from other journalism. In its emphasis on opinion, argument and analysis, it is much more like the cultural equivalent of the op-ed page, with the stylistic freedom that magazine writers enjoy more often than news reporters.

Arts journalism is a unique form of journalism, with The New York Times setting the highest standards. Many of the longer, reported pieces represent this journalism at its most ambitious, with reporters and editors collaborating to ensure that these pieces are as engaging and cohesive as the shorter reviews.

Aspiring arts journalists should note that while reviews and criticism (i.e. opinion pieces) provide the majority of work on the beat, reported features frequently command more attention both within the publication and among readers. The criticism contained within them distinguishes them as "arts"; the conception, reporting and editing make this "journalism" that ranks with the best of The Times as a whole.

For those aspiring to a career in arts journalism, this collection will help you learn from those who have ascended to the peak of their profession. "I don't think there's anything like it," explains visual arts critic Roberta Smith of working at The Times. "New York may not be the only center of arts in the world anymore, but to me it's still the world's center of criticism. You have your biggest reading public, on all fronts. And there's no other newspaper in the country that takes criticism as seriously as The Times does."

THE CHANGING TIMES

In presenting quality criticism on a wide range of arts published over the course of decades, this anthology will also show how The Times has changed with the times. The most recent and one of the most significant of these changes is technological. Long considered by many to be America's best newspaper, The New York Times (like most newspapers in a period of profound transition) now reaches far more readers through its Web site than through the printed page. To speak of it simply as a "newspaper" is an anachronism. It is a news gathering organization, a news site, a news brand.

The shift in emphasis from newsprint to Web site has some distinct advantages in the field of arts and culture reporting in particular. Through slide shows, concert tapings, interviews and other forms of technology that converge on the Web, The Times no longer simply describes a piece of visual art or a song; it can let its readers see or hear it for themselves. The Web's archiving capabilities help readers, who can search the site for articles and reviews on a specific artist or by a specific critic and find them conveniently grouped together.

Where too many news sites simply transfer print articles to the Web, The Times has taken increasing advantages of the features that technology affords, providing slide shows of arts exhibitions, interviews with musicians that incorporate the music, and other multimedia features that extend the realm of criticism beyond the printed page. The site also features blogs devoted to specific arts, which provide breezier, more conversational commentary and generate plenty of reader response in this era of journalistic interactivity. It offers dialogues between critics and question-and-answer sessions with readers.

Other significant shifts have more to do with demographics, diversity, generation and geography than with cyberspace. As with most newspapers, The Times was long dominated by white males (older ones, in the case of the arts), saddling the paper with a reputation for stuffiness and resistance to change. While female critics have provided a crucial perspective for some 30 years, racial diversity has not achieved similar balance. The Times has featured incisive staff criticism from African-American journalists including Kalefa Sanneh, Elvis Mitchell and the Pulitzer Prize–winning Margo Jefferson—each featured in this volume—only to see all of them leave its employment.

Once the upholder of cultural propriety, The Times has also become more responsive to popular culture in general, youth culture in particular and edgier artistry in whatever form. Now that the critics write for a national edition and an international Web audience, The New York Times increasingly ventures well beyond New York in its cultural coverage, though the vibrancy of its home city remains unchallenged as the cultural capital of the country.

Through the reviews, essays and articles that follow, you'll recognize just how much has changed at The Times. Are video games and postage stamps art? They wouldn't have been within the arts section of The Times a few years ago. Today, the popularity and cultural pervasiveness of the former lands it regularly on the front page of the arts section (as shown in this intro to a longer review), while the latter suggests that art is wherever a critic at The Times can make a case for it. In both cases, look at how the style of the review fits the spirit of the subject.

Selection I.1

The very idea of the video game as art—let alone featured on the front of The New York Times' arts section—shows just how much the coverage has changed in recent years.

Video Game Review | Grand Theft Auto IV
Grand Theft Auto Takes On New York
By SETH SCHIESEL

I was rolling through the neon deluge of a place very like Times Square the other night in my Landstalker sport utility vehicle, listening to David Bowie's "Fascination" on the radio. The glittery urban landscape was almost enough to make me forget about the warehouse of cocaine dealers I was headed uptown to rip off.

Soon I would get bored, though, and carjack a luxury sedan. I'd meet my Rasta buddy Little Jacob, then check out a late show by Ricky Gervais at a comedy club around the corner. Afterward I'd head north to confront the dealers, at least if I could elude the cops. I heard their sirens before I saw them and peeled out, tires squealing.

Published: April 28, 2008. Full text available at: www.nytimes.com/2008/04/28/arts/28auto.html?_r=1.

It was just another night on the streets of Liberty City, the exhilarating, lusciously dystopian rendition of New York City in 2008 that propels Grand Theft Auto IV, the ambitious new video game to be released on Tuesday for the Xbox 360 and PlayStation 3 systems.

***

Selection I.2

What is art? Whatever an arts critic can claim it is and build an argument for it.

ART
As Seen on Television: Sealed With a Simpson
By ROBERTA SMITH

The brilliant new stamps honoring America's first family of animation—the Simpsons—issued by the United States Postal Service in early May escaped my attention until the end of last month. That's when an accumulation of stampless unmailed bills forced an emergency trip to the post office.

There they were, Homer, Marge, Bart, Lisa and Maggie, each in a classic head shot against a little rectangular patch of electric color, projecting maximum psychic and visual power. There was no action, sound, plot or space to help them out, only color, line, scale and lots of personality. Really, are these not among the best American stamps ever?

Disregard our age's plethora of Simpsoniana: the juice cups, the lunchboxes, the toothbrushes. Contemplate the odds of progress within the limited format of the postage stamp and its tendency toward pomp and miniaturization. There's not much chance, but the Simpsons stamps make some headway. They pop. Here's why:

First, the peerless expressions, defined by Matt Groening's inimitable thickish line, are succinct encapsulations of each character. Homer is caught with mouth agape and tongue rippling: it's the panicked squawk, not the famous "D'oh." Marge purses her lips and looks confused, as if vaguely sensing one of Homer's clumsy scams. Bart wears his sweaty busted-again grin. Lisa is all sweet, I-tried-to-tell-you beneficence. Maggie's glare suggests that someone is stepping on her nightgown. Her pacifier has two motion lines, the only sign of movement in the stamps.

Second, the chromatic wattage is, as usual, extraordinary, even a bit shocking within the stamp genre. The Simpson palette has always

Published: July 7, 2009.

seemed as radical and subversive as the show's social commentary. It's similar in artifice to the innovative color of artists like Andy Warhol, Bruce Nauman and Matthew Barney. Five amped-up hues suffice: egg-yolk yellow, magenta, Dodger blue, darkened chartreuse and lavender, important bits of white (mainly eyes and teeth) and touches of red.

Subtle tonal distinctions are made. Homer's yellow head is seen against a slightly darker yellow background. Marge's hair is slightly darker than the blue behind Bart. Red defines only Homer's tongue, Maggie's pacifier, Marge's beads and the smidgeon of Bart's T-shirt.

Third, less is more. The "Simpsons" gestalt is boiled down to its essence, and so is stampness. The images are stripped of detail except for the letters USA and the number 44 (cents, the new first class). No fussy engraved textures, no identifying names. Color can take over and faces pop out. Like Richard Serra sculptures, only smaller and a whole lot cheaper, the stamps prove the adage that scale has nothing to do with size. They strike David-like blows against the Goliaths of American visual illiteracy.

It's not news that the Simpsons work almost as well off screen as on, but these images still amaze. Slowed to a standstill, deeply cropped and confined, the portraits single out for tribute both the family's indelible inmates and the breathtaking economy that brings them to life. I don't know whether to affix them to my delinquent bills or have them framed.

Part I

opinion: critical essays and reviews

AS WE'VE EXPLORED, OPINION BEGINS WITH A GUT REACTION. You like something or you don't—viscerally, instinctively. Your gut response isn't a matter of right or wrong. Critics can, do and should disagree on the merits of individual works of art. But gut reactions may well reflect how much experience you have in dealing with this particular art form. And that experience can help produce stronger arguments, with richer context and analysis leading to persuasive evaluation.

The selections in the following sections demonstrate that there are many ways that a critic can engage our interest. Some of them know a lot more than we do. They have more experience, a broader frame of reference. We read some critics because their styles are entertaining, even funny. We read some because we regularly agree with them, others because we regularly disagree but find their opinions provocative. We choose critics the way we might choose friends, enjoying the company of someone who has an engagingly conversational tone, an incisive intelligence and a self-deprecating wit. Sometimes we find reviewers more entertaining than whatever they're reviewing.

Some key elements are common to all arts criticism. Other qualities distinguish the individual arts. Here are some of the distinctions critics make, intuitive or not, that help shape both analysis and evaluation.

DEMOGRAPHIC

Hierarchical rankings of the arts traditionally have had as much to do with the audience for that art form as they do with intrinsic artistic value, and demographics underscore evaluative distinctions among different forms of art. What's considered to be "serious" or "fine" art has traditionally been art that attracts an elite, educated, often affluent audience. In decades past, coverage at The Times tended to cater more toward a cultural elite, giving more prominence to the symphony orchestra than the rock concert, for example. Such rankings have never been static, though, and the lines continue to blur.

Historically, the novel was initially dismissed as mindless, middle-class entertainment. Jazz and blues were regarded as threats to decent society, "race records" that inflamed primal urges. And neither movies nor television were once considered worthy of serious scrutiny.

Today, you can find graffiti and graphic novels covered in The Times with an appreciation once reserved for the gallery. Mystery thrillers and heavy-metal music have received the seal of critical approval as worthy of scrutiny. And younger, hipper, edgier art is far more integral to the cultural mix in the arts section than it was a few decades ago.

Your personal demographic will inevitably influence your response to art—your age, values, gender, religion, level of education, ethnicity, all of the elements that make you who you are. Your response to art reveals as much about you as it does about the art.

FORMAL

Some differences among the arts are formal; that is, they concern the form the art takes. Arts can be divided into the spatial and the temporal. Conceivably, you can absorb the whole of the spatial art at once, though it's likely that the longer you look at a painting or a photograph, the more you will see. On the other hand, temporal arts—the ones that progress over time—require a specific time span to apprehend the whole. You really can't come to terms with a novel or a piece of music until you've followed its progression from beginning to end—whereas a painting has a top and bottom, but no beginning or end. While film and television conventionally are temporal arts, some experimentalists have used both in gallery installations, emphasizing purely visual possibilities, blurring the line between the spatial (because they exist in space) and the temporal (because their images change over time, sometimes very slowly).

INVESTMENT

The investment required by a work of art also helps indicate its value. And different arts require a different sort of investment—sometimes money, sometimes time. This consideration is related to demographics, but is not synonymous. Some arts distinguish themselves by the price the work commands—from the many thousands to the many millions for certain paintings, or the high prices for an elaborate Broadway production. Other arts are more egalitarian—most movie tickets and music downloads cost the same whether the work is considered great art or mindless entertainment. Television criticism must deal with the investment required in time rather than money, applying different standards to a series that might require a commitment of months or even years than to a movie that represents a couple hours out of one's life.

In the chapters that follow, look for the keys common to all arts and culture criticism (description, analysis, context, evaluation). And then look for the elements that are distinctive, even unique, within each art form. The incisive review encompasses both.

the keys to quality criticism

LET'S GET THIS STRAIGHT FROM THE START: There is no formula for writing great reviews and critical essays. No critic starts with a checklist of elements, dealing with them one by one. The process of writing a review, of developing an argument from what begins as a gut reaction, is far more intuitive. It was only after I started teaching courses in arts and culture journalism (after 30 years or so of writing reviews, criticism, profiles, columns and trend features) that I codified what had been instinctual all along.

For most critics, the incisive review begins with a visceral response. You like something or you don't. You ask yourself why. Moving from the instinctive to the cerebral, you build an argument. Through the process of thinking and writing about the art, you might discover dimensions to the work, and to your response to it, that you hadn't realized before subjecting your gut reaction to critical analysis.

It's this cogitation, stylishly expressed, that makes the journey more important to the reader than the destination. Here are the four critical keys that unlock that response, that send us down the road. They are the elements that every writer and reader recognizes, often unconsciously, as essential to a review that proves more valuable than knee-jerk reaction or unreflective opinion:

- Description
- Context
- Interpretation
- Evaluation

Let's consider each of the four essential elements individually.

DESCRIPTION: WHAT IS IT LIKE?

Description precedes argument—not necessarily, or even usually, in the structure of a review, but in the sense that this is a starting point where all can agree. Those who love a piece of music and those who loathe it can both concur with the description of it as "slow" and "simple." Yet one critic's "meditative" is another critic's "boring." This is the distinction between descriptive and evaluative adjectives, and a crucial distinction it is.

The point where descriptive agreement leads to analytical and evaluative disagreement is the flashpoint of the argument. If we both agree that a piece of music is "noisy" (descriptive), but to me it's edgy and dynamic and full of life (positive) and to you it's a chaotic mess (negative), we've discovered something fundamental about the different qualities that each of us values in a piece of music in particular, and perhaps art in general.

Another example: Critics might agree that a particular movie is "fast paced." To the critic who believes that visceral thrills are all the justification such a movie needs, that the film functions like a roller coaster, this description will lead to interpretation and evaluation that are far different from the conclusions of a critic who dismisses "action flicks" as mindless entertainment. Such disagreements hint at broader critical arguments about the nature of the movie experience, the role of movies in the culture, or wherever the incisive critic wants to take such exploration.

Word choice is crucial in maintaining the distinction between descriptive and evaluative. "Simple" is generally descriptive (unless the critic is building a case that complexity is the hallmark of great art). "Simplistic" is usually pejorative—turning the same descriptive quality into a value judgment—and "simple-minded" even more so.

Both of us might recognize the "polish" of a piece of work, but what strikes you as "refined" seems more like "embalmed" to me. We've proceeded from agreement in description to polar opposition in evaluation. Once we recognize the points upon which we can all agree, we can analyze points of departure.

CONTEXT: WHERE AND HOW DOES IT FIT?

Beyond simply describing the work and evaluating it, the effective critic must also place it within a context for the reader—perhaps by showing how it relates to other works by the artist, other works within the genre or in other genres, or a larger cultural context within the society at large.

Context is something of a catch-all term, which we'll use here to refer to all background information about something beyond the specific work at hand. Each review might require a different balance and/or type of contextual background, depending on how much the readership is likely to know—or to want to know—about the artist and the type of art. If the reviewer is introducing the artist to the readership, more biographical context might be necessary than if the reader has followed the artist's career, in which case the review will likely focus much more on the new work.

Providing the proper amount of context is one of the trickiest challenges for a reviewer. A critic must gauge how much context he needs to provide a general readership without belaboring the obvious for readers who know a lot about the artist. If he defines a band's music as "death metal," does the term then need a few words of explanation? A few sentences? A few paragraphs tracing the evolution of the subgenre and how it fits within metal music, or rock music, or the culture at large? Too little might leave readers confused; too much will bore them.

If a reviewer categorizes visual art as "surrealist" or "abstract expressionist," how much knowledge can she assume on the part of the reader? Do such terms need to be defined—or more expansively explained—in every review?

As pop music critic Jon Pareles maintains in an interview that concludes the popular music chapter, "We write for a general reader rather than an avid music follower, so we make an effort to be straightforward and inviting."

When reading the reviews from The New York Times in the following chapters, analyze the amount and type or context within the review. Does the piece presume knowledge on the part of the readership—familiarity with the artist of the genre? If so, how much? Too much? Description, interpretation and evaluation refer specifically to the work being reviewed. Context is anything that doesn't; it is the information that puts the work into perspective.

INTERPRETATION: WHAT DOES IT MEAN AND/OR HOW DOES IT WORK?

Having described the piece of art and put it within a biographical/artistic/cultural context, the reviewer must explain how the work *works,* how the components cohere as an artistic whole. How does the soundtrack of a film complement the cinematography? (Not "how *well,*" for that is evaluation.) Why does this particular CD open with the sort of long ballad that other artists might save for the end? Are there figures in that Jackson Pollock canvas, and if so, what are they doing?

Description tells the reader what is there. Interpretation shows why it is there, at least from the reviewer's perspective. Interpretation helps build the argument that leads to evaluation—though, again, as we shall see, this doesn't mean that interpretation should precede evaluation within the structure of a review.

One place reviewers might be tempted to turn for help with the "why?" question is to the artists themselves. Doesn't the artist have a greater insight than anyone else into how and why a piece of art works? Not necessarily. Those who study criticism as an academic discipline should be familiar with the term *intentional fallacy,* the assumption that the expressed intent behind the art defines the art itself. Some art is as much of a mystery to the artist as it is to a viewership, leaving the analytical incisiveness of the critic to mediate. Some critics have built provocative cases based on interpretive evidence that the artist likely never intended (such as homoerotic undertones in the novels of Jane Austen, Mark Twain or Herman Melville).

Some artists are simply more voluble, eloquent or expansive in explaining, even justifying their art. Bono of the band U2 or director Quentin Tarantino will interpret themselves at such length that the critic is tempted to hear through their ears, see through their eyes. Critics can and should feel free to agree or disagree with the artist's interpretation. Novelist Thomas Pynchon and director Terrence Malick refuse to provide any interpretive clues, to say much of anything about the work, insisting (silently) that the art must speak for itself. Other artists simply aren't very good critics of their own work, lacking the analytical chops or the command of language (as anyone who has ever read an interview with Prince can attest). In any case, artist and critic have different roles. Artists create. Critics interpret and evaluate.

EVALUATION: IS IT ANY GOOD?

If so, why? If not, why not? This is more than an opinion, such as I like vanilla and you prefer chocolate; this is an argument, backed by interpretation, bolstered by context, informed by description. Fledgling critics often hedge about taking a strong evaluative position, or they declare an opinion without much of an argument to support it. The most powerful criticism—the kind that dominates this volume—neither pulls its punches nor flails wildly while trying to connect.

When reading the reviews in this volume, pay particular attention to how decisively a critic delivers an evaluation and how early in the review that evaluation comes. Such evaluation can take the form of a single adjective or adverb, or an entire paragraph. Confident critics—those who write with authority—take strong stands and leave little doubt for long in the reader's mind whether the review is positive or negative. Having taken the stand, the critic builds the argument with interpretation, context and description, showing not simply that the work is good or bad but *why* she believes it is so.

Critics arrive at different evaluations for a simple reason: They are different people. Men and women, conservatives and radicals, atheists and fundamentalists tend to respond differently to different types of movies, or to see different things in them. Older and younger reviewers tend to have different levels of comfort with the "shock of the new." Some critics prefer work that is polished and conventionally pretty; others have more of an affinity for the abrasive. "Disturbing" is a negative quality for some critics and high praise for others.

Timid critics worry about being wrong. There is no "wrong." Particularly with the most polarizing art, strong arguments can be made at either end of the evaluative extreme. Readers often get more from a provocative, counterintuitive evaluation with which they disagree than a more measured expression of conventional wisdom.

The critic who tries to please everyone ends up pleasing no one. A critic who isn't sure of his evaluative footing will tend to rely more on description (those elements, remember, with which we all agree) or biographical context. The results can read like the journalistic equivalent of play-by-play announcing.

"First the band did this song, then this one, then this one. . . ." Or, "the exhibition encompasses all sorts of paintings, beginning in the mid-19th century with blah blah and then proceeding into. . . ." Such description delays the evaluation as long as possible, or undercuts it entirely.

Equally timid and exasperating is the "on the one hand, on the other hand" review. Every critic knows the positive things and the negative things one can say about Madonna, or Stephen King, or Andy Warhol. The challenge is to provide a perspective that is vibrant and fresh, to let the reader experience the art and the artist through the critic's eyes.

Visual arts critic Roberta Smith describes opinion as "the main ingredient. That's the risk that a writer takes, similar to the risk that an artist takes. And opinions are just great fun to read."

The stronger the better.

 STORY**SCAN**

Selection 1.1

In the following review by Pulitzer Prize–winning book critic Michiko Kakutani, we can see how the four key elements establish a convincing argument that leaves no doubt about the critic's high regard for the novel, while acknowledging its flaws as well.

BOOKS OF THE TIMES
First Time for Taxis, Lo Mein and Loss
By MICHIKO KAKUTANI

The title of Lorrie Moore's heartbreaking new novel, "A Gate at the Stairs," comes from a song that her heroine, a college student and sometime musician, writes:

> Did you take off for Heaven
> and leave me behind?
> Darlin', I'd join you
> if you didn't mind.
> I'd climb up that staircase
> past lions and bears,
> but it's locked
> at the foot of the stairs.

Never mind the corny lyrics. And never mind the narrative stumbles this novel takes along the way to its searing conclusion: Ms. Moore has written her most powerful book yet, a book that gives us an indelible portrait of a young woman coming of age in the Midwest in the year after 9/11 and her initiation into the adult world of loss and grief. It is a novel that illustrates just how far Ms. Moore has come in the last two and half decades from her keenly observed but jokey 1985 collection of stories, "Self-Help," which showcased her gifts as a writer but also underscored her—and her characters'—emotional reticence, their reluctance to open themselves to deeply felt experiences.

recognizing flaws, but putting them in perspective

more early, strong evaluation

description

context

Published: August 28, 2009. Book reviewed: "A Gate at the Stairs." By Lorrie Moore.

again, flaw put
into perspective

analysis

context

analysis, with
an embedded
evaluation
("enormous
emotional
precision")

Although the characters in "A Gate at the Stairs" also have an annoying tendency to play coy little word games and make lame little jokes— it's a kind of nervous tic that enables them to detach themselves from threatening situations— Ms. Moore grapples in these pages with the precariousness of life and the irretrievable losses that accumulate over the years.

Like Alice McDermott's "Charming Billy" and "At Weddings and Wakes," this novel explores, with enormous emotional precision, the limitations and insufficiencies of love, and the loneliness that haunts even the most doting of families. While very funny at times, it is concerned at heart with the consequences of carelessness—of failing to pay attention to, or fight for, those one loves—and the random, out-of-the-blue events that can abruptly torpedo or transform a life.

The narrator of "Stairs" is one Tassie Keltjin, who is looking back on her 20th year. Having grown up on a small Midwestern farm, Tassie has never taken a taxi or an airplane, never eaten Chinese food, never seen a man wear jeans with a tie. Though her brother, Robert, who is desultorily thinking of joining the military, looks up to her as a focused, sure-footed college girl, she thinks of herself as lost, as lacking the ambitions of friends ("marriage, children, law school") and lacking an internal gyroscope that might lend ballast to her plans.

Enrollment at a small, liberal-minded Midwestern college (where political correctness is de rigueur, and students can take courses in things like wine tasting, war-movie soundtracks and Pilates) has made Tassie feel as if she'd been led out of a cave into "a brilliant city life of books and films and witty friends."

School has set her brain "on fire with Chaucer, Sylvia Plath, Simone de Beauvoir," and life in the university town of Troy has exposed her to the sophisticated ideas and ridiculous chatter of academic elites, who talk about things like animal rights and "the holocaust of chickens," and who describe education as an essentially "white" and "female" enterprise.

It's Tassie's part-time job as a nanny for a middle-aged couple, however, that will irrevocably alter her apprehension of the world. Sarah Brink runs a fancy restaurant called Le Petit Moulin, and her husband, Edward, is a cancer researcher. They have moved to Troy from the East and have just submitted adoption papers for a 2-year-old, mixed-race girl they have named Mary-Emma.

Tassie bonds with the little girl almost immediately, and when neighbors see them together, they often assume that she is the child's unwed mother. Soon Tassie's days have settled into a pleasant rhythm of classes, afternoon walks and play sessions with Mary-Emma, and evening dates with a handsome classmate named Reynaldo, who says he is from Brazil.

The previous four grafs are all description—detailing the plot without giving away too much.

Neither Reynaldo nor Sarah and Edward turn out to be who they say they are: revelations that Ms. Moore does a clumsy job of orchestrating (and in the case of Reynaldo, an absurd job of suggesting who he really is). In the hands of most writers such fumbles would instantly derail their story lines, but Ms. Moore is so deft at showing the fallout these discoveries have on her heroine that the reader speeds easily over the narrative bumps.

evaluation

Positive again puts the negative in perspective.

The lessons for Tassie, it turns out, have less to do with trust and betrayal than with the unforeseen costs of emotional inattention and romantic infatuation. She learns how bereavement can render one "passive, translucent and demolished"; how the accumulation of bad luck can strafe a person "to the thinness of a nightgown"; how love—for a man, a child, a sibling—fails to offer insulation from the calamities of everyday life.

description

If Ms. Moore, who started out as a short-story writer, demonstrates some difficulty here in steering the big plot machinery of a novel, she is able to compensate for this by thoroughly immersing the reader in her characters' daily existences.

context that underscores evaluation

evaluation

rest of graf is description, as is the following

With affection and a keen sense of the absurd she gives us bright, digital snapshots of flyover country where nearly every small town has a local Dairy Queen, where customers wait in lines, even in winter, and where the "whimsy and fuss" of homeowners' Christmas decorations— "penguins, palm trees, geese and candy canes all lighted up as if they were long-lost friends at a gathering"—provide a seasonal diversion for neighbors.

She gives us an indelible portrait of Tassie's family farm, where her mother has set up mirrors behind the flowerbeds to multiply the foxgloves and nightshade and phlox, and where her father has her don a hawk costume and run in front of his thresher to scare wildlife from its hiding places. ("Nobody wanted sliced mice in their salads," she wryly observes, "at least not this decade.")

evaluation

analysis

And most memorably, in this haunting novel Ms. Moore gives us stark, melancholy glimpses into her characters' hearts, mapping their fears and disappointments, their hidden yearnings and their more evanescent efforts to hold on to their dreams in the face of unfurling misfortune.

Where a less confident critic might have been tempted to write an "on the one hand, on the other hand" review, balancing the positive and negative evaluations, Kakutani effectively tips the scales, leaving no doubt that what's great about this novel outweighs its comparatively minor flaws. Throughout the chapters that follow, pay attention to how the critics of the various arts deal with the positive and the negative—how description, context and analysis coalesce into an evaluative argument. Each art has its distinctive properties, but these critical keys apply across the board.

popular music

● THE PIECES IN THIS SECTION HINT at the challenges that popular music coverage in The Times regularly faces. More than a dozen genres fit within this broad category—from rock to reggae, cabaret to hip-hop, jazz and blues to country and bluegrass, and then subgenres within those (and subgenres within subgenres). There are well-known acts who require coverage because of their news value, and unknown acts who merit coverage because their artistry deserves wider exposure.

A week that might see a half-dozen films and a couple of Broadway plays open will find the pop critic buried under a hundred or more new releases. Given the shift from CDs to downloaded cuts, and from record stores to social networking sites, the critic must pay even more attention to the Internet, where music often achieves viral exposure under the radar of both mainstream journalism and the music industry.

On the music calendar, most cities might have a major concert hall or two and a few clubs booking talent worth reviewing. The New York area, in contrast, has dozens to hundreds, depending on how wide the coverage casts the net. And there is national and international coverage as well: the big British artist consenting to an interview (if the biggest acts grant only a couple of interviews to launch a CD and concert tour, one will almost invariably be with The Times), the big festivals.

How does The Times keep up with it all? It doesn't. It can't. Nobody could. Even with the unlimited space the Web affords, there are only so many critics and so much time—and thus so many decisions that need to be made on the basis of gut, balance, intuition and experience.

THE CHANGING TIMES

Popular music (and popular culture in general, particularly that consumed by youth) was long relegated to second-class citizenship within coverage at The Times, which put greater emphasis on the so-called "fine arts." In the Sunday arts section, classical music consistently was featured more prominently than pop coverage. Rock and its offshoots were afterthoughts, kids' stuff. Not until the early 1970s did The Times hire its first full-time rock writer, Robert Palmer, who later became chief pop music critic from 1976 to 1988.

Yet even when The Times was paying comparatively scant attention to rock, one of the hallmarks of its musical coverage was the wide range of experience and expertise among its critics. John Rockwell, who preceded Palmer as chief pop critic, joined The Times as a classical music critic in 1972 and later served as dance critic. His critical acumen on both sides of the high-low cultural divide informed his criticism in all areas, helping to subvert that distinction in the process.

Likewise Palmer, though hired by The Times initially to write about rock, boasted a range that extended from the most traditional blues to the most avant-garde jazz. Where critics at many other publications often specialize in a specific form of music, today's Times critics continue to resist pigeonholing. The critics who provide The Times with much of its jazz coverage write plenty about rock and other forms of popular music as well, with chief pop music critic Jon Pareles showing a range beyond rock as great as that of his predecessors.

As the following selections suggest, Times music coverage—in comparison with coverage of other arts such as books, television and film—has been disproportionally provided by male critics, and white male critics at that. Ann Powers (now at the Los Angeles Times) was a rare woman featured prominently at The Times as a staff music critic. Sia Michel also joined The Times as a critic before her shift to pop music editor. This imbalance between genders isn't a problem merely or mainly at The Times, but has long been recognized within pop music criticism as a whole.

"It's not for lack of searching," says chief pop music critic Jon Pareles. "There have not been many slots—either on staff or as stringers—as a music critic, period. It's a job people (like me) tend to keep. Each time one has opened up, I have made a point of trying to add diversity."

(Aspiring female and minority critics take note: Other news organizations aspire to similar balance.)

FOUR TYPES OF POP MUSIC CRITICISM

Within coverage of popular music at The Times, critical commentary generally assumes one of four forms, described here from the shortest and least ambitious to the longest and most comprehensive.

CD Reviews

These are actually previews, because these generally run as a series of "Critics' Choice" capsules on Monday, before the release of the CD on Tuesday. While providing some critical context, these reviews of a few paragraphs each stick closest to the consumer guide model, advising fans of the artist and/or the genre, whether this new music is worth their while, and perhaps sparking the interest of newcomers to this sort of music as well. Compression presents a challenge; any experienced critic recognizes that it is tougher to write tightly than to ramble. Sunday's music section "Playlist" features even shorter, quirkier quasi-reviews by a Times critic or guest columnist.

This chapter includes a longer CD review than is typical at The Times— of "Loverly," by jazz vocalist Cassandra Wilson—in order to highlight the context underlying an argument that supports a strongly positive evaluation. Shorter reviews typically leave less room for context.

Concert Reviews

If these were merely reviews of a single performance, they would primarily interest those who attended or wish they had. The most vibrant concert reviews have a "you are there" quality, providing such atmospheric detail that the reader feels she can practically hear the music as part of the crowd, but they also provide plenty of background context on the artist as well as critical commentary on the music (its quality in general, beyond a specific performance).

Thus concert reviews can often substitute for CD reviews, focusing on the new music, how it differs from the old, etc. They can also serve as previews for music fans beyond New York, who might decide whether to buy a ticket for a concert by the same artist in their own city based on this review from earlier in the tour.

This chapter includes three very different live reviews: a prophetic one of Bob Dylan very early in his career, a piece that provides critical perspective on Green Day at a pivotal point in the band's career, and a longer piece on the Sugar Hill Gang that serves as a history of rap's formative years.

Profiles

As we'll see in Part II, profiles of artists often include so much critical commentary on their new music, along with critical context on their music as a whole, that such longer pieces can serve the function of a CD review/preview. Critics at The Times have far more space in a profile than they are generally accorded in a CD review, and criticism as well as reportage frequently informs these profiles.

Critical Essays

Typically the longest and most ambitious pieces of criticism at The Times, these present arguments that extend beyond a single artist or piece of work to explore trends and/or analyze how a style of music fits within the culture at large. This type of criticism distinguishes the music coverage at The Times and thus dominates the selections in this section.

When reading the following pieces, analyze how the four elements of criticism (description, context, interpretation, evaluation) interweave themselves within different pieces and different types of pieces. For example, in "The Rap Against Rockism," the longest and perhaps most provocative piece here, you'll see elements of live performance review, music criticism that could fit within a CD review, and plenty of context suggesting that the conventional wisdom about popular music is all too conventional and not nearly wise enough.

The piece builds a strong argument—one that makes readers think, whether they agree or disagree. That's what effective criticism, in whatever form, always does.

Selection 2.1

Well before there was much popular music journalism in The Times (or any-where else), Robert Shelton wrote what remains perhaps the most prophetic, star-making review ever published in a daily newspaper. Much of the writing is simply descriptive, more so than you'll see in most contemporary reviews, but the evaluation of what made Bob Dylan special at age 20 predicted the mercurial career to come.

Bob Dylan: A Distinctive Folk-Song Stylist: 20-Year Old Singer Is Bright New Face at Gerde's Club

By ROBERT SHELTON

A bright new face in folk music is appearing at Gerde's Folk City. Although only 20 years old, Bob Dylan is one of the most dis-tinctive stylists to play in a Manhattan cabaret in months.

Resembling a cross between a choir boy and a beatnik, Mr. Dylan has a cherubic look and a mop of tousled hair he partly covers with a Huck Finn black corduroy cap. His clothes may need a bit of tailoring, but when he works his guitar, harmonica or piano and com-poses new songs faster than he can remember them, there is no doubt that he is bursting at the seams with talent.

Mr. Dylan's voice is anything but pretty. He is consciously try-ing to recapture the rude beauty of a Southern field hand musing in melody on his porch. All the "husk and bark" are left on his notes and a searing intensity pervades his songs.

Slow-Motion Mood

Mr. Dylan is both comedian and tragedian. Like a vaudeville actor on the rural circuit, he offers a variety of droll musical monologues: "Talking Bear Mountain" lampoons the over-crowding of an excursion boat, "Talking New York" satirizes his troubles in gaining recognition and "Talking Havah Nagilah" burlesques the folk-music craze and the singer himself.

In his serious vein, Mr. Dylan seems to be performing in a slow-motion film. Elasticized phrases are drawn out until you think they may snap. He rocks his head and body, closes his eyes in reverie and seems to be groping for a word or a mood, then resolves the tension benevolently by finding the word and the mood.

He may mumble the text of "House of the Rising Sun" in a scarcely understandable growl or sob, or clearly enunciate the poetic poignancy of a Blind Lemon Jefferson blues: "One kind favor I ask of you—See that my grave is kept clean."

Published: September 29, 1961.

Mr. Dylan's highly personalized approach toward folk song is still evolving. He has been sopping up influences like a sponge. At times, the drama he aims at is off-target melodrama and his stylization threatens to topple over as a mannered excess.

But if not for every taste, his music-making has the mark of originality and inspiration, all the more noteworthy for his youth. Mr. Dylan is vague about his antecedents and birthplace, but it matters less where he has been than where he is going, and that would seem to be straight up. ●

Selection 2.2

We move from one of the earliest and most prophetic pieces of popular music criticism in The Times to one of the more contemporary and provocative. The generation that came of age with Bob Dylan, the Beatles and the Rolling Stones imposed (or at least accepted) certain standards of quality to which most of rock has adhered ever since. The next piece makes a powerful argument against the idea that the music of subsequent generations must submit to the rules of aging baby boomers. Just as in a trend story in the news pages, Kelefa Sanneh sets the scene with a (then) recent event and subsequently opens the piece to the bigger issues. In the fourth paragraph, he's careful to define his terms before launching a pointed attack on critical and generational orthodoxy. Whether or not you agree with Sanneh, he makes you question: Are you a "rockist"?

The Rap Against Rockism

By KELEFA SANNEH

Bad news travels fast, and an embarrassing video travels even ● faster. By last Sunday morning, one of the Internet's most popular downloads was the hours-old 60-second.wmv file of Ashlee Simpson on "Saturday Night Live." As she and her band stood onstage, her own prerecorded vocals—from the wrong song—came blaring through the speakers, and it was too late to start mouthing the words. So she performed a now-infamous little jig, then skulked offstage, while the band (were a few members smirking?) played on. One of 2004's most popular new stars had been exposed as. . . .

As what, exactly? The online verdict came fast and harsh, the way online verdicts usually do. A typical post on her Web site bore the headline, "Ashlee you are a no talent fraud!" After that night, everyone knew that Jessica Simpson's telegenic sister was no rock 'n' roll hero—she wasn't even a rock 'n' roll also-ran. She was merely a lip-synching pop star.

Published: October 31, 2004.

Music critics have a word for this kind of verdict, this knee-jerk backlash against producer-powered idols who didn't spend years touring dive bars. Not a very elegant word, but a useful one. The word is *rockism,* and among the small but extraordinarily pesky group of people who obsess over this stuff, rockism is a word meant to start fights. The rockism debate began in earnest in the early 1980's, but over the past few years it has heated up, and today, in certain impassioned circles, there is simply nothing worse than a rockist.

A rockist isn't just someone who loves rock 'n' roll, who goes on and on about Bruce Springsteen, who champions ragged-voiced singer-songwriters no one has ever heard of. A rockist is someone who reduces rock 'n' roll to a caricature, then uses that caricature as a weapon. Rockism means idolizing the authentic old legend (or underground hero) while mocking the latest pop star; lionizing punk while barely tolerating disco; loving the live show and hating the music video; extolling the growling performer while hating the lip-syncher.

Over the past decades, these tendencies have congealed into an ugly sort of common sense. Rock bands record classic albums, while pop stars create "guilty pleasure" singles. It's supposed to be self-evident: U2's entire oeuvre deserves respectful consideration, while a spookily seductive song by an R&B singer named Tweet can only be, in the smug words of a recent VH1 special, "awesomely bad."

Like rock 'n' roll itself, rockism is full of contradictions: it could mean loving the Strokes (a scruffy guitar band!) or hating them (image-conscious poseurs!) or ignoring them entirely (since everyone knows that music isn't as good as it used to be). But it almost certainly means disdaining not just Ms. Simpson but also Christina Aguilera and Usher and most of the rest of them, grousing about a pop landscape dominated by big-budget spectacles and high-concept photo shoots, reminiscing about a time when the charts were packed with people who had something to say, and meant it, even if that time never actually existed. If this sounds like you, then take a long look in the mirror: you might be a rockist.

Countless critics assail pop stars for not being rock 'n' roll enough, without stopping to wonder why that should be everybody's goal. Or they reward them disproportionately for making rock 'n' roll gestures. Writing in The Chicago Sun-Times this summer, Jim DeRogatis grudgingly praised Avril Lavigne as "a teen-pop phenom that discerning adult rock fans can actually admire without feeling (too) guilty," partly because Ms. Lavigne "plays a passable rhythm guitar" and "has a hand in writing" her songs.

Rockism isn't unrelated to older, more familiar prejudices—that's part of why it's so powerful, and so worth arguing about. The pop star, the disco diva, the lip-syncher, the "awesomely bad" hit maker: could it really be a coincidence that rockist complaints often pit straight white men against the rest of the world? Like the anti-disco backlash of 25 years ago, the current rockist consensus seems to reflect not just an idea of how music should be made but also an idea about who should be making it.

If you're interested in—O.K., mildly obsessed with—rockism, you can find traces of it just about everywhere. Notice how those tributes to "Women Who Rock" sneakily transform "rock" from a genre to a verb to a catch-all term of praise. Ever wonder why OutKast and the Roots and Mos Def and the Beastie Boys get taken so much more seriously than other rappers? Maybe because rockist critics love it when hip-hop acts impersonate rock 'n' roll bands. (A recent Rolling Stone review praised the Beastie Boys for scruffily resisting "the gold-plated phooey currently passing for gangsta.")

From punk-rock rags to handsomely illustrated journals, rockism permeates the way we think about music. This summer, the literary zine The Believer published a music issue devoted to almost nothing but indie-rock. Two weeks ago, in The New York Times Book Review, Sarah Vowell approvingly recalled Nirvana's rise: "a group with loud guitars and louder drums knocking the whimpering Mariah Carey off the top of the charts." Why did the changing of the guard sound so much like a sexual assault? And when did we all agree that Nirvana's neo-punk was more respectable than Ms. Carey's neo-disco?

Rockism is imperial: it claims the entire musical world as its own. Rock 'n' roll is the unmarked section in the record store, a vague pop-music category that swallows all the others. If you write about music, you're presumed to be a rock critic. There's a place in the Rock and Roll Hall of Fame for doo-wop groups and folk singers and disco queens and even rappers—just so long as they, y'know, rock.

Rockism just won't go away. The rockism debate began when British bands questioned whether the search for raw, guitar-driven authenticity wasn't part of rock 'n' roll's problem, instead of its solution; some new-wave bands emphasized synthesizers and drum machines and makeup and hairspray, instead. "Rockist" became for them a term of abuse, and the anti-rockists embraced the inclusive possibilities of a once-derided term: pop. Americans found other terms, but "rockist" seems the best way to describe the ugly anti-disco backlash of the late 1970's, which culminated in a full-blown anti-disco rally and the burning of thousands of disco records at Comiskey Park in Chicago in 1979: the Boston Tea Party of rockism.

That was a quarter of a century and many genres ago. By the 1990's, the American musical landscape was no longer a battleground between Nirvana and Mariah (if indeed it ever was); it was a fractured, hyper-vivid fantasy of teen-pop stars and R&B pillow-talkers and arena-filling country singers and, above all, rappers. Rock 'n' roll was just one more genre alongside the rest.

Yet many critics failed to notice. Rock 'n' roll doesn't rule the world anymore, but lots of writers still act as if it does. The rules, even today, are: concentrate on making albums, not singles; portray yourself as a rebellious individualist, not an industry pro; give listeners the uncomfortable truth, instead of pandering to their tastes. Overnight celebrities, one-hit-wonders and lip-synchers, step aside.

And just as the anti-disco partisans of a quarter-century ago railed against a bewildering new pop order (partly because disco was so closely associated with black culture and gay culture), current critics rail against a world hopelessly corrupted by hip-hop excess. Since before Sean Combs became Puff Daddy, we've been hearing that mainstream hip-hop was too flashy, too crass, too violent, too ridiculous, unlike those hard-working rock 'n' roll stars we used to have. (This, of course, is one of the most pernicious things about rockism: it finds a way to make rock 'n' roll seem boring.)

Much of the most energetic resistance to rockism can be found online, in blogs and on critic-infested sites like ilovemusic.com, where debates about rockism have become so common that the term itself is something of a running joke. When the editors of a blog called Rock-critics Daily noted that rockism was "all the rage again," they posted dozens of contradictory citations, proving that no one really agrees on what the term means. (By the time you read this article, a slew of indignant refutations and addenda will probably be available online.)

But as more than one online ranter has discovered, it's easier to complain about rockism than it is to get rid of it. You literally can't fight rockism, because the language of righteous struggle is the language of rockism itself. You can argue that the shape-shifting feminist hip-pop of Ms. Aguilera is every bit as radical as the punk rock of the 1970's (and it is), but then you haven't challenged any of the old rockist questions (starting with: Who's more radical?), you've just scribbled in some new answers.

The challenge isn't merely to replace the old list of Great Rock Albums with a new list of Great Pop Songs—although that would, at the very least, be a nice change of pace. It's to find a way to think about a fluid musical world where it's impossible to separate classics from guilty pleasures. The challenge is to acknowledge that music videos and reality shows and glamorous layouts can be as interesting— and as influential—as an old-fashioned album.

In the end, the problem with rockism isn't that it's wrong: all critics are wrong sometimes, and some critics (now doesn't seem like the right time to name names) are wrong almost all the time. The problem with rockism is that it seems increasingly far removed from the way most people actually listen to music.

Are you really pondering the phony distinction between "great art" and a "guilty pleasure" when you're humming along to the radio? In an era when listeners routinely—and fearlessly—pick music by putting a 40-gig iPod on shuffle, surely we have more interesting things to worry about than that someone might be lip-synching on "Saturday Night Live" or that some rappers gild their phooey. Good critics are good listeners, and the problem with rockism is that it gets in the way of listening. If you're waiting for some song that conjures up soul or honesty or grit or rebellion, you might miss out on Ciara's ecstatic electro-pop, or Alan Jackson's sly country ballads, or Lloyd Banks's felonious purr.

Rockism makes it hard to hear the glorious, incoherent, corporate-financed, audience-tested mess that passes for popular music these days. To glorify only performers who write their own songs and play their own guitars is to ignore the marketplace that helps create the music we hear in the first place, with its checkbook-chasing superproducers, its audience-obsessed executives and its cred-hungry performers. To obsess over old-fashioned stand-alone geniuses is to forget that lots of the most memorable music is created despite multimillion-dollar deals and spur-of-the-moment collaborations and murky commercial forces. In fact, a lot of great music is created because of those things. And let's stop pretending that serious rock songs will last forever, as if anything could, and that shiny pop songs are inherently disposable, as if that were necessarily a bad thing. Van Morrison's "Into the Music" was released the same year as the Sugar-hill Gang's "Rapper's Delight"; which do you hear more often?

That doesn't mean we should stop arguing about Ms. Simpson, or even that we should stop sharing the 60-second clip that may just be this year's best music video. But it does mean we should stop taking it for granted that music isn't as good as it used to be, and it means we should stop being shocked that the rock rules of the 1970's are no longer the law of the land. No doubt our current obsessions and comparisons will come to seem hopelessly blinkered as popular music mutates some more—listeners and critics alike can't do much more than struggle to keep up. But let's stop trying to hammer young stars into old categories. We have lots of new music to choose from—we deserve some new prejudices, too.

Selection 2.3

Long before rap replaced rock as the music at the cutting edge of popular culture, it was an underground New York phenomenon. Consider how Robert Palmer, the first critic hired by The Times to write specifically about rock and its offshoots, is able to show an appreciation that appeals to those who know a lot about hip-hop while providing the context for those who know little. This is more of an explanatory piece than one that lays down an argumentative gauntlet, though controversies over rap-as-art (and turntables as instruments) would subsequently rage.

Pop: The Sugar Hill Gang

By ROBERT PALMER

Rapping, a kind of rhythmic versifying with skeletal instrumental or unrecorded accompaniment, began in Harlem, the South Bronx and other black communities in the New York area. A white rock group, Blondie, has carried the rapping style into the national Top 10 with the hit single, "Rapture," but the champion rappers are the Sugar Hill Gang, Grand Master Flash and the Fabulous Five, and other groups that have sold large quantities of records but seldom perform for white audiences.

Rapping moved downtown for a night on Wednesday when the Ritz presented a cavalcade of rappers. The Sugar Hill Gang, whose "Rapper's Delight" was one of the first rap hits, headlined the show. The three men who do most of the group's rapping took turns declaiming rhymed couplets and chimed in as a unison chorus on key phrases while a tight band laid down funk rhythms that were heavily accented on the first beat of each measure. The band also accompanied Sequence, three women in glittering costumes whose raps were as fast and funny as those of the men.

Grand Master Flash and an assistant accompanied the Fabulous Five with a virtuoso performance on two turntables; Flash constructed bass and drum parts by repeatedly playing the first few bars of records by Queen & Chic; he created extravagant special effects by stopping records with his hand while they were playing, while they were spinning, a technique that resulted in a regular, percussive skidding sound. "What you've just beared witness to is seven men and two turntables," one of the group's rappers told the predominantly white, enthusiastic crowd. "Think about it."

The Funky 4 Plus 1 provided even more food for thought. The group's five rappers chanted in crisp unison and traded phrases in a kind of whiplash call and response. They were able to inject some personality, and some new rhymes and couplets, into what has already become a fairly standardized idiom, and they were as disciplined as a crack drill team. Their lone disk jockey provided minimal accompaniment by repeating bass figures and drum parts from various funk and disco records. Basically, the Funky 4 Plus 1 provide a kind of rhythmic noise. Melody and harmony have no place in their music, which rides on an irresistible dance beat and various cross rhythms.

The evening featured several surprise guests, including Andy Hernandez from Dr. Buzzard's Original Savannah Band, who rapped over the instrumental track of his latest recording, the delightful "Me No Pop I." The Coconuts, who are Mr. Hernandez's associates in the

Published: March 13, 1981. Full text available at: www.nytimes.com/1981/03/13/arts/pop-the-sugar-hill-gang.html.

group Kid Creole and the Coconuts, also performed a short set of
their own and demonstrated conclusively that they are not spectacular
dancers.

Rapping is probably familiar to most New Yorkers as an intru-
sive noise on the subway or in the park—the noise that comes out
of blaring cassette players and portable radios. But as the Ritz show
demonstrated, rapping has a much broader appeal than one might
have anticipated. It's an intriguing test of the performer's verbal ingenuity and rhythmic exactitude, and it's fine.

***

Selection 2.4

While the previous review used one concert to introduce an emerging genre of music, the next one finds a band at a pivotal point in its transition from punk to pop, anticipating the greater mainstream success Green Day would subsequently achieve. It captures the flavor of the night in question, but the context and evaluation extend well beyond a single performance. Jon Pareles writes more vividly (check his verbs and adjectives) than in some of the earlier pieces included here, putting more of his own personality into the review in the process.

POP REVIEW
Suburban Listlessness As Caught by Green Day
By JON PARELES

Twenty years after punk-rock was born, it has triumphed in ways no one expected. It has survived not by conquering cities, where its speed and noise emerged, but by infiltrating the suburbs, where its supercharged message of seething boredom and aimless resentment find receptive ears in high schools and malls. Punk prevails not as revolutionary music—the hope of its British wing—but because it's bratty.

Green Day, a three-man band from the San Francisco Bay area, has seized the punk moment; the group's first major-label album, "Dookie" (Reprise) has sold three million copies. The band performed at the Nassau Coliseum on Friday night for an elated crowd of squealing young girls and uproarious high-school slam-dancers, all singing along on lines like "Call me pathetic, call me what you will" and "Sometimes I give myself the creeps."

Seats had been removed to turn the arena's entire floor into a mosh pit. People who had bleacher tickets rushed security guards to leap over a barrier and join the crush. Billie Joe, the band's guitarist, urged, "Please look out for the smaller people," and "Don't let anybody get hurt." Later, when a topless woman climbed on a companion's shoulders, he first said, "Mom, put your clothes back on," then admonished nearby boys not to grope her. But it was a happy melee.

Green Day's lyrics veer from torpor ("I'm not growing up, I'm just burning out") to complaint ("Are you locked up in a world that's been planned out for you?"), and its songs are unapologetically catchy. From bands like the Ramones, the Buzzcocks and All, Green Day has learned how to write fast, tuneful, major-key songs, and it delivers them with pure punk drive. Billie Joe's speed-strummed guitar

Published: December 5, 1994.

chords, Mike Dirnt's loping or pummeling bass lines and Tre Cool's explosive drumming are all strong enough to do justice to an encore of the Who's "My Generation." Billie Joe sometimes sings in an affected English accent, but he carries melodies and enunciates words, putting him on the pop end of the punk-rock spectrum.

Yet Green Day holds on to enough punk rebelliousness to make the band uncomfortable as arena-rock entertainers. It brought along two opening acts, Die Toten Hosen, a German band that plays first-generation punk songs, and Pansy Division, a San Francisco band that uses punk-rock tunes for raunchy, funny, assertively gay lyrics: "We're queer lovers in your face today."

Looking out on a crowd that was almost uniformly dressed in T-shirts and flannel shirts tied around the waist, Green Day tried to mock the audience's conformity. Billie Joe raised a finger; the fans copied him. He played a mock arena-rock guitar solo, making self-congratulatory faces, and drew applause. He cued the crowd to clap along nowhere near the beat; he slowed down the band and swayed with upraised arms, but grew disgusted when the audience took the arena-rock routine even further and held up flaming cigarette lighters. Punk-rock is here to stay; punk independence may need a refresher course.

Selection 2.5

This combo concert review offers an audacious linking of two artists who did not play together and might initially seem to have little in common beyond generation and gender. Yet an astute critic (of the same gender) finds so much more than initially meets the ear. Note how much context from their previous music she builds in, appropriate for careers of such duration. Even performance reviews can present an argument.

CRITIC'S NOTEBOOK
Pop Godmothers: Burnished by Experience
By ANN POWERS

Maybe it never really changed, but the popular music business has unequivocally returned to judging female artists by their pounds of flesh. Yards of young midriff define the female presence in pop, overshadowing not just talent but personality as well. This is sad, not only because it shuts out those with better voices than abs, but also because it makes sexuality dull, as false and uniform as the scent of deodorant.

Published: September 13, 2000.

It's time for a resurgence of brazen women to recharge the mainstream with some rock 'n' roll oomph. Two senior advisers for this much-needed offensive offered their services on Saturday night in Manhattan, showing how pop's girl androids might free their humanity.

Marianne Faithfull, who appeared at the Sylvia and Danny Kaye Playhouse at Hunter College, emerged in 1965 as a mod Britney Spears, an ingenue most valued for her looks. She was a model and a consort to Mick Jagger, playing the girlish ideal. Then in the 1970's she practically destroyed herself with heroin. With the release of her punk-influenced 1979 album, "Broken English," she became a rock phoenix, rising with a new, rugged voice and a genius for music that strips away romantic illusion.

Koko Taylor, who played at B. B. King's Blues Club and Grill, has been a raw-voiced oracle since she rose to fame, also in 1965. She never had conventional beauty to fall back on, vocally or physically. As virtually the only female blues belter competing with the men on the South Side of Chicago, she fit in by cultivating earthiness. Her very existence defied the notion of the ladylike, and she turned that difference into a strength, a sign of her honesty.

Ms. Faithfull, 54, and Ms. Taylor, 65, have developed their challenging approaches separated by the gaps of race, class and feminine convention. On Saturday, Ms. Faithfull offered her usual anthem, John Lennon's brainy polemic "Working Class Hero"; Ms. Taylor echoed the sentiment in the far more plain-spoken Willie Dixon stomper, "Big Boss Man." During another of her trademark songs, Ms. Faithfull evoked the conflicts caused by desire by repeating the title word until it became a spell: "Guilt, guilt, guilt." Ms. Taylor worked similar magic with more humor as she finished her version of "Hound Dog." She growled: "Bowwow! Bowwow!"

Strip away the bohemian aura enveloping Ms. Faithfull and the raunchy-mama stereotypes that surround Ms. Taylor, however, and the same brave project is revealed. In concert these women risked ugliness to find grace in uneven reality. Their voices are wrenched by use, and they pushed them as hard as they ever have. No matter that their bodies show the mark of time, too; they adorned themselves in sexy clothes and moved with the abandon of women who fully own their own sexuality. It is striking how radical their choice to express themselves unhesitatingly still seems.

Ms. Faithfull, who has played the gown-clad diva in recent years, exploring the songbook of Brecht and Weill, was in full rocker mode in a filmy flowered shirt with a plunging neckline, trousers and moppy hair. Her salty mood may have been enhanced by the support of a tight, inspiring band, especially Greg Cohen on bass and Smokey Hormel on guitar. At times she plopped into a chair and just observed her band mates soloing; her immersion in the music gave her a break from her diva-fabulous persona.

She surveyed her rich career, including a few of the songs she recorded in her gamine days, like the Merseybeat charmer "Come and Stay With Me," written by Jackie DeShannon with the help of Jimmy Page. Her smoke-cured voice added depth to the song's sunniness.

Ms. Faithfull also had fun with material from her current album, "Vagabond Ways" (Instinct). "Incarceration of a Flower Child," a Roger Waters song that Pink Floyd never managed to record, is her new showpiece. She fell to her knees to relate this caustic story of a hippie dream gone disastrous, which seemed almost autobiographical. She poured as much into the album's title track, a streetwalker's tale that she wrote with David Courts. Ms. Faithfull has sometimes been overwhelmed by the melodrama her music generates, but this evening she had fun with it, flaunting the jaded humor that lifts her out of the fray.

As Ms. Faithfull went into her encore, Ms. Taylor was taking the stage in Times Square. She also had a fine band, led by the suave guitarist Vino Louden. Like Ms. Faithfull, she went full speed into songs from a new album, "Royal Blue" (Alligator), and old favorites, including her classics "I'd Rather Go Blind" and "Wang Dang Doodle."

Instead of artful irony, Ms. Taylor used party songs like "Blues Hotel" to leaven the pain of her confessions. Drenched in sweat, she rode the flow of pain into pleasure into pain that is the blues. Her face showed that changing current, transforming in an instant from a show-biz smile to a fierce mask of concentration.

Ms. Taylor's powerhouse contralto has not completely survived decades of hard labor. Sometimes she would aim for a note and just a rasp would come out; the effect was like a misfired gun. This made her intention all the more profound. This far from ideal performance was full of a quality female musicians are rarely even allowed to display: the courage to live in the rough.

Selection 2.6

Though the Powers piece pairs two artists from elsewhere who just happen to be playing New York, the city's own music remains the particular province of The Times. Here a perceptive and eclectic critic (who also covered classical and dance for the newspaper and served as editor of the Sunday arts section) analyzes three of the city's seminal rock artists from a particularly New York perspective. In writing about Lou Reed, Patti Smith and Television, he attempts to show that their music "suggest[s] things about not only their creators but, implicitly, about New York rock in general."

Three Faces of New York Rock

By JOHN ROCKWELL

Lou Reed, Patti Smith and Television are all crucial forces in 1970's New York rock-and-roll, and all of them have new records out now. None is likely to sweep the top of the sales charts. But all three are fascinating, and suggest things about not only their creators but, implicitly, about New York rock in general.

Mr. Reed might seem an unlikely father figure; his image of perverse wickedness is not exactly paternal. Still, ever since nearly a decade ago with the Velvet Underground, the seminal underground rock band for which he composed and sang, Mr. Reed has lurked in the shadowy background of the scene. He is a principal inspiration— and occasional representative—of glitter rock, punk rock, new-wave rock and progressive rock. He also has overt ambitions as a poet, and as such is very much part of the link between the New York avant-garde arts community and rock that Miss Smith and Talking Heads (currently recording their second album) also represent.

But Mr. Reed's status has been achieved despite, or perhaps partially because of, the extreme variability of his work as a solo artist. That variability expresses itself not only in terms of different styles but of a wide range of quality. In general his music has seemed to evolve from the leaden primitiveness and poetic declamation of the Underground days toward a denser, almost jazzish kind of progressiveness, akin to what David Bowie and Brian Eno are now turning out. But along the route of that development, Mr. Reed has swung so wildly between the poles of cynical, commercial reductions of his ideas and aggressive experimentation that he has sometimes left his fans completely confused: A two-disk set called "Metal Machine Music" was purchased by innocent rockers who then discovered a screaming onslaught of grating, overdubbed fragments of sound, unrelated to "music" of any kind as conventionally conceived.

"Street Hassle," Mr. Reed's new disk, is one of his strongest in years. It manages to sound reasonably commercial and yet to be full of interesting experimentation, as if Mr. Reed were finally beginning to make some sort of productive synthesis of the warring tensions within himself. The defiantly tuneless singing and the grimness of the themes will limit its appeal to the mainstream market, no doubt. But like the others being considered here, that isn't (or shouldn't be) Mr. Reed's main concern. New York underground rock is an art form that at its best can exercise a reasonable amount of impact on the society as a whole—enough to keep the artists decently well off and to sustain the large record companies' interest in them. If somebody breaks through and has a hit, fine, but to strive for that would be fatal.

Published: April 16, 1978.

This confusion of art and popularity has been one of the reasons that Patti Smith's direction in the past couple of years has seemed unsure (another, more tangible reason was a broken neck). Miss Smith wants it all: She wants to be a loner American artist-outcast (nicely suggested by a ranting speech to that effect on her new "Easter" album that is almost drowned out by impatient rhythmic clapping from a live audience, and which precedes one of the strongest songs on the record, "Rock n Roll Nigger"). But she also wants to be the "field marshal" of rock and to have hits, and some of her interviews have gone rather far in denying her artistry in an attempt to appeal to "the kids."

Her first album, "Horses," struck this admirer as a wonderful document indeed. She and others felt John Cale's production sounded thin. But it captured the actual sound of her band, which had a teasing sinuousness that the following two albums lacked, and it allowed the rapt declamation of her poetry and chanting to emerge unimpeded. Her second disk, "Radio Ethiopia," was generally considered a precipitous decline from that standard—although as a crazed, raucously uncommercial, semi-Moroccan, Rimbaud-ridden freak-out it had its virtues, and there are some fine songs on it.

"Easter" is a better record than "Radio Ethiopia"; certainly it is more ostensibly commercial in that the songs are clearly defined, and Jimmy Iovine's production is both true to the thumping basics of rock and to Miss Smith's singing. To this taste, however, she is still mistaking her own greatest gifts: It's not the band we want to hear, especially now that Richard Sohl, the wonderful keyboard player, has left the group. They're O.K. as backup for her, but she's the show. Too often these days on this disk and in live performance, she fails to maintain the verbal and declamatory control that marked her best work two and three years ago, and too often her songs become merely awkward vocalizations of the band's journeyman rock. In addition, she doesn't always display her own delightful sense of humor on the disk (in that respect the song "Rock n Roll Nigger" compares ironically to Mr. Reed's mordant "I Want to Be Black" on "Street Hassle").

Still, she remains a noble force in American rock, as both a symbol and an actuality, and the best material here is well worth encountering. One hopes her own rhetoric hasn't put her, her record company and the public in the position of judging the ultimate success of "Easter" by its sales. Patti Smith remains a fascinating American artist, just like she says she is, and one trusts that this will be far from the last step in her musical evolution.

Television is led by a composer, singer and guitarist named Tom Verlaine, who not only co-wrote a number of Miss Smith's songs but was her lover for a while. The quartet's first album, "Marquee Moon," was widely prized last year as one of the finest products of mid-1970's New York rock, and the group's second disk, "Adventure," is just as good.

Partly that's because, so far at least, Mr. Verlaine has found a style (a formula, if you wish) in which he can express himself and into which he can probe deeply, without being tempted into unfocused experimentation. Part of the problem that Mr. Reed and Miss Smith face—and which any rock composer must one day encounter—is that stylistic evolution can be particularly difficult in rock because of the inherent simplicity of the form and because fans grow used to hearing a particular idiom. Mr. Reed has been around long enough and is sufficiently venturesome that he simply has to change direction periodically; Miss Smith is restless by her very nature. Mr. Verlaine is still a largely unknown force to the general public and can still contentedly explore the style he has already forged. With this disk he proves that he can work fruitfully within that style, and even develop it suggestively. Where he goes into his third, fourth and fifth LPs remains to be seen.

The style so far is built on an often plodding but steadily effective rhythm section (somewhat akin to that of Crazy Horse with Neil Young) consisting of Fred Smith, bass, and Billy Sica, drums. Over that Mr. Verlaine sings, and he and Richard Lloyd, the other guitarist, engage in high-flying, ornamented, arpeggiated guitar duets—sometimes augmented by keyboard work from Mr. Verlaine. The result is fierce, sometimes exciting, sometimes haunting. Mr. Verlaine has a strangulated voice, but on this new disk especially it has its definite charms, and it's certainly personal. In addition, one should mention the chunky, abrupt phrasing and the delicate, almost koto-like effects that some of the songs suggest. The lyrics aren't easily deciphered without a printed text, and the key phrases that do emerge have a markedly suggestive quality.

Ultimately, "Adventure" is the most powerful record of these three. That doesn't mean Tom Verlaine is necessarily going to be considered by rock historians a more important figure than Lou Reed or Patti Smith—he hasn't been around as long as Mr. Reed, and to this taste at least, he hasn't quite reached the heights Miss Smith has achieved at her very finest. But he's made two wonderful albums, with every promise of more to come.

Selection 2.7

Like Rockwell and other critics from The Times, Ben Ratliff can apply his critical instincts to a variety of music. But jazz is his specialty, and here he uses context to support a very enthusiastic evaluation of a performer who has also crossed genres and blurred categories, but here returns to the jazz songbook. From his descriptions of the interplay, you can practically hear this music sing and swing.

CRITIC'S CHOICE
New CDs: Cassandra Wilson "Loverly"
By BEN RATLIFF

When Cassandra Wilson made the all-standards album "Blue Skies" in 1988, such jazz tunes were a little more sacred than they are now. There was an innovation-versus-tradition argument in progress. Ms. Wilson was then an impossibly hip young singer making her name with a radical fringe that merged jazz improvisation with complicated funk (imagine that!). For her to record songs like "I'm Old Fashioned" and "Polka Dots and Moonbeams"—with a straight-ahead rhythm section, treating the songs with due respect and scat singing— amounted to decent frisson. It was a lovely record, too.

Great songs are always in short supply, but in the very best jazz, material becomes negligible. The band takes over and does whatever it does, dominating over authorship. Many always knew this, but more know it now, and know it deeply. So "Loverly," Ms. Wilson's new record that is nearly all jazz standards, isn't conceptually jarring. But it's good to see how far she, and we, have come in 20 years. And for whatever reasons—don't give the songs all the credit—it's her best work in a long time.

Back on "Blue Skies" you could hear Ms. Wilson assuming a crouch, meeting the demands of the songs. (She armed herself, too, with some of Betty Carter's passionate phrasing. Good for you if you can do that.) Now she lets the songs come to her. Years of getting close to pop and touring with a hand drummer have accustomed her to finding a groove and a vamp first; the song can wait. And apart from the normatively swinging first and last songs of "Loverly"—"Lover Come Back to Me" and "A Sleepin' Bee"—the song does wait. Ms. Wilson and her band, with piano (Jason Moran), guitar (Marvin Sewell), bass (Lonnie Plaxico or Reginald Veal), drums (Herlin Riley) and percussion (Lekan Babalola), figure out their rhythmic strategies up front, in a soup of barrelhouse piano, postmodernism, Cuban and African influences, folk and funk. It's slow, chic and often extremely good.

The song list includes Lerner and Loewe's "Wouldn't It Be Loverly?" from "My Fair Lady"; one original, an Afro-Cuban chant called "Arere"; "Dust My Broom," representing blues; and "St. James Infirmary," representing, I guess, where jazz, folk and pop met a long time before Ms. Wilson started making records.

The rest are more like a jazz student's idea of standards. There are two well-prepared duets, both killers: "Spring Can Really Hang You Up the Most," with acoustic guitar, and "The Very Thought of You," with acoustic bass.

Published: June 9, 2008.

Much of the music transmits the feeling that the engineer pressed the record button in the middle of a jam session in which everyone was happily hanging behind the beat. Occasionally you hear some kind of clinking, maybe from Ms. Wilson's bracelet; she gooses the rhythm section with grunts, the way she might on a gig, or wanders off microphone and sings a few lines to the walls. Naturalism is the idea, but this is a beautifully constructed record, from Mr. Moran's blenderized, genre-defying piano solos to Ms. Wilson's judicious phrasing, using the full range of her double-smoked voice.

Selection 2.8

An incisive critic must do more than render verdicts on artists and music, as this argument on changes in the industry attests. Jon Pareles conveys a strong sense of the past, present and future of music as a commercial commodity. This excerpt represents about one-third of a longer piece.

MUSIC
Songs From the Heart of a Marketing Plan
By JON PARELES

In "Creator," the rawest track on Santogold's debut and self-titled album, the singer Santi White boasts, "Me I'm a creator/Thrill is to make it up/The rules I break got me a place up on the radar." It's a bohemian manifesto in a sound bite, brash and endearing, or at least it was for me until it showed up in a beer commercial. And a hair-gel commercial too.

It turns out that the insurgent, quirky rule breaker is just another shill. Billboard reported that three-quarters of Santogold's excellent album has already been licensed for commercials, video games and soundtracks, and Ms. White herself appears in advertisements, singing for sneakers. She has clearly decided that linking her music to other, mostly mercenary agendas is her most direct avenue to that "place up on the radar."

I know—time for me to get over it. After all, this is the reality of the 21st-century music business. Selling recordings to consumers as inexpensive artworks to be appreciated for their own sake is a much-diminished enterprise now that free copies multiply across the Web.

While people still love music enough to track it down, collect it, argue over it and judge their Facebook friends by it, many see no reason to pay for it. The emerging practical solution is to let music sell something else: a concert, a T-shirt, Web-site pop-up ads or a brand.

Published: December 28, 2008. Full text available at: www.nytimes.com/2008/12/28/arts/music/ 28pareles.html.

Musicians have to eat and want to be heard, and if that means accompanying someone else's sales pitch or videogame, well, it's a living. Why wait for album royalties to trickle in, if they ever do, when licensing fees arrive upfront as a lump sum? It's one part of the system of copyright regulations that hasn't been ravaged by digital distribution, and there's little resistance from any quarters; Robert Plant and Alison Krauss croon for J. C. Penney and the avant-rockers Battles are heard accompanying an Australian vodka ad.

The question is: What happens to the music itself when the way to build a career shifts from recording songs that ordinary listeners want to buy to making music that marketers can use? That creates pressure, subtle but genuine, for music to recede: to embrace the element of vacancy that makes a good soundtrack so unobtrusive, to edit a lyric to be less specific or private, to leave blanks for the image or message the music now serves. Perhaps the song will still make that essential, head-turning first impression, but it won't be as memorable or independent.

***

A Conversation with . . . **Jon Pareles**

CHIEF POPULAR MUSIC CRITIC

© The New York Times

A writer, critic and editor for the seminal Crawdaddy! and Rolling Stone as well as The Village Voice, Jon Pareles joined The New York Times in 1985 after three years of freelancing for the paper. He has been the chief pop critic since the late 1980s. With experience encompassing both alternative and mainstream publications, Pareles has long been one of the most respected critics in popular music. He combines a thorough grounding in music tradition that extends well beyond rock with an ear that remains open to the fresh and challenging, whatever the genre. This is an edited transcript of an e-mail interview.

With the wide range and sheer amount of popular music in New York, who at The Times decides what gets covered and who covers it?
The critics (me, Ben Ratliff, Nate Chinen, Jon Caramanica), pop reporter (Ben Sisario) and the pop editor (Sia Michel) decide. We're all constantly trawling through the new and interesting, and we make decisions on a pretty improvisational basis. We meet biweekly and e-mail all the time.

Sia Michel is the best all-around editor, from copy to interview negotiation, that I've ever worked with, hands down. She assigns and edits all features, daily and Arts & Leisure, working with critics, reporters and freelancers. When a critic comes to her with a good reason for doing a story, she hones the idea and helps it get done. For the Monday CD reviews, Sia makes the preliminary list and the critics choose from it or add to it. She's also aware of stories in other sections, like Business, Style or The New York Times Magazine.

In The Times tradition the chief critic is in charge of the concert reviewing schedule, which means that I (though sometimes Sia when I'm traveling) cull a list of potential concerts and send it to the other critics once a week, choosing the ones I want and sometimes nudging them to cover something. The two mostly-jazz critics who know that field better often add things. All the critics check off what they want to do, also adding things they're aware of. If there are conflicts, I make the decision, usually on the basis of seniority, but there is plenty to go around.

There's a hierarchy, but it's rarely invoked. To use an annoying word, the process is collegial. The Times, and I, trust the critics to know what's worth covering. We do like to vary who covers recurring events, so that even though I'm the chief pop critic, I don't cover Bruce Springsteen or Madonna every time around. I learn something from reading the other critics, and the reader gets variety.

How is covering music for The Times different than writing about it for a music-specific publication such as Rolling Stone? Or for a newspaper in a different city?
We write for a general reader rather than an avid music follower, so we make an effort to be straightforward and inviting. There are fewer inside references (No "It's like Slint meets dubstep"). And of course there's no profanity, which can demand some artful workarounds.

What has always surprised people about New York Times coverage—and this dates back at least to the time when John Rockwell and Robert Palmer were chief pop critics, and perhaps to when Robert Shelton plugged a guy named Dylan—is that we don't just cover the biggest things, but also music on numerous fringes. If a critic thinks it's interesting, we find a way to cover it, even if it's something as short as a Sunday Playlist item or a Weekend listing. It's different, strangely enough, from the music magazines I worked for long ago, which were always thinking about chart positions and reader demographics. We have less space, perhaps, but more freedom. We recognize the long tail. That's due to the nature of popular music, always bubbling up from some subculture, and also from the general policy of trusting the critics and reporters to know what's worth covering.

As for different cities, New York is the world's magnet city and America's media city. So we are always awash in possibilities, and we're always juggling big national-scale events with local ones. New York is also such a global city that, ideally, we would cover music in every community—and we do try to, with varying degrees of success. Papers in other cities have fewer concert choices nightly and less access to stars than The New York Times does, so we have both more possibilities and more triage. When I read newspapers from elsewhere, I see more stories with local angles and more coverage of local scenes. We can't be local boosters in the same way.

Since a lot of popular music is aimed at a younger audience, what critical standards do you apply when you plainly are not part of the target demographic?
There's a longer discussion I'll skip about the whole flawed idea of a target demographic. After all, rock 'n roll is all about what happens when the wrong demographic gets a hold of something and runs with it.

No, I'm not a teenage girl, but then again I never was. Still, I can recognize a well-made tune, a clever (or clichéd) lyric, an ingenious arrangement, a bright musical idea in general. I remember what it was like to be a lovesick high-schooler, an angsty college kid and some other target demographics, though not a ghetto kid or a good ole boy, which doesn't prevent me from enjoying hip-hop or country music. I also have a perspective that comes from, yes, decades of listening to popular music. Pop isn't a secret code only decipherable by target-demographic insiders (though they may have more clues). It's an attempt to communicate widely and often loud.

I'm really just trying to figure out the music for myself and then explain it clearly to the reader. I don't try to force 21st-century pop into some baby-boomer aesthetic. I'm fascinated, and often moved, by music made today for today's conditions. I'm also bored or left cold by a lot of it—just as I have been in previous decades. Yet I have always loved the way music can react instantaneously to or even predict the here and now, and I savor living in the present. I don't expect my take to be in any way definitive. I provide an individual reaction, which people are free to endorse or discount. A critic can't use someone else's ears or instincts.

There have been profound technological changes in the ways in which music is created and distributed. Do these changes affect the way you cover it as well?
Technology and popular music are inseparable, and I can only begin to enumerate the changes—most of them good—that digitization has brought to the job. I can get an album in minutes. I can take it anywhere. I can see videos and all of a performer's other public faces, as well as what matters to the fans. I can check facts instantly. And on the production side, the Web version of The New York Times provides new formats for sharing information, from podcasts to blogging—which, of course, also makes it possible to work nonstop feeding the blog. It's all a work in progress.

At some other publications, critics seem to have specialized beats—rock, jazz, country, hip-hop, whatever. Why do critics at The Times have more freedom to transcend categorical strictures?
It goes back to letting the critic decide what's worth covering. Few listeners stay entirely in one niche, and frankly, I don't trust a critic who does; it would be putting on blinders. (Just consider the number of genres referenced in a well-produced hip-hop album.) Practically speaking, there aren't that many of

us to cover a huge spectrum of music, and when someone asks for an assignment, I assume he has something to say about it.

How do you envision your readership?

Impatient, curious, literate, argumentative, with many different levels of involvement in music, from professional musicians to occasional listeners. Obviously they are reading because they want to know what's worth their ear time, or maybe to figure out what their children or parents are listening to. I'm sure that, like any writer, I reflexively and narcissistically assume that my reader is like me. But there's a reality check on that: I'm out nightly among all sorts of different people. I listen to them and talk to them, and I also want them to understand what I write if they choose to read it.

I get reader response from high-school students and septuagenarians and many people in between. Some are incredibly well-informed; some thank me for helping them discover something; some offer sidelights or reminiscences; some disagree vehemently. Let a hundred schools of thought contend.

What are the differences between the way a professional critic responds to music and the way a really passionate, knowledgeable fan does?

Critics are generalists (or dilettantes) and passionate fans are specialists. I don't expect to be as well-informed as some fans. I'm usually less starstruck and more analytical (though some fan bases are far more nit-picking). I do try to get the point of the music, and to make sure the facts are ironclad.

How do you keep up with everything? It isn't like being a movie critic, where there might be seven or eight releases on a busy week.

I don't keep up with everything. I just try. And I hope that the piles of unlistened-to CDs on my floor and downloads occupying my hard drive shouldn't have been my alternate priorities.

It's improvisational. One old-school thing—playing a show in New York—is probably the surest way to get my attention while I'm making the schedule. But I try to stay informed about everything else, too. And I open my own mail, so I do glimpse just about every new release. But I get 10 to 30 CDs every day, and I can only hear a fraction of that music.

How can an aspiring journalist best prepare for a career as a popular music critic?

I don't know if there are careers as popular music critics anymore, given the wreckage of music magazines and the shrinkage of newspapers. But assuming such careers still exist after graduation, the fundamental things apply: Listen and write and edit and rewrite. Learn to describe clearly and to build an argument. Get some historical background and context. One good exercise, for a real critic as opposed to a fan, is to listen to something popular that you dislike, figure out how it works and why it affects people, and also figure out and explain (persuasively) why you dislike it. And, whenever possible, leave your target demographic behind and listen to something way out of your niche. Maybe even dance to it.

MAKING**CONNECTIONS**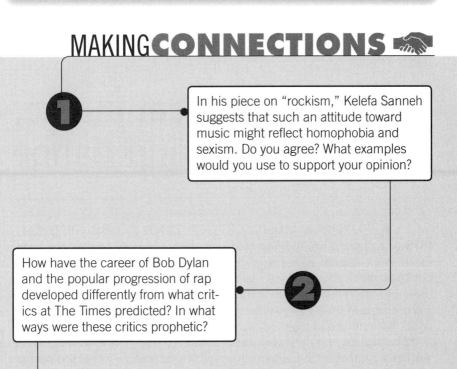

1 In his piece on "rockism," Kelefa Sanneh suggests that such an attitude toward music might reflect homophobia and sexism. Do you agree? What examples would you use to support your opinion?

How have the career of Bob Dylan and the popular progression of rap developed differently from what critics at The Times predicted? In what ways were these critics prophetic? **2**

 3 This chapter includes one piece from an African-American male (Kelefa Sanneh) and one from a white female (Ann Powers). The rest are all from white males. Are there any differences in attitude or perspective that you can see in these pieces, based on race and gender?

 4 Try the challenge suggested by Jon Pareles: "Listen to something popular that you dislike, figure out how it works and why it affects people, and also figure out and explain (persuasively) why you dislike it." Do it in such a way that doesn't suggest that you are inherently smarter than the people who like it. Does writing about this music change how you think or feel about it?

classical music, opera and dance

● POPULAR MUSIC CRITICS TEND TO BE GENERAL-
ISTS—English majors and pop culture mavens who may or may not know
much about musical theory. In fact, some of the musicians they cover may
not know much about musical theory, either. Classical musical critics, at least
those who aren't faking it, need to be specialists, grounded in theory, technique
and centuries of tradition, just like the music they cover. Many classical music
critics have studied or majored in music; few pop music critics have.

The challenge for the classical music critic is to apply his knowledge to the
work in ways that are illuminating for experienced readers yet not too confusing for the uninitiated. In the pieces that follow, analyze how well-versed you
need to be in the subject to find the writing of a particular piece engaging, the
argument provocative.

Another difference between pop and classical music coverage is that
the former is typically more concerned with the new—the new sensation,
the new hit, the next big thing. In classical music, tradition weighs a lot
more heavily, with the critic frequently mediating between the comfortingly
familiar and the shockingly fresh. In many of the pieces that follow, you'll
find that ongoing tension, a tug of war between the past and the future of
classical music.

The opening essay in this chapter directly addresses that tension by examining the implications of a "dying tradition," one steeped in the standards of
a couple of centuries ago. Orchestras and operas are expensive cultural insti-
tutions that rely on subscriptions and subsidies from wealthy patrons, many
of whom prefer to hear composers they know or musical values they find
familiar. When they think of classical music, they think of Beethoven, Brahms
and Bach.

Within that tradition, an expressionist such as Arnold Schoenberg or an
avant-garde composer such as John Cage might still seem unacceptably radical,
a half-century or more after his emergence. By contrast, the contemporary
audience for visual art has no problem accommodating Picasso and Pollock as
well as Rembrandt and Da Vinci, seeing the progression as part of a continuum.
In literature, 20th-century modernists such as Joyce, Fitzgerald and Faulkner

found widespread acclaim for fiction that responded to different places and different eras than that of Dickens.

Another of this chapter's selections shows how considerations of time and place have changed perceptions of Stravinsky, putting him in a different cultural context. "The Rite of Spring," a composition that initially sparked outrage, has become accepted within the tradition. An orchestra, opera or tradition-minded dance company must walk a tightrope in terms of repertoire: Daring to veer too much toward the new, it risks alienating a constituency; relying too much on the old, it becomes a relic, a museum piece. Again, here's that tug of war between the past and the future, mediated by the critic.

Where "The Rite of Spring" brought outrage to the classical music hall, in recent years some classical composers and performers have stepped outside the conservatory with music that has found favor with younger fans. Phillip Glass (reviewed here), Steve Reich and the Kronos Quartet are just a few of the artists who have straddled the divide between classical and popular music. A review by Allan Kozinn of new music shows artists who are all but obliterating that line.

Pop artists including Paul McCartney, Elvis Costello and Rufus Wainwright have dabbled in classical forms, to mixed/negative reviews from classical critics and general befuddlement from pop fans. Twyla Tharp has found inspiration for choreography in the music of Billy Joel and Bob Dylan, and has collaborated with David Byrne, formerly of Talking Heads. (This chapter also encompasses dance, where there's a similar tension between the old and new, though some dance troupes emphasize only the latter while many ballet companies lean toward the former.)

Meanwhile, the star power of some classical artists extends well beyond classical music. The only piece here not written by a classical critic provides an appreciation of Luciano Pavarotti, exploring his popular impact rather than the intricacies of his artistry—and that piece ran on the op-ed page of the paper. Notice the ways that this piece differs from those written by classical critics, and how its intended readership might differ as well.

The Times employs classical music critics specifically to cover orchestras, chamber music, opera, et al. and dance critics who specifically cover dance. Most other papers don't have that luxury (or sometimes even the luxury of covering classical music at all). At some, dance falls within the beat of the classical music critic; at a few, the theater critic also covers dance. Either approach makes some sense, depending on the qualifications of the critic.

Whatever specialized knowledge this beat requires, the initial response is visceral. In analyzing this gut reaction and arriving at an evaluation, the knowledgeable critic must then determine how much weight to give the composition, the conductor (or, in dance, the choreographer) or the orchestra (or dancers). Then he or she develops that argument in a manner that is engaging for the general reader and incisive for the classical devotee.

Selection 3.1

From rock music to the novel, critics often find themselves decrying the death of a form or celebrating a rebirth. The concern is even more crucial in classical music, which reaches a smaller audience and is popularly defined by tradition. This analysis from Edward Rothstein's "Connections" column (similar to the "Critic's Notebook" employed elsewhere in The Times' arts coverage) additionally shows how a book can provide a springboard for a piece of criticism that isn't a book review. Here he tackles the biggest question of all: If the classical tradition is dying, why should anyone care?

Connections
Classical Music Imperiled: Can You Hear the Shrug?
By EDWARD ROTHSTEIN

The sounds of a dying tradition are painful, particularly if the tradition's value is still so apparent, at least to the mourners, and still so vibrant to a wide number of sympathizers. Those melancholic strains can sometimes be sensed only on the edge of awareness, sounding like faint drones, heard only in moments of silence. But they are all the more distressing if the imminent demise seems a result of previous carelessness or willful neglect.

That is how I often think of the Western art-music tradition—the classical tradition—these days, and though I once tended to whine about its problems with cranky optimism, now even a stunning performance seems like a spray of flowers at a funeral.

O.K., this is a bit too melodramatic. There is no need after all to act like an extra in "A Song to Remember," or any other cinematic biopic from an era when names like Chopin or Beethoven could still command box-office attention, an era when émigré film-score composers imported the symphonic tradition into Hollywood.

I also don't idealize the idolatry that once enshrined the long 19th century of music (roughly 1785–1915) that forms the heart of the Western art-music tradition. But it is astonishing how little is now sensed about what might well be lost with it. And traditions do come to an end. The reading of ancient Greek and Latin—once the center of an educated person's life—now seems as rarefied as the cultivation of exotic orchids.

The title of Lawrence Kramer's new book, in fact, is exactly right: "Why Classical Music Still Matters" (University of California). It is the kind of title that would not have been used a generation ago, when debates about the musical scene might have involved titles more like "Why Contemporary Composers Don't Matter" or "Why Audiences Are Stuck in the Past."

Published: July 2, 2007.

What has changed is not how much the tradition means to its devotees, but how little it means to everyone else. From being the center of cultural aspiration, art music has become almost quaintly marginal; from being the hallmark of bourgeois accomplishment ("Someday you'll thank me"), music lessons have become optional attempts at self-expression; from appearing on newsmagazine covers, maestros now barely rate boldface in gossip columns.

Prescriptions have been plentiful, but so many years have gone by without significant music education in the schools and musical commitment in the homes, and so many ears have gotten used to different sounds and minds to different frames of references, that the question has changed from "What can be done?" to "Why should anything be done at all?"

Why, in other words, should we care? After decades of arguments asserting that different cultures just have different ways of expressing themselves, that distinctions and assertions of value are tendentious, and that Western art music deserves no pride of place in a multicultural American society, it may be that even the problem is no longer clearly seen. The premises have shifted.

Unfortunately I don't think the answers Mr. Kramer gives will make the difference, if any answers even can. Mr. Kramer—who teaches English literature and music at Fordham University and whose lyrical and suggestive studies of music and 19th-century culture have been fascinating contributions to recent musicology—sees the problem clearly enough. But in trying to explain the value of this repertory and its unique status he writes more like an introverted lover than an extroverted judge, more like someone gazing at its marvels from within than someone determined to articulate its virtues to a skeptical outside world.

"No other music tells us the things that this music does," Mr. Kramer writes, but those things don't entirely become clear in his retelling. This is not his weakness alone. When proselytizing for a nonverbal tradition, something is always lost in translation, and Mr. Kramer is sometimes too precious and allusive, given the magnitude of the task.

Nevertheless it is worth giving him close attention, and getting acquainted with his modes of expression ("Classical music allows us to grasp passing time as if it were an object or even a body"), because of the strength of his insights. He sees the ways melody (a "treasured, numinous object") and its troubled fate become the focus of attention in so much of this music, the ways dramas of loss and recovery seem to be played out again and again, and the ways music and film reveal each other's preoccupations.

He suggests, for example, why Rachmaninoff's Second Piano Concerto plays so central a role in the film "Brief Encounter." (It portrays "a deep subjectivity immune from manipulation or constraint by external forces," he says, expressing the yearning of the narrator who recalls her star-crossed love affair.)

In Mr. Kramer's explorations, though, one thing becomes clear: how many kinds of narratives can be extracted from the classical repertory. Theodor W. Adorno's criticism serves as a model, examining music as an emotional, intellectual and political drama in sound. A Beethoven symphony becomes an account of attitudes toward political authority and war, or an exploration of subjective feeling in a threatening world. "An American in Paris" by Gershwin has an "undertone of dissatisfied reflection" underneath the "prevailing high spirits," suggesting the fading spirit of the Jazz Age. The music Mr. Kramer calls classical becomes a kind of philosophical program music, recounting complex interactions between ideas and feelings.

The music's ability to sustain these kinds of readings—and be illuminated by them—is a more profound achievement than it might seem. Music of this period is shaped in the form of a narrative. Even technically—in terms of harmonic movement or (as Mr. Kramer suggests) melodic processes—a 19th-century composition is literally a story in sound, telling the picaresque adventures of a theme. But it is a story so abstract that it can attract extraordinarily different metaphorical retellings. It reaches so widely because of this openness; it reaches so deeply because of its taut construction.

The stories this music tells—which involve, as Mr. Kramer notes, tales of fate and circumstance, loss and confrontation—are dramas in which listeners have found their personal experiences and sentiments echoed in sound. Many compositions are public demonstrations, displaying all the grand scale and force of communal ritual, and were written for the newly developing concert halls.

There, for the first time, the bourgeois audiences could hear something of their own lives enacted in symphonic splendor—the dramas of desirous, independent citizens, yearning, struggling, loving, brooding, recognizing, regretting, learning—ultimately bound into a single society by the more abstract society of intertwined sounds reaching their ears. Those musical stories are still our own, although in the tradition's waning years we may, unfortunately, no longer feel compelled to listen.

Selection 3.2

Like the previous piece, this review tackles large questions, but this one is grounded in a single night's opera performance. Though a pop composition from 1980 might seem historical to pop audiences (classified as "classic rock"), the minimalism of Philip Glass and Steve Reich still challenges common perceptions of classical music. Note the distinction between "daring simplicity" and "simplistic." This piece includes all the essential elements of a performance review, but Anthony Tommasini provides a lot of context with his focus on audience response.

Music Review
'SATYAGRAHA': Fanciful Visions on the Mahatma's Road to Truth and Simplicity
By ANTHONY TOMMASINI

This is a fitting time to revisit Philip Glass's opera "Satyagraha," a landmark work of Minimalism. I take Mr. Glass at his word that when "Satyagraha" was introduced, in Rotterdam in 1980, he was following his own voice and vision, not firing a broadside against the complex, cerebral modernist composers who claimed the intellectual high ground while alienating mainstream classical music audiences. Happily, that divisive period is finally past.

Metropolitan Opera patrons, mostly bound by tradition, might not seem a likely source of Glass fans. But when Mr. Glass appeared onstage after the Met's first performance of "Satyagraha," on Friday night, the audience erupted in a deafening ovation.

"Satyagraha" (a Sanskrit term that means truth force) is more a musical ritual than a traditional opera. Impressionistic and out of sequence, it relates the story of Mohandas K. Gandhi's fight for the civil rights of the Indian minority in South Africa from 1893 to 1914. The staging—created by Phelim McDermott, director, and Julian Crouch, associate director and set designer, for the Met and the English National Opera, where it was seen last year—makes inventive use of fanciful imagery, aerialists, gargantuan puppets and theatrical spectacle to convey the essence of a self-consciously spiritual work.

Without knowing the events of Gandhi's struggles in South Africa you would have little idea what is going on, starting from the opening scene. Gandhi, portrayed by the sweet-voiced tenor Richard Croft in a heroic performance, lies on the ground in a rumpled suit, his suitcase nearby. The moment depicts an incident when Gandhi, as a young lawyer en route to Pretoria and holding a proper first-class ticket, was ordered to take his place with the Indians on board and, when he resisted, was pushed from the train onto the platform.

But this abstract production takes its cues from Mr. Glass, who was not interested in fashioning a cogent narrative. What continues to make the opera seem radical comes less from the music, with its lulling repetitions of defiantly simple riffs, motifs and scale patterns, than from the complete separation of sung text from dramatic action, such as it is.

The libretto, assembled by the novelist Constance DeJong, consists of philosophical sayings from the Bhagavad-Gita, the sacred Hindu epic poem. Mr. Glass honors the text by keeping it in the original Sanskrit and setting every syllable clearly. This production dispenses with Met Titles on the theory that the audience would actually be distracted by paying attention to the words, which at best serve as

Published: April 14, 2008.

commentary. Instead key phrases in English are projected on a semi-circular corrugated wall that forms the backdrop of the production's gritty and elemental set.

"Satyagraha" invites you to turn off the part of your brain that looks for linear narrative and literal meaning in a musical drama and enter a contemplative state—not hard to do during the most mesmerizing parts of the opera, especially in this sensitive performance. For example, in the hauntingly mystical opening scene when Gandhi reflects on a battle between two royal families depicted in the Bhagavad-Gita, Mr. Croft, in his plaintive voice, sang the closest the score comes to a wistful folk song while undulant riffs wound through the lower strings.

That the impressive young conductor Dante Anzolini, in his Met debut, kept the tempos on the slow side lent weight and power to the repetitive patterns. At times, though, during stretches in the opera when Mr. Glass pushes the repetitions to extremes, as in the wild conclusion to the final choral scene in Act I, the music became a gloriously frenzied din of spiraling woodwind and organ riffs.

Even in this breakthrough work Mr. Glass does not come across as a composer who sweats over details. He tends to rely on default repetitions of formulaic patterns, the only question being how often to repeat a phrase. Sometimes the daring simplicity just sounds simplistic. When he does work harder, fracturing the rhythmic flow or injecting some pungent dissonance into his harmonies, I am more drawn in.

In this regard Mr. Glass is different from another founding father of Minimalism, Steve Reich, whose music is just as repetitious as Mr. Glass's. But Mr. Reich has always had an ear for ingenious, striking and intricate detail.

Sometimes, with its aerial feats and puppetry, the Met production relies too much on stage activity. Still, it's quite a show. Mr. McDermott and Mr. Crouch have assembled a group of acrobats and aerialists called the Skills Ensemble, who produce magical effects. In one scene they form a huge puppet queen clothed in newspaper who goes to battle against a hulking puppet warrior assembled from wicker baskets. The use of simple materials is meant as homage to the poor, oppressed minorities for whom Gandhi gave his life.

Because Gandhi relied on the news media of his day to support his agitation for human rights and published his own journal, Indian Opinion, newspapers are a running image in the production. Actors fashion pages into symbolic barriers for protests. At one point, in despair, Gandhi disappears into a slithering mass of people and paper.

The cast entered into the ritualistic wonder of the work and the production despite solo and choral parts that are often formidably hard. It's almost cruel to ask male choristers to sing foursquare, monotone repetitions of "ha, ha, ha, ha" for nearly 10 minutes, as Mr. Glass does. Yet the chorus sang with stamina and conviction.

Besides Mr. Croft, other standouts in the excellent cast included the soprano Rachelle Durkin as Gandhi's secretary, Miss Schlesen; the mezzo-soprano Maria Zifchak as his wife; the bass-baritone Alfred Walker as Parsi Rustomji, a co-worker; and the baritone Earle Patriarco as Mr. Kallenbach, a European co-worker and ally. You are not likely to hear the long, ethereal sextet in the last act sung with more calm intensity and vocal grace than it was here.

Ultimately, despite its formulaic elements, "Satyagraha" emerges here as a work of nobility, seriousness, even purity. In the final soliloquy, timeless and blithely simple, Gandhi hauntingly sings an ascending scale pattern in the Phrygian mode 30 times. To some degree the ovation at the end, after a 3-hour-45-minute evening, was necessary. The audience had to let loose after all that contemplation.

Selection 3.3

This largely contextual piece ran under the same main headline along with more performance-specific reviews. Stravinsky, the composer whose most famous work sparked riots upon its debut, found an unlikely home in Los Angeles. Note how a change of place and the passage of the decades change the cultural context in which an artist is viewed.

MUSIC
Stravinsky: A Rare Bird Amid the Palms: A Composer in California, At Ease if Not at Home
By BERNARD HOLLAND

LOS ANGELES—It is both astonishing and perfectly normal that Igor Stravinsky passed nearly half of his mature life here. Astonishing, given the distance, both geographic and spiritual, from the St. Petersburg of his youth and the Paris of his first fame; normal, when we place the path of his composing career alongside this low-lying, near-endless tide of urban Southern California.

Los Angeles, after all, is where Julia Jean Mildred Turner became Lana and a part of history. When asked, this city acts as a shower bath, washing away an old life with the turn of a handle and asking no questions about the new clothes acquired afterward. Stravinsky changed musical identities at least four times, his nationality twice.

It has been said by people who do not wish it well that Los Angeles has no past and no future, only a present. The charge is untrue; the place is more. Yet for some the lure of the city is, indeed, its capacity for instant transformation. Stravinsky must have felt at ease if not at home. Whereas the career of Beethoven or Wagner was one long thread of becoming, Stravinsky led a musical life of seemingly disconnected

Published: March 11, 2001.

nows. He was challenged by the moment, eager to compete with the style or trend in front of him at the time and then to master it.

First he engaged the world of his teacher Rimsky-Korsakov: Russia's late-19th-century intersection of the Romantic and the primitive. Stravinsky successively flattered it ("The Firebird"), sharpened its aim ("Petrouchka"), then blew it to smithereens ("The Rite of Spring").

Against this music, how do we measure pieces like "The Soldier's Tale," coming just a few years later, in 1918: tight, glaring, dry-eyed, boogying its way through off-center rhythms and uneven meters? The Octet is a curt dismissal of personal sentiment and Expressionist fever, yet by 1930 Stravinsky had written the "Symphony of Psalms," the most chastely touching of all 20th-century religious works. When serialism began to sweep the musical world, Stravinsky was there to elevate Anton Webern to sainthood and turn out pieces like the "Canticum Sacrum" and "Requiem Canticles."

Taken in toto, the Hollywood film is Los Angeles's profound gift to culture, even if its artifacts, taken individually, often float giggling into space. Yet there is also here a strong and binding life of the arts, in which Stravinsky shared and which he used to his advantage. World War II generated colonies of distinguished émigrés. Europeans like Thomas Mann, Arnold Schoenberg, Franz Werfel, George Balanchine and Arthur Rubinstein all came, dazed both by the horrific events in their homelands and by the seductive flora and tropical breezes of Southern California.

Otto Klemperer was the music director of the Los Angeles Philharmonic when Stravinsky made his first visit, in 1935, five years before moving there. Esa-Pekka Salonen now directs the orchestra, and he has been remembering a distinguished neighbor with a month-long series of Stravinsky concerts and events, to be replicated in part next weekend at Lincoln Center.

A curious pilgrim follows a colonnade of three-story palm trees along Doheny Drive, across frenetic Sunset Boulevard and up the narrow winding street to 1260 North Wetherly Drive. The Stravinsky house is small—white stucco and wood—on rising ground and sheltered by green growth around it. The interior, we are told, was artful clutter: the furniture was worn; the books were many. North Wetherly was the site of Stravinsky's first sustained domestic happiness after the lingering illnesses and deaths of his first wife and his older daughter, and his subsequent marriage to Vera de Bosset Sudeikina in Bedford, Mass. Two of Stravinsky's four children eventually came to America: Soulima, teaching piano at the University of Illinois, and Milene, settling in Los Angeles.

The Stravinsky friends were polyglot, international and many. There were the Russian and German enclaves, but also a detachment of British writers, like W. H. Auden, Christopher Isherwood, Dylan

Thomas (who shared the composer's taste for hard spirits) and, especially, Aldous Huxley, with whom Stravinsky spoke in French.

Years later, Mr. Salonen considered buying the house, which had fallen on hard times. The conductor noted the carpet indentations where the great man's pianos had stood, the hook where a goat had been tethered (Stravinsky liked the milk) and the built-in couch where Thomas had slept off more than a few over indulgences. An aspiring composer himself, Mr. Salonen wisely feared the presence of ghosts.

Klemperer and others performed Stravinsky's pieces at the Philharmonic. The composer himself appeared as pianist and conductor. Even the gaping Hollywood Bowl embraced the Stravinsky of "The Firebird." The publisher Boosey & Hawkes eventually provided him a comfortable annual retainer, and there were the constant tours and travels for a man less famous than Clark Gable but not too far behind.

This month and last, the peripheral events around town have included small dramatizations ("A Word With Igor" at the Los Angeles Central Library), panel discussions on Stravinsky's influence here ("The Eclectic Stravinsky" at the Armand Hammer Museum at U.C.L.A.) and reminiscences of recording sessions and concerts from those who were there.

A recent program of the Los Angeles Philharmonic at the Dorothy Chandler Pavilion offered instructive contrasts: the ballet score "Agon," the little opera "Mavra," in concert form, and "The Rite of Spring." "Mavra" is one-act Pushkin, Stravinsky's rustic little stab at Russian folklore.

"Agon," conforming to its title, is a contest between the tonal and the not-so-tonal. It is music of Stravinsky's old age: the temperature has cooled; the detachment from the audience and from practical performance problems is pronounced. "Agon," indeed, is ballet music of extraordinarily complicated stops and starts, and asymmetrical counterpoint. The Los Angeles players had a hard time with it. Run-of-the-mill ballet orchestras must find it defeating.

What a different world is "The Rite of Spring," this wild beast of a piece that even after 88 years and thousands of performances, still tears at the listener's viscera. It speaks to the young, and an unusually youthful audience stomped and yelled with enthusiasm.

The evening began with Stravinsky's eerie harmonization and arrangement of "The Star-Spangled Banner," a basic American artifact heard through distinctly distant ears. Stravinsky's oblique little act of wartime patriotism offers proof like no other that this great man, although among us, was not one of us.

He was to move once again, at the very end of his life, this time to New York, where he died in 1971. Los Angeles had evidently lost its pull. Was it the smog of which the great man complained, or was it a tired sensibility's need for the extremes of the seasons? Maybe Stravinsky moved just to move. New York was one more place not to belong.

Selection 3.4

As we shift here to ballet, the tug of war that dominates this chapter remains the same. Note how Alastair Macaulay advances his central argument, expressed through the opening exclamation and the lead paragraph as a whole, through descriptions of a lot more pieces than you're likely to find in a classical music review. Yet the descriptive summaries never succumb to play-by-play; they are offered in the service of a general thesis.

DANCE REVIEW
What Audiences Haven't Seen Before
By ALASTAIR MACAULAY

SAN FRANCISCO—Novelty as cause for celebration! In ballet, an art so often stuffed with the same old chestnuts, it takes real courage to promote creativity rather than conservation. Diaghilev remains the exemplar here, but in this regard the United States has led the world for several decades. The concept of presenting a multiple-program bonanza of new choreography goes back to the 1972 Stravinsky Festival of New York City Ballet. That event included old works too, but its wealth of innovation became the stuff of legend. At least four of the new works choreographed then have gone into international ballet repertory.

One of that festival's dancers was Peter Martins, who now runs City Ballet. In 1988 he staged its American Music Festival along the same lines, and then, starting in 1992, he began a series of occasional, somewhat festival-like spring Diamond Projects, each of which has produced multiple new works within weeks. Another of those 1972 dancers was Helgi Tomasson. Since 1985 he has run San Francisco Ballet, which is now reaching the climax of its 75th-anniversary season by presenting a New Works Festival that bids to rival City Ballet in the new-choreography stakes.

Ten world premieres by 10 choreographers are occurring over three nights; some of the scores are commissioned, and these programs will continue for just over two weeks. Since the choreographers include Paul Taylor, Mark Morris, Christopher Wheeldon, James Kudelka, Jorma Elo, Stanton Welch and Yuri Possokhov, the season is automatically of national and international significance.

The festival began on Tuesday with a gala-type account of Program A (most of the audience was in evening dress): a triple bill of Mr. Possokhov's "Fusion," Mr. Wheeldon's "Within the Golden Hour" and Mr. Taylor's "Changes." "Fusion" and "Within the Golden Hour" feature handsome décors and costumes and are set to

Published: April 24, 2008.

attractively interesting music; both show their creators extending their ranges and adding to their craft.

"Fusion" is an East-meets-West ballet. Set mainly to jazz-related music by the British composer Graham Fitkin, but opening with Middle Eastern-sounding music composed by Rahul Dev Burman, as arranged by the Kronos Quartet, it includes four men dressed approximately as (sometimes whirling) dervishes; four women who might be modern odalisques; and four other men whose bare-armed look is more Western. Above, a row of small screens hang like flags; James L. Ingall's lighting changes them from orange to blue and back again. (At one point dervish movement is projected onto some of them.)

Though separate style ingredients are shown—the dervishes bend their thoraxes in and out like bellows; the women (on point) have jumps and positions with winged arms—this is, as the title indicates, a melting pot ballet. Both women and men even get to do, daffily, the same little pelvic wiggles. There are male-female pas de deux and single-sex group dances, but the emphasis is on flow, on overlap, on coexistence. It's not without structural intelligence, and all of it is mildly agreeable.

"Within the Golden Hour" shows from first to last that Mr. Wheeldon's gifts of construction are more complex and skilled: it's generally beautiful. The music, by the Italian composer Ezio Bosso, is an appealing series of strings-only numbers, sometimes featuring solo violin and viola, and in parts drawing on Baroque material (in the manner of Tippett's delectable "Fantasia Concertante on a Theme of Corelli"); the costumes are in sensuous shades of green, amber and blue (with women wearing dresses over tights of the same color).

Magpielike, Mr. Wheeldon includes—as he often has before— choreographic devices better known from a wide range of other dancemakers, including Mr. Taylor (perhaps for the first time) and, certainly, Frederick Ashton (a favorite Wheeldon source, especially in his American commissions). There are 14 dancers, used in various groups, arranged to frame and separate four distinct pas de deux. Of these, the second is for two men, bright, brisk and winning; sharing the same material; moving together but without physical contact.

In each of the three other duets, however, man partners woman. The focus, here as in other Wheeldon male-female pairings, is almost always on the lines and shapes shown by the woman, so that we may hardly realize that the guiding impulse comes as a rule from the man, who pushes or pulls, lifts and lowers, turns and steers her. Each duet successfully establishes and sustains its own different mood.

Though all the women (Katita Waldo, Sarah van Patten and Maria Kochetkova) are responsive and handsome, I couldn't help wishing, here as in previous pieces, that Mr. Wheeldon would allow even one of them some serious signs of independence. There are memorable lifts, but these tend to be ends in themselves, without real expressive integrity, dynamically shaped as if they should be applauded. The larger group dances are entirely well shaped, and the ending—everyone joining into a machinelike group that pulsates from side to side—is the work's masterstroke.

Because Mr. Possokhov and Mr. Wheeldon have evidently enriched their own lexicons and capabilities, I ought to applaud them here more than I do. For the same reason, perhaps I should applaud Mr. Taylor less than I do them, for there's hardly a jump or lift or pose in his new "Changes" that he hasn't often shown before. Unlike "Within the Golden Hour," "Changes" doesn't end on a wow note but instead recapitulates its opening scene, as the curtain falls.

Yet "Changes" reminds me how, in 1988, Mr. Taylor's contribution to City Ballet's American Music Festival ("Danbury Mix") was, brilliantly, set to the most imaginatively original of all American composers, Charles Ives, and so went to the heart of that festival's idea. Likewise, "Changes" addresses a core era of San Francisco history: the 1960s. Danced to songs by the Mamas and the Papas, it recreates, in affectionate but near-cartoon terms, the nonconformist liberalism of Haight-Ashbury and the Berkeley campus.

We see the haircuts, the fashions, the dances (the hitchhike, the mashed potato, the Watusi) of that era; we see the characters, the actions (dope-sharing is mimed), the vitality and the surprising innocence. Mr. Taylor, as is his wont in these circumstances, rehearsed it with his own company; his former star Patrick Corbin then taught it to 11 San Francisco dancers. And seldom if ever have any performers who were not Taylor specialists ever caught the features of the Taylor style so well, always using their weight and three-dimensional physicality to make the movement strong, always filling a phrase sharply against its music.

In "California Earthquake" Courtney Elizabeth is a wild and liberated star who keeps, literally, knocking a crowd dead. In "I Call Your Name" Pauli Magierek dances radiantly with four men who lift her, upend her but always show that she is queen bee. Aaron Orza and Benjamin Stewart make "Dancing Bear" a work of childish dreams and adult protectiveness. And in "California Dreams" the ensemble surges, rotates and throbs in a joyously mixed paean. Forty years on, Mr. Taylor's "Changes" has given San Francisco images of itself in the 1960s, the very time when it seemed to change world culture.

Selection 3.5

Ultimately the question of whether a work is old or new isn't as important as whether it's any good. Here's an example of a funny review that even those who know nothing about dance would find more entertaining than the performance. Alastair Macaulay takes an idea he might have tried for a single paragraph and sustains the tone for the whole piece. Instead of simply expressing his disdain, he makes it funny, in a manner that drips with irony.

Dance Review | Los Vivancos
They Are Men, Hear Them Roar
(and Stomp, Tap, Break Dance and Pirouette)

By ALASTAIR MACAULAY

On Sunday night in Battery Park, at the end of one of those late-summer evenings when the view across the harbor to the Statue of Liberty makes you wonder if Venice and St. Petersburg have so very much more to offer, the River to River Festival presented Los Vivancos, seven Spanish brothers, as part of its Evening Stars series. The program advised us that "the backbone of the show is flamenco, and it is augmented by a variety of musical and dance disciplines, including some of the more graceful movements from the martial arts, break dancing, ballet, theater and the circus."

However, each Vivancos seemed to this observer to be delivering the same extended proclamation, as follows: "Just look how I brood, how I smolder, how I frown, how I suffer. Am I not gorgeous? I am even more gorgeous than my brothers. See how I drum my heels into the floor; see how I sweat; I am a real man. Applaud me!

"I am such a stud, and so moody; I am on fire for you. Yes, these spotlights show how fast my knees tremble while I tap my feet: what could be more exciting? Look! I just did four pirouettes while falling off balance. I do big ballet jumps too—I can quote phrases from the ballet 'Don Quixote'—and all to get you going. And so what if I don't straighten my legs? I am much too unbelievably virile for that. Do you like these short shirts we wear and the way they ride up to show our stomachs? Applaud me!

"As you see, as you hear, we Vivancos play musical instruments and we mix flamenco with tap, ballet, break dancing, acrobatics. O.K., we do not do any of these things with true refinement, but admit it! We are men! This is dance as rock concert, yes, but so much more artistic. Does not our intense artistry drive you wild with desire?

"Yes, you guessed it, now we start to remove our clothing, for you alone. Look at these arms, these shoulders, these gleaming abs, so chiseled, so desirable: what men we are, and how completely hand-some. Now I rotate my wrists—so glamorous, such true flamenco—and I let you admire my pecs almost as much as you want.

"Ah! This is my big solo. I never do more than one phrase at a time. After each phrase I demand your applause, and I breathe hard to show you how much my art torments me. I know what you like. No tights were ever tighter than these. Do you not adore my rhythm, my crescendo?

Published: September 9, 2008.

"Now do you not worship this intensely artistic number where two of us wear cream-colored tail coats and dance in unison? How we pose, strut, storm, swirl. We are peacocks! And now we are matadors! I remove my coat, press it to my cheek (so meaningful, so sincere), then dash it to the ground. I am Man, and oh! so manly.

"No, this is not real sweat. Whenever I go into the wings, I put water into my hair so that I can return and shower the stage with moisture when I do. How manly, how hard-working this makes me seem, yes? And how civilized: in this duel number, I and my brother play fragments of Paganini, Dvorak, Bach to the same loud rock beat and with the same flamenco flourishes: is this not tasteful? See our passion, our ardor, our game that we two men resent and admire each other at the same time. Our Spanishness, our pride, our honor: are these not sensational?

"Now in this final number I and my brothers descend—bare-chested—into the audience. And you stand to applaud us! Who could resist us? Did we hear someone say, 'The end of the world will be like this?' Yes! Maybe it will. We are Los Vivancos. Our virility is total."

Selection 3.6

As we continue with circus and spectacle, here's a piece about opera tenor Luciano Pavarotti as popular phenomenon, written by a nonclassical critic, appearing as an op-ed column rather than in the arts section. Both the broader readership and the cultural concerns are significantly different; note the subtle ambivalences of the evaluation.

Tenor of the Times

By DAVID HAJDU

On Sept. 13, 1994, Luciano Pavarotti and Bryan Adams stood side by side before a symphony orchestra assembled on a vast outdoor stage in Modena, Italy, Mr. Pavarotti's hometown, and they performed a duet of "O Sole Mio." Mr. Pavarotti, beaming, sang the hoary old heart-stopper beautifully, almost as if he had not done it several jillion times before. Mr. Adams croaked and giggled and clutched the microphone in palpable terror. The performance, which was televised internationally and later released on video, survives on YouTube. Watching it now, in the wake of Mr. Pavarotti's death from pancreatic cancer, one can only marvel at the incongruity of the scene and wonder what in the world was that rock star doing in the company of that guy Adams?

Luciano Pavarotti was, among many things—perhaps above all—a rock star, regardless of the fact that the music he sang happened

Published: September 8, 2007.

The New York Times

to be opera or, on occasion, folk or popular music in the operatic mode. To recognize this is not to deny his profound gifts as an artist or to diminish his importance as the most beloved tenor of the post-war era. He was blessed with a stunningly gorgeous voice, pure yet unmistakable, which he employed with ardor in the service of beauty and joy. He brought countless listeners, including this one, to rapture.

In addition, as waves of encomiums in recent days have reminded us, his enormous appeal gave Mr. Pavarotti an evangelical dimension. More than anyone since Enrico Caruso, we are repeatedly told, Mr. Pavarotti brought opera to the masses. This is true, but not the whole truth: more than anything, what Mr. Pavarotti did was bring mass culture—particularly the sensibility of the rock 'n' roll age—to the world of opera.

He came to see his work as a mission of outreach. In this, he was carrying on a tradition as old as opera itself. Performers, promoters and civic leaders have worked for centuries to connect opera with the populace. In the American Old West, every frontier town worth its tumbleweed erected an opera house between the Wells Fargo station and the saloon. In the early 20th century, every vaudeville bill had a "class" act—a soprano or a vocal duo who would sing excerpts from an aria or two between the magicians and the jugglers.

Mr. Pavarotti, following the lead of his hard-driving, open-eyed manager, Herbert Breslin, veered away from full-scale operas in traditional halls and branched into the recital business, where his buoyant personality could flourish and his indifference to acting and his reluctance to learn new roles would not be significant liabilities. Mr. Breslin pushed him into the mold of rock stardom, and he fit nicely. Mr. Pavarotti was the first opera star to be booked in Madison Square Garden, and he became an arena attraction, the aria Elvis. He played Vegas; he did "The Tonight Show"; he was the musical guest on "Saturday Night Live"; he starred in a Hollywood movie, "Yes, Giorgio."

Although the singer and manager parted ways acrimoniously, Mr. Pavarotti stayed for the rest of his career in the mold set by Mr. Breslin. He expanded his audience through his arena tours with Plácido Domingo and José Carreras, and through a series of concerts with rock and pop singers including James Brown, Celine Dion, Meat Loaf and the Spice Girls, not to mention Bryan Adams.

What was it about Luciano Pavarotti that made him so popular among people who otherwise showed no special affection for opera? He had a peasant quality that made up for his performing an art usually associated with a cultured elite. He had a robust earthiness that signified authenticity, especially to Americans of the postwar era who prized ruralism and took vernacular artists to be truer, more legitimate, than trained urban professionals. Mr. Pavarotti, who never mastered reading music, was a largely intuitive musician, and that seemed to come across to his advantage.

He was, if not larger than life, larger in size than most humans. Indeed, he was practically the embodiment of an opera-hater's parody conception of a male opera singer—so huge he could hardly support his own weight, robustly Italian, blustering, flamboyant and oddly child-like. With his heavy beard and long, wavy hair, his enormous eyebrows permanently cocked in seeming puzzlement, and his habitually broken English, Mr. Pavarotti seemed almost like a character from a Warner Bros. cartoon come to life, ready to sing a chorus of "Kill the Wabbit!" All this, I suspect, may well have helped him endear himself to a public inured to pop stars who look and act very much like cartoons and self-parodies.

Never much disposed to the acting side of opera, Mr. Pavarotti learned in time to play Pavarotti, regardless of the character he was supposed to be. He drew from his own personality, like a popular singer, and his sensibility was exuberant, boyish, inclined to emotional extremes, and not very reflective. The kind of opera he gave us was, on the whole, a music of voluptuous emotion, little darkness, and not much thought. There was melodrama but little drama; there were out-cries of pain, but scarcely any doubt, no melancholia.

The opera of Mr. Pavarotti was always thrilling and rarely chal-lenging. It was something less than opera in the fullness of its dramatic potential. Still, it had a beauty that was practically unnatural in its per-fection. It always made me happy, and it was grand, like the man who made it.

Selection 3.7

The chapter returns full circle with the same tension between old and new, tradition and innovation, as it pertains to opera, employing the news peg of a big announcement from one opera company to examine the issue in a broader context. Tommasini is not only predicting audience reaction but examining his own. Here is the way in which opera moves forward, and here are the risks.

MUSIC
In Charting Its Future, City Opera Chooses an Adventurous Path
By ANTHONY TOMMASINI

The most vibrant performing arts institutions strive to find a balance between hewing to a historic mission and branching into new territory. If done right, which usually means gradually, adventurous initiatives and dynamic change can be not just artistically enriching but smart business as well.

But the recent announcement from the New York City Opera about its plans for the next two seasons suggests that this essential 65-year-old company, called the People's Opera by Mayor Fiorello La Guardia, is poised for a near-complete makeover. Its very iden-tity could change under its new leader, Gerard Mortier, the brilliant, unabashedly provocative director of music festivals and opera com-panies in Europe. Clearly, though Mr. Mortier does not officially become the City Opera's general and artistic director until the fall of 2009, he has been pivotal to the company's plans for next season, which looks to be a nonseason.

As widely reported, the New York State Theater will undergo major renovations. The work will be scheduled so that New York City Ballet can essentially continue its offerings. But the City Opera

Published: June 4, 2008.

will be without a home for the 2008–9 season. This displacement, compounded by financial shortfalls, has forced the company's hand.

To present staged productions in locales around the city would have resulted in an unsustainable deficit. Instead, in place of the roughly 120 staged performances it routinely presents each season, the City Opera will offer 90-minute concerts in each borough as well as panel discussions, lectures and opera movies. There will be only one opera, in concert performances: Barber's "Antony and Cleopatra," starring the company's longtime prima donna Lauren Flanigan.

There's not much of a theme to this collection of offerings, but the concerts look intriguing, with programs focused on Messiaen, Stravinsky, Britten and Debussy, giants whose operas will be produced in Mr. Mortier's inaugural season. The idea is to whet the audience's appetite for the contemporary fare Mr. Mortier intends to champion.

The problem is that such events serve that purpose best when presented in conjunction with a production of a challenging opera, as the San Francisco Opera showed when it staged the premiere of John Adams's "Doctor Atomic" in 2005. In preparation for the opera itself, audiences in the city could attend panel discussions about the physicist Robert Oppenheimer and the world-changing development of the nuclear bomb, and hear Mr. Adams speak about his new opera and preside over performances of his music.

Mr. Mortier is making the best of a bad situation. But will City Opera regulars drift away during this season without staged opera? The company will be counting on re-emerging in 2009 with a refurbished profile.

Mr. Mortier has promised bold, cutting-edge productions of landmark 20th-century operas. Stravinsky's "Rake's Progress" will be presented at an off-campus site to be determined, and a new staging of Philip Glass's "Einstein on the Beach" will inaugurate the renovated house. There will be imported productions, like the English National Opera's stark and haunting staging of Britten's "Death in Venice" starring Ian Bostridge as Aschenbach, a hit in London. There will also be new productions of Debussy's "Pelléas et Mélisande," Janacek's "Makropulos Case" and, at long last, the first New York staging of Messiaen's challenging five-hour masterpiece, "St. François d'Assise," which Mr. Mortier wants to present in the Park Avenue Armory.

A season focused on formidable 20th-century works will excite many opera lovers, including me. The programming makes a statement that a people's opera does not have to play it safe and be afraid to challenge audiences. Besides, over the last couple of seasons at the City Opera, disappointing box-office receipts for standard fare have indicated that the company cannot rely on appealing productions of "Carmen" to keep the lights on.

Yet will there be something as well for Puccini lovers, for aficionados of Handel, for the regulars who have been crucial to the City Opera over the years? At its best, the company has staged engrossingly updated productions of staples with winning young casts. On March 20, for example, PBS's "Live From Lincoln Center" presented the City Opera's "Madama Butterfly," an abstract, austerely beautiful production by Mark Lamos with two very attractive and vocally rewarding leads: the Chinese soprano Shu-Ying Li as Cio-Cio San and the American tenor James Valenti as Pinkerton.

Like his predecessor Paul Kellogg, Mr. Mortier understands that the City Opera cannot be the Metropolitan Opera Lite, simply a more affordable and approachable place to hear standard repertory. And with Peter Gelb at the Met working overtime to reinvigorate that company with theatrically innovative productions, not to mention a multimedia outreach effort that has shaken up the international opera world, it is more essential than ever that the City Opera have its own identity.

One problem is that over the last two decades the Met has introduced into its repertory compelling productions of most of the 20th-century works Mr. Mortier will offer in his inaugural season, the exceptions being "St. François d'Assise" and "Einstein on the Beach."

Mr. Mortier is going to bring another major change. The company will essentially be shifting to the "stagione" system of presenting works. Many companies, like the Met, are repertory houses, in which a large number of productions circulate throughout the season, with a different show each night. Stagione houses present one production at a time for a limited run, sometimes with a little overlapping. The advantages are obvious: a company gets to focus all its attention, and its promotional machinery, on a single show. The drawbacks are also obvious: there are many more dark nights for the theater, when the cast of the current production is resting up.

Again, for New York to have a stagione house is an interesting departure. It will certainly set the City Opera apart from the Met. But this is a lot of change for a single company and its audience to absorb at once.

As someone who has been exasperated by the stodginess of many American orchestras and opera companies, I find it odd to be worried about whether the City Opera is going too far too fast. Mr. Mortier is banking on the idea that when the City Opera presents "Einstein on the Beach" or "Death in Venice," these will be events that no opera fan or theatrically curious New Yorker will want to miss. It's an exciting and precarious gamble.

Selection 3.8

Finally, this essay offers the most radical vision for the future of classical music, from a classical critic who doubles as the Beatles' expert at The Times, and who seems very open to inspiration beyond the typical confines of the recital hall. Note how someone who loves both classical and rock has been dismayed at most attempts to combine the two. Can classical music mean this as well as Beethoven?

Mining Pop for Avant-Garde Inspiration

By ALLAN KOZINN

Something odd and fascinating is happening at the borders of classical music and pop right now. Particularly in new-music circles, young musicians are searching for repertory in the pop avant-garde.

There were inklings of this in the early 1990s, when arrangements of Frank Zappa pieces turned up in programs by the Meridian Arts Ensemble, the American Composers Orchestra and, in Europe, Ensemble Modern and the Ensemble Intercontemporain. But that seemed only modestly remarkable. Zappa, after all, had been composing symphonic works since the late 1960s, and these transcriptions of his rock works shared the spirit of those scores. And transcriptions of Jimi Hendrix songs by the Kronos Quartet, and Nirvana tracks by the Bang on a Can All-Stars, seemed amusing stunts, offered as encores.

More recently the pianist Christopher O'Riley has devoted full CDs to transcriptions of songs by Radiohead and the melancholy songwriter Nick Drake; and Alarm Will Sound, the inventive chamber orchestra, has been fascinated with electronica, having recorded an album of its own transcriptions of Aphex Twin's brashly amusing pieces and gone on to arrange works by Autechre, Mochipet and Preshish Moments, as well as proto-electronica oldies by the Beatles ("Revolution 9") and Varèse ("Poème Électronique").

Alarm Will Sound played a concert of these pieces at Le Poisson Rouge a couple of weeks ago and has a second transcribed-electronica (acoustica, as the group puts it) CD due in the fall. Mr. O'Riley is about to release a new disc with songs by Nirvana, Radiohead, Pink Floyd and other groups and will perform them at the Highline Ballroom on Aug. 24.

Suddenly, it seems, something new is happening: When they play this music (and they play more conventional repertory as well), Alarm Will Sound and Mr. O'Riley are a Bizarro World version of Arthur Fiedler and the Boston Pops. Granted, where symphonic pops orchestras typically take million-selling hits and coat them in sugary strings and lithe winds—in effect, eviscerating them—Mr. O'Riley and Alarm Will Sound aim for something closer to the spirit of the dark-hued and often rhythmically or harmonically complex originals they seem drawn to.

Given a choice, I prefer this new model, but I've never understood the appeal of symphonic pops. As a fan of symphonic music I find pops programs embarrassingly lightweight, and as a fan of rock I find the wimpy arrangements pops orchestras play execrable.

I guess I'm an original-instrument guy at heart. It's not just me. Leonard Bernstein loved the Beatles and other rock composers:

Published: August 9, 2009.

he played snippets of their music at the piano in his Young People's Concerts, and in one of his last interviews he compared the songs of John Lennon and Paul McCartney to those of Schubert. But you wouldn't have caught him waving a baton at the New York Philharmonic as it poured out a treacly, bright-eyed version of "I Want to Hold Your Hand."

I don't think you'd catch Alarm Will Sound playing that kind of thing either. It is no accident that the one Beatles song in its repertory is the group's least popular (if most adventurous) piece.

Mr. O'Riley has the tougher job. In reducing Radiohead's inventive palette to the keyboard, he risks making the music sound like Chopin or Debussy, with Radiohead themes substituted for the originals. Sometimes he succumbs. But when his arrangements work—in "Airbag" and "Black Star," where he suggests the sonic grandeur of the originals if not the timbres, or in the gentle "Exit Music (for a Film)"—they put the music's disquieting essence in an unusual perspective and tell you something about its structure that you can miss in the kaleidoscopic originals.

Yet there is something to be said for the kaleidoscope, and you shortchange it at your peril. In that regard Alarm Will Sound has its limitations too. Electronica tends to draw on disparate sources, many so electronically modified that approximating them persuasively with orchestral instruments is impossible. It can be fascinating to watch Alarm Will Sound make the effort. At its Poisson Rouge concert it created effects by rubbing sheets of paper together before the microphones, and with percussion instruments large and small.

In "Revolution 9" it may have helped that Lennon sampled classical works (a Vaughan Williams choral piece, a climactic chord from Sibelius's Seventh Symphony). I admired the ingenuity of Matt Marks's arrangement, which captured most of the notes, sounds and idiosyncratic spoken sections of the Beatles track. Missing, though, was the mixing-board virtuosity that gives this piece its cinematic eeriness and makes it a visceral evocation of a revolution in progress. In the end the best you could say was "Nice try."

I have nothing against Mr. O'Riley's interest in Radiohead and company or Alarm Will Sound's fascination with electronica (and off-the-edge nonelectronic rock groups like the Shaggs). I wish their versions uniformly worked better than they do. But you find yourself suspecting that Marshall McLuhan was right after all: where this music is concerned, at least, the medium is the message.

Still, I have a suggestion for these performers. Now that they have undoubtedly caught the attention of Radiohead, Aphex Twin and others in their borrowed repertory, why not commission those musicians to write works specifically for them and for the instruments they play? That would expand the repertory in a useful way and let the composers stretch as well.

MAKING**CONNECTIONS**

1 What is the relationship between the "classical music" that most of these pieces concern and what Allan Kozinn terms "new music"? Are these different genres or part of the same continuum?

In David Hajdu's appreciation, he asks, "What was it about Luciano Pavarotti that made him so popular among people who otherwise showed no special affection for opera?" Does he answer the question? If so, how? Is Pavarotti's popularity a sign of his greatness, an artistic flaw or both? **2**

3 Alastair Macaulay's review of Los Vivancos takes an entirely different tone from other reviews. Is this effective satire or critical overkill?

4

As stated throughout, many of these pieces concern the challenge of keeping the offerings fresh and new while pleasing audiences who prefer traditional work. Explain how at least three different writers address this problem. What do you think the solution is?

visual arts

IN NO CULTURAL AREA DOES The Times distinguish itself more from other general-interest journalism than in covering the visual arts. Where most newspapers devote scant or no attention, The Times highlights such coverage with its Friday fine arts section as well as daily reviews and pieces in its Sunday arts section. New York is the nation's capital for the visual arts, and The New York Times is its paper of record.

Critiquing the visual arts is also the area where fledgling critics—at least those who aren't art majors—are generally least comfortable. As with classical music and the other fine arts, the visual arts require more of a specialist's than a generalist's knowledge. But most students are fans of some form of music and can shift at least some elements within that frame of reference (virtuosity, dynamics, emotional impact) to a form of music with which they're less familiar.

With the visual arts, neophytes often aren't sure where to begin. In some cases they can't help wondering whether a painting or sculpture or video installation even qualifies as art at all. As with other forms of criticism, the response starts with a gut reaction. For a professional critic, this reaction is conditioned by an encyclopedic knowledge of artistic progression and legacy, a recognition that all art is in some ways a response to art that has come before and that we need to know where art has been in order to know where it's going.

There are different but sometimes related questions we face with each of the visual arts: Is the painting realistic or abstract? Does the photograph reflect, interpret or alter reality? Is the piece of sculpture representational? How well does the architecture fit within its surroundings, serve the function of the building with its form and generate aesthetic pleasure?

So where does the fledgling critic start? Let's return to the elements of criticism introduced early in this volume, for it's in the field of visual arts that these signposts provide the clearest step-by-step path toward a critique. First, description: What *is* this painting, photo, sculpture or architecture? How can we describe it so that the reader can see it through our words? What size, colors, textures, shapes?

Next, context. This step might take some research, requiring the student to learn what the professional critic would already know from decades of experience. If this is an exhibition of work by a single artist, where does this artist fit among her contemporaries? Who are her influences? What is she inspired by or rebelling against? Often, a publicity kit distributed to journalists in conjunction with the exhibition is a good place to start, though rarely will it provide the last word.

If this is an exhibition of work by different artists, what is the organizing principle? Are these all painters from a certain period, a certain place, a certain "school"? What is the commonality, and where are the differences?

Next, interpretation. How does it work? What does it mean? If this is nonrepresentational art, or art that aims for a childlike simplicity, or art that makes us question the very notion of what art is, how does what's on the canvas (or in the photo, sculpture or architectural design) support such an analysis?

Finally, evaluation. As with other artistic genres, professional critics are more likely to make strong evaluative statements early in their critiques, while novice critics might take more space with description and hedge their bets on analysis. No matter what your instinctive response might be, Pablo Picasso, Jackson Pollock and Andy Warhol are likely to survive an amateur critic's withering scorn with their reputations intact. That doesn't mean you can't mount an argument against the work of any of them. Just make sure it's an informed analysis that an intelligent readership will find provocative and illuminating; don't give anyone a reason to dismiss you as ignorant.

In the interview that closes this chapter, Roberta Smith, a visual arts critic for The Times, describes her process: "The first thing is listening to your gut. The second thing is accumulating this vast storehouse of experience and knowledge, which I think is mostly empirical. And the third thing is your understanding of your craft as a writer and what the responsibilities of that are—which for me at least are compression and taste, a distinctive tone and pleasure for the reader."

As you read the following pieces, look for the evidence of the critic's "storehouse of experience and knowledge," and determine how much knowledge the critic demands of her readers to follow her arguments. It's a tricky balance to engage the interest of the knowledgeable and the general reader alike.

Selection 4.1

This headline could encompass the chapter, for every art review must see through new eyes, offering the reader a fresh vision. Not only does the perspective on one of the world's most renowned painters change with the changes in the cultural context, but it changes with the viewer and with each viewer's own changes. Here, with an "economic slump" similar to the one Rembrandt experienced, Pulitzer Prize–winning art critic Holland Cotter finds plenty new to say about an artist about whom we might have thought everything has been said.

ART
In the Gloom, Seeing Rembrandt With New Eyes
By HOLLAND COTTER

In the 17th century the Netherlands was the most prosperous country in Europe. Then at midpoint of the century, partly because of a draining war, the bubble burst. The Dutch art market, at its zenith, collapsed. People thought, "Oh, it's just a phase." It wasn't. The golden age of Dutch art was over.

Rembrandt was hit especially hard. A decade earlier he had been a star, with a client waiting list a mile long. Amsterdam, like New York today, was a town of culture-craving burghers who had to have—had to have—a Rembrandt in their homes. So he turned himself into an art machine, piled on assistants to finish off work, and became very rich.

He also grew careless. He mortgaged himself to the hilt. In addition to making art, he sold it, not only dealing his own work but that of other artists. He bought a Rubens and flipped it at a markup. He flogged paintings by his apprentices that looked very much like his own.

With the economic slump, everything fell apart. Creditors banged at the door; clients disappeared. He was broke, out of fashion, a loser. If other artists believed it was just a matter of time before the Dutch market recovered, my guess is that Rembrandt did not. At least he didn't paint as if he did. He had lost too much. He went his own way.

I thought of this on a visit to the Metropolitan Museum of Art's Dutch painting galleries a few days ago. I hadn't spent time with these pictures since the Met's "Age of Rembrandt" show in 2007, which had, to be honest, sated my appetite for this art.

But art changes all the time, according to what's going on around it. Now I was looking at Dutch painting from inside an economic collapse, with a market on the rocks, and a Gilded Age revealed as fool's gold. The art looked different.

I was particularly struck by how different the Rembrandts appeared, but then I always am. They're like friends you've known for so long and so well that you figure there can't be any surprises, but there are. They're never quite the same twice.

I don't experience this with Vermeer. The Vermeers I carry around in my head correspond pretty closely to those I re-encounter on the wall. Is it because each composition is so precisely resolved, each object so exactly placed, each figure so cleanly shaped

Published: January 9, 2009.

that they fix themselves in the mind the way rhymed poetry or worked-out thoughts do? I don't know, but with Rembrandt it's not the same.

For example, I tend to remember the sitter in his portrait of the ebony worker Herman Doomer (1640) as a young man, though he's not. With his smiling eyes and wide-brimmed hat, he has a youthful look, but he was in his mid to late 40s when the likeness was painted. In later portraits Rembrandt seems to age his sitters prematurely. But in this one, done when his life and career were still flying high, no.

Seeing the picture called "The Toilet of Bathsheba" (1643) also took me by surprise, maybe because a later Bathsheba picture, the one in the Louvre dated 1654, stays so firmly in mind. Both related to the same biblical story: a beautiful young wife is preparing for a liaison with her lover, King David, which will lead to the death of the husband she is betraying.

In the Louvre painting the nude woman is lost in sad reverie, as if already filled with regret for what she is about do. The mood of the Met picture is almost the opposite. Here, while getting a pedicure and a comb-out, she fondles one of her breasts and gives us a smug, seductive glance. The waiting David is faintly visible in a distant tower. The peacock of pride broods in a corner of her room.

Some people consider Rembrandt a sentimentalist, but he can be as tough as nails, as he is in this picture. By the time he painted it, fortune had already delivered some shocks: his wife, Saskia, had died a year earlier, and he was immersed in a protracted fight with her family over the inheritance she had left for their son Titus. Still, his career was solid and his life was afloat.

Then it wasn't. In 1649 his servant and lover Geertge Dircx sued him for the equivalent of palimony. His new mistress, also a servant, Hendrickje Stoffels, testified on his behalf, and Dircx was jailed, but the whole business was badly destabilizing. He was borrowing large chunks of cash to pay off extravagant loans, and brokering iffy art deals.

The economy tanked; the art market vanished. He was forced into bankruptcy; a court sold his house and possessions, including his art collection. The only bright light was Stoffels's steady presence and his art, which he kept making because it was all he knew how to do.

The Met has a 1660 portrait of Stoffels, but it is not by the same artist who made Bathsheba as a self-adoring little operator and gave Herman Doomer eternal youth. Living in near-poverty, public reputation shot, with nothing to gain or lose, Rembrandt was painting in a fresh way because he was painting mostly for himself.

The color in the Stoffels portrait is unspectacular: shades of tawny brown with flicks of red like ruby chips. The brushwork is loose and undescriptive. Technically the picture is unfinished, but it's as complete as it needs to be to deliver the image it does: a devastatingly candid and loving portrait of woman, not young, leaning forward from darkness into light.

Now even when he was working on commission, he went his own way, as he does in "Woman With a Pink" (early 1660s). I've seen this portrait I don't know how many times over the years. If I was asked what my favorite Met painting is, this one would rank high. But on this visit the unnamed sitter looked only half-familiar, like a friend who, since the last meeting, had aged or grown. It was as if she had had some kind of changing experience, or I'd had one.

I remembered the face as narrow, recessive and feline. But it's not: it's oval, with a vulnerable wide forehead and owlish eyes. I remembered her sitting in front of a gold-framed painting, but forgot the gold-dust mist that rises from low behind her. (X-rays indicate that the figure of a child was originally painted here, then painted out.) And I had completely forgotten how vivid the pink carnation is: real, aromatic, fresh-picked. No wonder she holds it the way she does: straight up, in the light, as if saying, "Just look at this."

In the end the picture fits a type. It's a conventional burgher portrait of a specific person in a specific setting, of a kind Rembrandt had painted, to his considerable profit, many times. But now he feels free to leave some conventions out and make things up, to dress his bourgeois sitter like a sibyl or queen, to illuminate her with compassion like light. One result is a picture like an ember fire: low, but warm and long-burning.

I'm not saying hard times alone produced this painting. Rembrandt and art are so much more complicated than that. But when he was put to the test by circumstance, he somehow turned catastrophe into opportunity; turned his weakness into strength. From almost nothing—a little paint, a stretch of cloth, a freed-up mind and an unembarrassed heart—he made this.

Selection 4.2

This review offers a detailed examination of a gut reaction, one that can be deepened and enriched through the repeated viewings that the scale and intensity of this modernist painter's work demand. The critic wisely urges the reader to "give the art time." Though Michael Kimmelman, chief art critic for The Times (now based in Berlin), provides plenty of critical context, watch how he warns about letting the biography overly influence the evaluation.

ART REVIEW
In Joyous Colors, a Hint of Joys Lost
By MICHAEL KIMMELMAN

I'll probably be going back and back to the Joan Mitchell show at the Whitney this summer to get another shot of pleasure. The impact of her works, especially the later ones (she died of lung cancer 10 years ago, at 66), is so immediately intoxicating that a natural reaction is to distrust the art. Paintings this suave and sure-footed must be glib and manipulative, you may be excused for telling yourself.

Distrust your distrust. All the stories circulated over the years about Mitchell's incredibly nasty, drunken nature, besides possibly serving as cathartic acts of revenge by abused former friends and acquaintances, implicitly acknowledge what the art may fail to convey at a glance, namely, a desired, anticipated tragic aspect. Tales of Mitchell's troubled personality indirectly lend these objects of instant joy a hint of gravitas.

I said at a glance because if you give the art time, its emotional range does reveal itself, not just in terms of anger and pain but in subtler terms, more difficult to pin down and frequently more profound. Even the "Grande Vallée" paintings of the mid-1980's, maybe her most exuberant series of pictures, prove the point. Lush, opulent fields of nearly blinding colors, these works seem entirely paradisiacal. It takes awhile for your eyes to adjust to their light, then perhaps you may notice the shade of melancholy, a certain afterimage, which can bring late Bonnard to mind. Memory wafted on perfumed breezes of orange and jasmine: the "Grande Vallée" series was inspired by a friend of Mitchell's, the composer Gisèle Barreau, who described a flowery valley where she used to play as a girl in Brittany, a lost Arcadia that Mitchell fantasizes about in these abstracted landscapes.

Wisps of pink rise and hover against a blue field streaked with black in "La Grande Vallée VI." Silence and warmth pervade these pictures, the warmth and silence of a partially dreamed-up past, which is sweeter and more precious because it is gone or never was. Mitchell was coping with the death of her sister, and she had her own desperate fears about dying. ("Painting is the opposite of death," she once said. "It permits one to survive.") But you really don't need to know her biography to intuit the hopeful, elegiac strain. Life is never so sublime or sad as it is in art and in the recollection of a long-ago, wished-for childhood.

I have started at the middle of Mitchell's story. The Whitney exhibition, organized by Jane Livingston, surveys a four-decade career of resolute, circumscribed consistency. (It is supplemented by excellent shows at four commercial galleries.) Mitchell was born in 1926 into affluence in Chicago, the daughter of a willful father, a doctor and

Published: July 5, 2002.

amateur artist, with whom she felt competitive. Marion Strobel, her mother, wrote poetry and, with Harriet Monroe, edited Poetry magazine, which was the first to publish Pound and Eliot. Eliot and Dylan Thomas visited the house. Thornton Wilder read Joan and her sister poems at bedtime. Poetry was Mitchell's lifelong inspiration.

She arrived in New York in the mid-1940's, a student of Hans Hofmann for a day. She fled his class without enrolling, saying she couldn't understand a word he said, but she became deeply indebted to his work in later years. She quickly absorbed the influences of Kandinsky, Pollock, Gorky, Kline and de Kooning. She was never an innovator, and she never said she was. She joined a movement on the upswing, carved out a space for herself within it, stuck with it when others didn't and never doubted its basic value.

You see the indebtedness to Pollock, Gorky and de Kooning in works like "Cross Section of a Bridge" (1951) and "Ladybug" (1957): the skittering gestures; the interlaced skeins of drips and slashes; the restlessness; the flashes of bright color and occasional horror vacui; the forward-thrusting layouts, a Cubist holdover; and the centrifugal energy held in check by rigorous architecture.

But you also see a specific virtuosity—a deft handling of many different sorts of lines—that was her own.

The painter Grace Hartigan once complained that Mitchell, in her early years, was too calculated, not impulsive enough, for Abstract Expressionism, and it's true that Mitchell did plot every stroke before she laid it down. "The freedom in my work is quite controlled," Mitchell acknowledged. But so was Pollock's. Like him and the other big boys of the New York School, she painted with willed authority. And for a while she was accepted as one of them, a star. In that respect she never really struggled for recognition, although, self-pitying and combative, she always complained that she did—until the New York art world, fickle as usual, finally did begin to turn the spotlight elsewhere by the late 1950's.

At which point she decided, for a combination of professional and personal reasons (among them, a long, tumultuous relationship with the painter Jean-Paul Riopelle), to spend more and more time in France. Mitchell's art went through stages there. There are ferocious paintings of clotted splatters and drips in the early 60's. Then hovering shapes appear in muted green, gray and blue. They're masses of pigment that suggest trees or parts of landscapes—somber physical presences perceived as if through a mist or haze. Atmosphere is injected into the paintings, but it's a thick air, as if heavy-hearted. Mitchell called these works "black paintings," even though there's almost no black in them.

They give way by the early 70's to more vividly colored multi-panel paintings in which increasing varieties of shapes and lines jostle. Hofmann's influence is clearest here. Like other balletic kinds of abstraction, including his, Mitchell's art was about opposition and balance: opposing forces held in tense, momentary equilibrium. When the pictures failed, they yielded to chaos and decoration. When they succeeded, there was a kind of informal harmony that suggested nature. You see this in the complex paintings of the 70's like "Blue Territory," "Clearing," "Salut Tom" and "La Vie en Rose." Fields, beaches, violets and begonias. Suggestive landscapes are marked out in broad, shallow depths.

I used to wonder about these 70's paintings, which seemed transitional. A good retrospective, among other things, forces you to think twice about art you thought you knew. At the Whitney, I recognize my error.

Mitchell lived in Vétheuil, a town near Paris, where Monet lived for a while. To her death she denied his influence, which was undeniable. Like other expatriate Americans, she was probably predisposed toward a French aesthetic and toward Monet before she decided to live there, then she increasingly accepted Monet's style: his lyricism and what you might call his unapologetic elegance.

Seeing Mitchell's later paintings at the Corcoran Gallery in Washington in 1988, in the last big Mitchell show, gorgeous pictures, it seemed obvious how far she tried to push Monet into the late 20th century. Sun flooded through the Corcoran's skylights on canvases that redoubled the light.

Some of these late paintings now look to me almost like enlargements of details from earlier pictures, the strokes isolated and bolder, like late de Koonings in their reductiveness, but with an easier and more varied touch: sometimes suggesting bursting streamers; sometimes hectic squiggles, black and green against pastel colors (peach and lemon), as in "Faded Air I," a diptych. Its strong diagonal expertly binds the two panels by an intricate knot. The work is about sunflowers, Mitchell volunteered, which "look so wonderful when young, and they are so very moving when they are dying." Hence, perhaps, the faint trace of nostalgia, another afterimage, delicately implied.

Nathan Kernan, a poet who collaborated with Mitchell on a portfolio of prints she made at the end of her life, in a catalog accompanying a Mitchell show at the Cheim & Read Gallery, recounts the time, shortly before she died, when she asked him to select poems to read at a friend's funeral. When he read Rilke's "Entrance" to her, she said, "Save that one for me."

So he did, for her memorial at the Whitney 10 years ago.

> With your eyes, which in their weariness
> barely free themselves from the worn-out threshold,
> you lift very slowly one black tree
> and place it against the sky: slender, alone.
> And you have made the world. And it is huge
> and like a word which grows ripe in silence.
> And as your will seizes on its meaning,
> tenderly your eyes let it go.

Mitchell's work, over time growing ripe, too, leaves its own mark after your eyes let it go.

Selection 4.3

The passage of time provides much of the context in a review of an exhibition that demands a career reassessment. Photography had to fight for legitimacy as art, and color photography in particular was dismissed as snapshots. In the case of William Eggleston, consider how Cotter explains the ways "we see the work more clearly now." Appreciate the deft interweaving of analysis and biography, as the art reflects the artist.

"Memphis," a photograph from about 1969, by William Eggleston. Corcoran Gallery of Art/
Eggleston Artistic Trust. Courtesy of Cheim & Read, New York.

Art Review | William Eggleston
Old South Meets New, in Living Color
By HOLLAND COTTER

Thirty years ago photography was art if it was black and white. Color pictures were tacky and cheap, the stuff of cigarette ads and snapshot albums. So in 1976, when William Eggleston had a solo show of full-color snapshotlike photographs at the august Museum of Modern Art, critics squawked.

It didn't help that Mr. Eggleston's pictures, shot in the Mississippi Delta, where he lived, were of nothings and nobodies: a child's tricycle, a dinner table set for a meal, an unnamed woman perched on a suburban curb, an old man chatting up the photographer from his bed.

That MoMA's curator of photography, John Szarkowski, had declared Mr. Eggleston's work perfect was the last straw. "Perfectly banal, perfectly boring," sniffed one writer; "erratic and ramshackle," snapped another; "a mess," declared a third.

Published: November 7, 2008.

Perfect or not, the images quickly became influential classics. And that's how they look in "William Eggleston: Democratic Camera, Photographs and Video, 1961–2008," a retrospective at the Whitney Museum of American Art that is this artist's first New York museum solo since his seditious debut.

Naturally we see the work more clearly now. We know that it was not cheap. The dye transfer printing Mr. Eggleston used, adapted from advertising, was the most expensive color process then available. It produced hues of almost hallucinatory intensity, from a custard-yellow sunset glow slanting across a wall to high-noon whiteness bleaching a landscape to pink lamplight suffusing a room.

And compositions that at first seemed bland and random proved not to be on a 2nd, 3rd and 20th look. The tricycle was shot from a supine position so as to appear colossal. The woman on the curb sits next to a knot of heavy chains that echoes her steel-mesh bouffant. The affable guy on the bed holds a revolver, its barrel resting on his vintage country quilt.

Although unidentified, these people and others were part of Mr. Eggleston's life: family, friends and neighbors. The retrospective—organized by Elisabeth Sussman, curator of photography at the Whitney, and Thomas Weski, deputy director of the Haus der Kunst in Munich—takes us through that life, or what the pictures reveal of it, on a tour that is a combination joy ride, funeral march and bad-trip bender. Patches of it feel pretty tame now, but whole stretches still have the morning-after wooziness of three decades ago.

Mr. Eggleston is a child of the American South. He was born in Memphis in 1939 and spent part of his childhood living with grandparents on a Mississippi cotton plantation. His family was moneyed gentry; he has never had to work for a living. Self-taught, he was already seriously taking pictures by the time he got to college (he went first to Vanderbilt, later to the University of Mississippi); his encounter with the work of Henri Cartier-Bresson and Walker Evans pushed him along.

By his own account, unless he is working on commission his choice of subjects for pictures is happenstantial. He shoots whatever or whoever is at hand. The earliest picture in the show, from 1961, is of a prison farm adjoining his family's plantation. Murky and grainy, it could be a scene from the 19th century; the prisoners are all black. Then come any-old-thing images of post–World War II strip malls and suburbs; almost everyone is white.

Although Mr. Eggleston rejects the label of regional photographer, he was, at least initially, dealing with the complicated subject of a traditional Old South (he says the compositions in his early pictures were based on the design of the Confederate flag) meeting a speeded-up New South, which he tended to observe from a distance, shooting fast-food joints and drive-ins almost surreptitiously, as if from the dashboard of a car.

Around 1965 he started to use color film, and his range expanded. He moved in close. The first picture he considers a success is in the show. It's of a teenage boy standing about arm's length from the camera. He's seen in profile, pushing carts at a supermarket. His face is slack, his eyes a little glazed, his body bent in an effortful crouch. He's ordinary, but the golden sunlight that falls on him is not: it turns his red hair lustrous and gilds his skin. A prosaic subject is transformed but unromantically; lifted up, but just a little, just enough.

In 1967 Mr. Eggleston made a trip to New York, where he met other photographers, important ones, like Diane Arbus, Lee Friedlander and Garry Winogrand, learning something from each. Although he has a reputation for being remote, even reclusive, he also has a public persona as a dandyish hell raiser, a kind of exemplar of baronial boho. In any case he has never lacked for art-world connections. Mr. Szarkowski was one; another was the curator Walter Hopps, who became a friend and traveling companion beginning in the 1960s and '70s.

These were the Merry Prankster and "Easy Rider" years, when road trips and craziness were cool, and Mr. Eggleston set out on some hard-drinking picture-taking excursions. He also embarked on repeated shorter expeditions closer to home in the form of epic bar crawls, which resulted in the legendary video "Stranded in Canton."

Originally existing as countless hours of unedited film and recently pared down by the filmmaker Robert Gordon to a manageable 76 minutes, it was shot in various places in 1973 and 1974. (The new version is in the retrospective.) Mr. Eggleston would show up with friends at favorite bars, turn on his Sony Portapak, push the camera into people's faces and encourage them to carry on.

And they did. Apart from brief shots of his children and documentary-style filming of musicians, the result is like some extreme form of reality television. Your first thought is: Why do people let themselves be seen like this? Do they know what they look like? You wonder if Mr. Eggleston is deliberately shaping some tragicomic Lower Depths drama or just doing his customary shoot-what's-there thing, the what's-there in this case being chemical lunacy. For all the film's fringy charge there's something truly creepy and deadly going on, as there is in much of Mr. Eggleston's art. You might label it Southern Gothic; but whatever it is, it surfaces when a lot of his work is brought together.

Images of gravestones and guns recur, but the real morbidity comes indirectly, like mood, through association. A little girl stands outside a playhouse reminiscent of a Victorian mausoleum; a young man sits in the back of a car, dazed, like a zombie from "Night of the Living Dead." Houses look empty, meals abandoned; an oven stands open, as if inviting entry; a green-tiled shower suggests an execution chamber.

In many of these images color has the artificial flush of a mortician's makeup job. This effect achieves its apotheosis in a series of commissioned photographs from 1983 of Elvis Presley's Graceland. Mr. Eggleston depicts the singer's home as an airless, windowless tomb, a pharaonic monument to a strung-out life embalmed in custom-made bad taste.

But then there are moments of utter old-fashioned beauty, natural highs. You're outdoors in the farmlands of Jimmy Carter's Georgia, in a series of pictures commissioned by Rolling Stone before the 1976 election. Or you're standing under mountainous clouds on a piece of wide, flat earth that is Mr. Eggleston's family land.

Probably no one asked for this picture. He took it because he takes pictures a lot, and that's where he was with his camera that day. The clouds just happened, the way clouds do.

As a group Mr. Eggleston's more recent pictures, in the series called "The Democratic Forest," add to, rather than develop or depart from, what came with that giant step he took in the '60s and '70s. There are more images of pop-cultural glut, unsavory home cooking and soulful skies. There is also more obvious artfulness as his travels take him to Europe and Asia and onto film sets at the invitation of directors like David Lynch, Gus Van Sant and Sofia Coppola, all of whose work he has profoundly influenced.

The color has grown lusher than ever and the angle of vision indirect as we see reality layered on, refracted through glass, in mirror reflections. The world is still chipped and scarred, but cleaner. The subjects in the pictures feel lingered over. The stoned, on-the-road, trapped-in-yesterday rawness is gone. Some of these new pictures really are banal and a little boring, in part because the mess of life gets left out.

This isn't surprising. Part of being a long-term traveler is that you get comfortable; you relax. You stop living on adrenaline, stop bracing for jolts to the system. The irritated alertness conducive to a certain kind of art subsides. At some basic level the world is less strange and you're less of a stranger to it, unless you deliberately derange yourself or hit the road again, or adjust yourself to a new now.

Mr. Eggleston, who lives in Memphis, is now on a project with Mr. Lynch; beyond that, I don't know what his plans are. The America he presented to such shocking effect more than 30 years ago is now full color—not black and white, not North and South—in every sense. The national soul is still as delirious and furious, but maybe a little more sober, or about to become so. I wonder what one of our finest living photographers will continue to make of it.

Selection 4.4

The Twin Towers of the World Trade Center occupied a place of significance in the New York skyline long before they became the tragic symbol of 9/11. Compare and contrast these two appraisals of an early model of the towers—"the best new building project that New York has seen in a long time," as the first Times architecture critic (and a Pulitzer Prize winner) described it in 1964—and the controversy surrounding what will take their place at ground zero.

Big but Not So Bold; Trade Center Towers Are Tallest, But Architecture Is Smaller Scale

By ADA LOUISE HUXTABLE

The towers are pure technology, the lobbies are pure schmaltz and the impact on New York of two 110-story buildings and auxiliary structures with a projected population of 130,000 workers and visitors using a city-size amount of services is pure speculation. These are the three areas in which an undertaking of the size and scale of the World Trade Center must be evaluated: engineering, design and planning.

As engineering, the buildings' roots are in Chicago in the eighteen-eighties, where technology and esthetics combined for that uniquely American contribution to art and urban life, the skyscraper. By the nineteen-thirties it had shaped the Manhattan skyline and the 20th century.

However, even as the World Trade Center is dedicated, the palm is going back to Chicago, where the Sears Tower will be still higher and even more advanced in its tall building technology.

Megalomania and Economics

In the sixties, new developments in framing techniques that increased strength and rigidity and decreased bulk and cost made megalomania compatible with economics. Don't knock the 20th century, when art finally equaled man's aspirations.

Big buildings are beautiful by accident—through sheer size and drama—and by design.

As design, the World Trade Center is a conundrum. It is a contradiction in terms: the daintiest big buildings in the world. In spite of their size, the towers emphasize an almost miniature module—3 feet 4 inches—and the close grid of their decorative facades has a delicacy that its architect, Minoru Yamasaki, chose deliberately. The associated New York architects are Emery Roth and Sons.

Published: April 5, 1973.

The module is so small, and the 22-inch wide windows so narrow, that one of the miraculous benefits of the tall building, the panoramic view out, is destroyed. No amount of head-dodging from column to column can put that fragmented view together. It is pure visual frustration.

Mr. Yamasaki is a modest size, and he talks insistently of "human scale." He believes this miniaturization "humanizes" the huge buildings and relates them to the man in the street. Because the delicate aluminum grid covers the closely spaced columns of a load-bearing exterior wall, he claims structural justification.

But the most beautiful skyscrapers are not only big, they are bold; that is the essence and logic of their structural and visual reality. They are bone-beautiful, and the best wear skins that express that fact with the strength and subtlety of great art.

These are big buildings but they are not great architecture. The grill-like metal facade stripes are curiously without scale. They taper into the more widely-spaced columns of "Gothic trees" at the lower stories, a detail that does not express structure so much as tart it up. The Port Authority has built the ultimate Disneyland fairytale blockbuster. It is General Motors Gothic.

Still, there are things to be grateful for. Whether one likes the style or not, the Port Authority simply did not raise hack speculative standards to the ultimate power. It tried for something special. And those lobbies are gloriously high and spacious, if dubiously grand.

The third factor, planning, is bringing the big building increasingly under attack in cities today. It is being looked on more as monster than as marvel. The tall building is recognized not as an isolated object, but as an element of the environment.

How They Work

Because the open spaces and circulation areas around the World Trade Center are still clutter and rubble, these buildings cannot be considered yet as a total complex or measured in the all-important terms of how they work in their surroundings.

Belatedly, questions are being raised about energy use and pollution, and all those city troubles that a city-size structure complicates. The World Trade Center will take 80,000 kilowatts of electricity a year, for example, or 20 per cent of Con Edison's growth.

The skyscraper has become a sophisticated problem in environment. And that is how the World Trade Center will ultimately have to be judged, rather than for its esthetic effect on the skyline, or its status value. Survival, not vanity, is the issue now.

Selection 4.5

This piece in particular encompasses so much more than the art of architecture, delving into social, cultural and political implications rather than restricting itself to the aesthetic.

AN APPRAISAL
A Tower of Impregnability, The Sort Politicians Love
By NICOLAI OUROUSSOFF

The darkness at ground zero just got a little darker. If there are people still clinging to the expectation that the Freedom Tower will become a monument to the highest American ideals, the current design should finally shake them out of that delusion. Somber, oppressive and clumsily conceived, the project suggests a monument to a society that has turned its back on any notion of cultural openness. It is exactly the kind of nightmare that government officials repeatedly asserted would never happen here: an impregnable tower braced against the outside world.

The new design by David Childs of Skidmore, Owings & Merrill is a response to the obvious security issues raised by the New York Police Department, specifically the tower's resistance to car and truck bombs. The earlier twisted-glass form, a pastiche of architectural visions cobbled together from Daniel Libeskind's master plan and various Skidmore designs, lacked grace or fresh ideas. The new obelisk-shaped tower, which stands on an enormous 20-story concrete pedestal, evokes a gigantic glass paperweight with a toothpick stuck on top. (The toothpicklike spire was added so that the tower would reach its required height of 1,776 feet.)

The temptation is to dismiss it as a joke. And it is hard not to pity Mr. Childs, who was forced to redesign the tower on the fly to meet the rigid deadline of Gov. George E. Pataki. Unfortunately, the tower is too loaded with meaning to dismiss. For better or worse, it will be seen by the world as a chilling expression of how we are reshaping our identity in a post–Sept. 11 context.

The most radical design change is the creation of the base, which will house the building's lobby and some mechanical systems. Designed to withstand a major bomb blast, the base will be virtually windowless. In an effort to animate its exterior, the architects say they intend to decorate it in a grid of shimmering metal panels. A few narrow slots will be cut into the concrete to allow slivers of natural light into the lobby.

Published: June 30, 2005.

The effort fails on almost every level. As an urban object, the tower's static form and square base finally brush aside the last remnants of Mr. Libeskind's master plan, whose only real strength was the potential tension it created among the site's structures. In the tower's earlier incarnation, for example, its eastern wall formed part of a pedestrian alley that became a significant entry to the memorial site, leading directly between the proposed International Freedom Center and the memorial's north pool. The alley, flanked on its other side by a performing arts center to be designed by Frank Gehry, was fraught with tension; it is now a formless park littered with trees.

The interior, by comparison, holds a bit more promise for the hopelessly optimistic. Visitors will enter from north and south lobbies, where they will have to slip around an interior partition set just beyond the revolving doors—yet another concession to security concerns. If the configuration of windows could somehow be improved, one could imagine, with some effort, a sealed cathedral-like room with heavenly light spilling down.

But if this is a potentially fascinating work of architecture, it is, sadly, fascinating in the way that Albert Speer's architectural nightmares were fascinating: as expressions of the values of a particular time and era. The Freedom Tower embodies, in its way, a world shaped by fear.

At a recent meeting at his Wall Street office, Mr. Childs tried to deflect this criticism by enveloping the building in historical references. The height of the tower minus its spire (1,368 feet) matches the height of the taller of the former World Trade Center towers and is meant to re-establish a visual relationship to the nearby World Financial Center, which was exactly half that height. The fortresslike appearance of the base was partly inspired by the Strozzi Palace in Florence, the relationship between the base and the soaring tower by Brancusi's "Bird in Space" sculpture.

But the tower has none of the lightness of Brancusi's polished bronze form, let alone its sculptural beauty. And the Strozzi Palace's rough stone facade is beautiful because it is a mask: once inside, you are confronted with a courtyard flooded with light and air, one of the Renaissance's great architectural treasures. What the tower evokes, by comparison, are ancient obelisks, blown up to a preposterous scale and clad in heavy sheaths of reinforced glass—an ideal symbol for an empire enthralled with its own power.

This obsession with symbolism extends all the way up to the tower's spire. Mr. Childs has long been itching to reposition the original spire, which, as Mr. Libeskind envisioned it, had to be set at the edge of the tower to echo the outstretched arm of the Statue of Liberty. In the new version, the spire rises out of the center of a tension ring mounted atop the building, an abstract interpretation of Liberty's torch and a concept that, like Mr. Libeskind's, has more to

do with pandering to public sentiment than with any big architectural idea.

All of this could be more easily forgiven if it were simply due to
bad design. But ground zero is not really being shaped by architects;
it is being shaped by politicians. Soon after the new security requirements were announced, it became clear that the entire building would
have to be redesigned. That could have been seen as a last chance to
repair what had become a confused master plan, one that had little
connection, except in the minds of Mr. Libeskind and Governor
Pataki, to the original. Instead, the quality of the master plan has been
sacrificed to the governor's insistence on preserving hollow symbolic
gestures.

Absurdly, if the Freedom Tower were reduced by a dozen or
so stories and renamed, it would probably no longer be considered
such a prime target. Fortifying it, in a sense, is an act of deflection.
It announces to terrorists: Don't attack here—we're ready for you.
Go next door.

Selection 4.6

*In the interview at the end of this chapter, Roberta Smith talks about how
pop art blurred the distinction between pop and fine art, and how her own
reviews tend to focus on the immediacy of the visual experience (perhaps at
the expense of historical context). This review illuminates both concepts, with
a single-word evaluation that is both early and strong: "terrific."*

ART REVIEW | ROY LICHTENSTEIN
The Painter Who Adored Women
By ROBERTA SMITH

"Roy Lichtenstein: Girls," at the Gagosian Gallery, presents
12 of Lichtenstein's early paintings of the female creatures otherwise
known as women. Based on cartoons and mostly blond, they are
anonymous, beautiful and often unhappily bothered, usually by men.
Or, if you like, by boys.

Title aside, the show is terrific. Just when you thought you'd
seen enough Pop Art to last a lifetime, this selection proves otherwise.
It reveals Lichtenstein honing his indelible yet impersonal style, and it
can be seen in one of New York's most painting-friendly architectural
settings. And ultimately only an ogre would deny that Lichtenstein's
portrayals in some way glorify the American woman by giving innocuous images of her generic concocted self and her roiling emotions
such blazing formal power.

Published: June 11, 2008.

After all, as Dorothy Lichtenstein, the artist's widow, remarks in an interview in the show's catalog, "Roy adored women." And the anonymity of his subjects has exceptions. The smiling woman in "Sound of Music" is clearly Julie Andrews about to burst into song as musical notes stream through the window—although her cheer is undercut by the sharp black shadow that divides her face into areas of red and blue, not unlike the stripe of green in Matisse's Fauve portrait of his wife in a hat.

These paintings are themselves bursts, hot flashes of composition, America, humor and color galvanized and made one by pictorial intelligence. Because their visual machinations are perfectly obvious, they make normally arcane terms like form and formalism exhilaratingly accessible. Basically we watch them work.

Mrs. Lichtenstein notes that Lichtenstein painted on an easel that allowed him to turn each canvas so he could be sure that its power operated in all orientations. It had to work abstractly, in other words, in a way that couldn't be missed.

Dating from 1962, 1963 and primarily 1964, the cartoon-based images here are dominated by industrial-strength red, yellow and blue, generously contoured with black lines. The onslaught of color and the seeming dumbness of the images are interrupted by the black-on-white balloons of speech or thought (or, sometimes, music), which have a complex visual and cognitive role in the Garbo-talks vein.

The paintings that lack them can seem too mute, but stillness is their point. In "Blonde Waiting," you feel the seconds tick against the silence as a woman with an Angie Dickinsonesque mop of yellow hair intently watches a yellow alarm clock beside a yellow bedstead, wondering just how late Mr. Right is going to be. The silence turns film noir in "Little Aloha," where the main colors are black and dark blue and one of Lichtenstein's few nonblondes casts a come-hither look from the shadows.

But even without the balloons or musical notes, white is an essential element in these paintings. It is visible in highlights, like the woman's tears of happiness in "Kiss V," a compact, nearly quartered composition that must have benefited especially from Lichtenstein's rotating easel. But mainly white is filtered through the scrims of Ben-Day dots. Lichtenstein's cultivation and manipulation of the dot pattern is one of the show's main subtexts.

In the earliest works here—"Forget It! Forget Me!," "Little Aloha" and even the classic "Masterpiece" (where the female lead speaks the prophetic words "Why, Brad darling, this painting is a masterpiece!")—the dots are faint and uneven, not quite pulling their weight. But they quickly gain size and substance and diversify. For example, women's lips are often rendered not in solid red but in

Ben-Day stars, stripes or little bow-tie shapes that stand out from the Ben-Day dots of the faces.

The Ben-Day dots allow Lichtenstein's painting to look both more and less artificial. They signify mechanical reproduction, but they also add suggestions of light and reflection, shifting colors and variations in touch. The reflections would eventually lead to Lichtenstein's many portrayals of mirrors, but first they seem to have spawned ceramic sculptures and works in porcelain enamel on steel, a small selection of which is included in the Gagosian show. On their shiny surfaces, fake reflections and shadows—like the aggressive, tattoolike scattering of Ben-Day dots on "Head With Red Shadow"—compete with real ones.

Mrs. Lichtenstein's catalog interviewer is, perhaps appropriately, the latter-day Pop artist Jeff Koons, who as usual alternates a golly-gee robotic air with genuine perceptions. Sometimes he blends the two, as when he says: "I always loved how Roy's work really challenges life force because it tries to compete with life force in the realm of the artificial. He would try to have the artificial keep up and challenge the power of life."

This is another museum-quality show from Larry Gagosian's gallery, and, as is often the case here, everything has a double function, like serving up artists that any dealer would like to represent. Not only is there Mr. Koons's interview with Mrs. Lichtenstein; Richard Prince, who just left the Gladstone Gallery and is about to have a show at Mr. Gagosian's gallery in Rome, contributes a small inserted brochure. It juxtaposes each of 22 steamy pulp-fiction covers of books (all titled with female first names) with a Lichtenstein woman painting. The illustrations of scantily clad, curvaceous femme fatales would seem to be the last thing Lichtenstein had in mind.

What he had in mind was form, a transformation of the terms of real and fake that, as Mr. Koons suggests, was beyond either, a thing in itself. This show makes especially clear how Lichtenstein's work functions as a kind of primer in looking at and understanding the grand fiction of painting: the thought it requires, its mechanics, its final simplicity and strangeness. These great paintings convey all this in a flash of pleasure, compounded by the thrill of understanding.

Selection 4.7

These opening paragraphs of a longer piece by Smith take art beyond the museum or gallery into the public arena, with a punchy lead that introduces an exploration of what has changed, and why, in outdoor sculpture and the art world's changing response to it.

Anish Kapoor's reflecting "Cloud Gate," an abstract public art piece nicknamed the Bean,
at the Millennium Park in Chicago. Peter Wynn Thompson for The New York Times

ART
Public Art, Eyesore to Eye Candy
By ROBERTA SMITH

Art adores a vacuum. That's why styles, genres and mediums left for dead by one generation are often revived by subsequent ones. In the 1960s and '70s public sculpture was contemporary art's foremost fatality—deader than painting, actually. The corpse generally took the form of corporate, pseudo-Minimalist plop art. It was ignored by the general public and despised by the art world.

At the time many of the most talented emerging sculptors were making anything but sculpture. Ephemeral installations, earthworks and permanent site-specific works were in vogue, and soon the very phrase "public sculpture" had been replaced by public art, an amorphous new category in which art could be almost anything: LED signs, billboards, slide or video projections, guerrilla actions, suites of waterfalls.

But over the past 15 years public sculpture—that is, static, often figurative objects of varying sizes in outdoor public spaces—has become one of contemporary art's more exciting areas of endeavor and certainly its most dramatically improved one.

To be sure, this new public sculpture is not always good. (Damien Hirst's "Virgin Mother" at Lever House comes to mind.) If this kind of work may not be batting much above .300, hits are happening, showing art's ability to reach larger audiences (as it satisfies its core one) and to create a communal experience that is in some ways akin to movies or popular music in its accessibility.

Published: August 24, 2008. Full text available at: www.nytimes.com/2008/08/24/arts/design/24smit.html.

Some recent successes have included Rachel Whiteread's 1993 "House," a concrete cast of the interior of a London terrace house; Mark Wallinger's 1999 "Ecce Homo," a life-size figure of Jesus crowned with thorns, hands bound, standing amid the din of Trafalgar Square in London; Takashi Murakami's wicked aluminum and platinum leaf Buddha shown in the atrium of the IBM Building in New York in the spring; and Anish Kapoor's abstract "Cloud Gate," nicknamed the Bean, at Millennium Park in Chicago. Freely mixing elements of Pop, Minimalism, conceptual art and realism, these pieces also often benefit from new technologies and materials that make them dynamic and provocative. (Jean Dubuffet's giant, cartoony "Group of Four Trees," at 1 Chase Manhattan Plaza in Lower Manhattan, is a marvelous, unsung ancestor, but then it arrived in 1972, when sculpture was in an uproar.)

Certain artists may do their best work in the public arena. The Kapoor Bean's giant, mercurylike dollop of brilliantly polished steel gives the phrase plop art robust new life and converts this artist's sometimes glib involvement with reflective surfaces into an enveloping experience both humorous and almost sublime. From outside, the Bean's curving exterior casts distorted reflections of its world—plaza, sky, city, people—back at us. It makes itself seem larger than it is by making us seem smaller, but its distortions change with every step we take, tilting the world this way and that, as if the universe were slightly adrift.

✳✳✳

A Conversation with . . . **Roberta Smith**

ART CRITIC

© The New York Times

With a passion and wide-ranging appetite for the visual arts, Roberta Smith started her career by contributing to arts magazines. She served as senior editor for Art in America and art critic for The Village Voice before joining The New York Times in 1986. This is an edited transcript of a telephone interview.

How do you train or prepare yourself for a career as an arts critic?
The story I always tell is that my mother decorated her house a lot and always wanted to know what I

thought of things. So I was raised in a situation where looking at things and having opinions was approved, encouraged. I began by writing whatever I was told to write about by an art magazine, for next to nothing. At a certain point, I really liked it, and I realized that I needed to get into a more journalistic situation. So that's when I went to The Village Voice for four years before I went to The Times. And that's when I really felt like I was doing it, and it was the right thing for me to do.

I think if this is your ambition, you read a lot of criticism, and you find out who you like and think about why that is, and you immerse yourself in your subject. When you're first writing criticism, you're kind of winging it. You have an idea and a basic amount of confidence, or even arrogance. But it takes a tremendous amount of exposure to your subject.

You're always exercising your critical facility. Even though being a critic can be kind of an alien, weird thing to settle on, you realize that you've been doing this all the time, and all you have is your gut. The first craft you learn is kind of a psychoanalytical one. You learn to listen to yourself. That unit that you have—your mind, your body—which I call a kind of critical facility or instrument, is constantly feeding you information. So what you learn is to make it conscious. And then you learn to articulate it to yourself. And then you learn to articulate it to your readership.

So the first thing is listening to your gut. The second thing is accumulating this vast storehouse of experience and knowledge, which I think is mostly empirical. And the third thing is your understanding of your craft as a writer and what the responsibilities of that are—which for me at least are compression and taste, a distinctive tone and pleasure for the reader. And in among all that has to be opinion.

There was a study done a few years ago at Columbia University that most arts reviewers didn't seem to think that opinion was very important. But that's the main ingredient. That's the risk that a writer takes, similar to the risk that an artist takes. And opinions are just great fun to read. That's the real pleasure, in seeing someone say, this, not this; that, not the other thing.

The greatest kind of writing for me is the writing that in a few words not just makes me think of something differently, but experience it differently. It's like a light going off. Like, "Oh my god, I've seen that, and I've never seen it put into words."

With the encyclopedic knowledge the critic accumulates, are you writing for a general reader or a very art-savvy reader?
I assume I'm writing for people who are interested. But I also think it fluctuates with your subject. Sometimes your subject might be more esoteric. But I don't see myself as, say, teaching. I see myself demonstrating the exercise of opinion, showing how to experience something. I don't have a particularly strong academic background, so most of what I know I've learned on the job. So I don't even know if I could write in a specialized way.

But the thing that they tell you about The Times is that it's like a super-market, where people don't buy from every section. So you have a kind of self-selected readership. I take as much knowledge for granted as the average sportswriter. But my basic task is, I just want to get people out of the house. I want to get them interested enough so they'll say, "I've got to see this," whether it's a positive or negative review. Because there are so many different ways for something to be interesting to experience. I really want to talk about what it's like to be in front of the object.

With all the art in New York, who decides what will be reviewed and who will review it?
We have a kind of pecking order of critics. The Times sees as its mission to cover everything that's big—just like Broadway shows or movies. So anything in a museum we try to cover, and major shows. Then there are smaller insti-tutions, like alternative spaces. And at the paper we have what we call wish lists. So you make a list of what you would like to review in a given month, or, for lack of a better word, a semester. And things get divvied up, according to a schedule. And then with the gallery reviews you tend to get what you asked for unless somebody else wants it too.

You first write about what you know a lot of people will want to see. Then you write about things, at least from my choices, that you think will be really valuable for them to see. So it's an extremely imperfect science how things get chosen. I don't know how the other guys do it, but I read every piece of my mail, to look for press releases or announcements that seem intriguing.

How does being an arts critic for The New York Times differ from being one at a different publication or in a different city?
I don't think there's anything like it. New York may not be the only center of arts in the world anymore, but to me it's still the world's center of criticism. You have your biggest reading public, on all fronts. And there's no other news-paper in the country that takes criticism as seriously as The Times does. And gives us as much space, as much freedom, and basically respects critics. The advantage we have (over magazines with long lead times) is that we're in print while the things we're writing about are on view. And that is a matter for me of life and death.

I can't imagine doing what I'm doing anywhere else but New York. It's just the seriousness of this audience. And that's really a sad thing, in terms of our national culture and our national psychology. Because I think access to the arts and experience with the arts is really crucial to human happiness. If you don't understand what's possible in life, art is one way you find out.

After moving from The Voice to The Times, were you aware of having more influence, writing for a different reader or writing with a different tone?
Kind of all and none of the above. I'd say The Voice is like a guerrilla camp, and The Times is like an extremely well-run army. There's this incredibly

well-organized hierarchy of the writers, the editors, the copy desk, and being involved with that process is really exciting for me and has been part of my education.

But The Voice was really important for me because it made me understand this thing of the readership, which has to be your first responsibility. In the art world, I'd sort of thought I was the spokesperson for the artist. But once you have this readership with which you have this bond, it's like a truth serum for me. You can't be worried about whether you're pleasing the artist; you have a different understanding of your responsibility.

With The Times, I initially thought I should be careful. I've been given this really big gun. And I could hurt somebody. So I feel like my writing pulled back a bit. But then I realized when I was sliding quietly into galleries that I'd given a bad review to that they were still happy to see me. And it was kind of deflating in a way. But it was also liberating, like I could say what I want.

In terms of power, being an art critic is not like being a theater critic or a movie critic. Museums are one thing, but the gallery scene is really big here, and galleries are free. So theater and movie critics are helping people decide how to spend their money. The one thing I say about power is that you earn power. I get a certain amount of visibility at The Times, but I have to live up to it. Your readers give you power. There are plenty of people who have very little effect, who aren't really read. If you start thinking about power, it'll show up in your writing, and you'll lose it.

Do you apply different aesthetic standards to outsider or folk art than you do to the work of more conventionally trained artists?
I think it's complicated because it's so subjective. And you sort of start in the same place, with your experience. There are so many trained artists that now sort of look outsider-ish, and there are so many outside artists who are absolute masters. But in both cases, or in all cases, the first thing you're looking for is something that has a degree of newness. Something you haven't experienced before. And part of the reason of building up this mental image bank of experience is that you can immediately measure it. It's possible for outsider art to be just as convention-bound and unoriginal as the work of a trained artist. So I don't make that much of a distinction.

Do you make a distinction between fine arts and popular art and culture?
Yes, to a certain extent. The distinction for me is between a certain kind of intimate, handmade, artisinal experience that I don't think popular culture has.

But I think the relationship of popular to high culture has become so com-plicated since—well, basically since pop art, in my area. But in both cases, you're still looking for a kind of originality. And anything can convince you that it's a kind of high art. I think these categories clarify things in a way, but when you're a creator, they're just there to be transcended. If you design a chair that is so great it convinces 80 percent of the people who look at it that it's art, it really doesn't matter whether you wanted to make art or just wanted to make a chair.

What's the difference between a professional art critic and someone who sees a lot of art, loves it and knows a lot about it?
And they're also meeting deadlines? That's the difference. It's kind of a cliché, but we're all critics. In every discipline, everybody has a vote. And the way you vote just takes different forms. I vote by writing about something. Other people vote by buying tickets to concerts or buying art. Some people vote on their blogs. And some people just vote by being in a bar and talking about something. This discourse is the life's blood.

Let's end with my running a couple of clichéd artistic responses past you: First, "I don't know much about art, but I know what I like."
Well, in a way, that's what I've been talking about. That's where we all start. We start not knowing much, and you have to rely on your own reaction. And even as you know more and more, that's all you have to rely on. But that cliché to me conventionally reflects a closed mind. Because if you really know what you like, you're constantly examining that, and what you like is going to change.

How about the other common response: "My kid could paint or draw that"?
It's like the monkeys locked in a room that could have probably done Shakespeare. There's a chance that your kid could have done it, and we all have reactions like that, which is basically saying, "That's not art." But the more you know, the more you understand why that's possibly not true. Art is complicated in that way, because in some ways it's an incredibly special-ized activity, yet everybody has a certain capacity for it. Everybody has one good photograph, one good pot, one good abstraction in them. It's great if you've got a kid who can make that. And it's great if a trained artist can convey something of that childlike exuberance in their work. That's the life force of art.

MAKING**CONNECTIONS**

1 How does art from centuries ago reveal itself in new ways with the passage of time in Holland Cotter's reassessment of Rembrandt? Find a piece of famous art from ages ago and examine how it might speak differently to our time than it did to its time.

Both Cotter's piece on William Eggleston and Roberta Smith's on public art examine how work that was widely disparaged is now celebrated. How and why does this change take place? Can you think of any contemporary work (in the field of visual arts or elsewhere) that has yet to achieve legitimacy but might well do so in years to come? **2**

3 The two pieces on the Twin Towers—before and after—offer very strong evaluative opinions on filling that space. Why have both projects been controversial? What concerns do architecture reviews have beyond visual aesthetics?

How has this chapter changed your conception of the way that critics deal with these questions: What is art? What is good art? Is beauty simply in the eye of the beholder, or are there critical standards that aren't totally subjective?

5 Examine the endings—the kickers—to these pieces. What is the best? Why? What could be punchier?

theater

● IN AMERICA, THEATER IS PRACTICALLY SYNONY-MOUS WITH BROADWAY. And no critics wield greater influence over the success or failure of a Broadway production—or any other New York theater—than those at The New York Times. The chief theater critic has long been considered the most powerful critic at The Times, likely in New York, perhaps the country. For books, music, movies, even art, other voices compete for authority. But for readers who want to know whether a play is worth the money and time—and for some who even plan annual vacations around which shows to see—The Times serves as the measuring stick.

Not that The Times has an emperor's thumbs up/thumbs down power over which productions shall live and which shall die. Fortunately for Andrew Lloyd Webber and Disney, some theatrical productions are critic-proof, just like some movies, books, pop CDs and TV shows. But the serious theater-goer—the one who prefers provocative fare on a regular basis rather than the once-a-year, razzle-dazzle splurge—might spend hundreds of dollars a month on theater (particularly since Broadway tickets have crossed the three-figure threshold) and wants to make a judicious investment. An incisive, enthusiastic review from The Times can make all the difference between a long run and a quick close.

"Awareness of this position could be paralyzing if you let it be," chief critic Ben Brantley acknowledges in the interview that concludes this chapter. "So it's an awareness that you store only in the back of your mind, where it casts a sense of responsibility on what you write without suffocating it."

Brantley doesn't limit himself to New York theater. He files (and blogs) annually from London. The Times typically covers significant developments in other theater hubs such as Chicago and Los Angeles as well.

You might think that reviewing theater would have the most in common with reviewing film, since both involve actors and directors, scripts and sets. Actually, in some respects the theater review has more in common with reviews of concerts or even dance recitals. (At papers without the resources of The Times, a critic might cover both theater and dance, or a single critic might be responsible for all such cultural offerings.)

A movie remains the same every time it's shown. But live performances offer the possibility of differences, however subtle, each night. This is why many arts sections that use a rating system (whether stars or letter grades) for movies and recordings (which The Times doesn't) aren't as likely to do so for concerts or performances of plays.

Theater has often been described as an actor's medium. No matter how much control the director asserts during rehearsals and previews, onstage the actor communicates directly with the audience. And it's a different sort of acting than you see in films, for the actor must project to the last row of what are often very large theaters. You can't have the subtleties of a close-up that you have in film, where a twitch of the lip or an averted glance can express more than dialogue. For those in the front row of a theater, everything's a close-up; for those farther back, nothing is.

For these and other reasons, some movie stars stumble when they attempt a Broadway performance (though their presence in the cast may sell tickets), while some acclaimed stage actors never make the leap to film stardom. A few actors succeed at both, calibrating their performances for the differences in medium.

As with movie remakes, some Broadway productions are revivals. For those, the context in a review typically includes how the new production compares with earlier ones—not just whether it's better or worse, but also how it's different. The comparisons might involve the different actors and director, a different approach to the material or differences in audience perception, because of the passage of time. In this chapter, for example, we open with reviews of two productions of Samuel Beckett's "Waiting for Godot," described as "a mystery wrapped in an enigma" upon its first New York staging in 1956 and heralded as the "greatest of 20th-century plays" in 2009.

In this case, it was the times that changed more than "Godot." Other productions, however, take radical liberties in order to keep pace with the culture. With Shakespeare remaining a rite of passage for actors and directors alike, some productions stay as faithful as possible to the manner in which the plays were presented during the Bard's time. Others insist that the production must be as true to these times as he was to his, in order to communicate most powerfully with contemporary audiences. A critic can make arguments on either side.

Lighting, staging, pacing, sets, costumes—all fall within the critic's purview. Like a concert review, an atmospheric theater review can make the experience of being there come alive, showing how some productions thrive in the majestic expanse of a Broadway palace, while others are perfectly suited for the bare bones production of an off-Broadway theater that is little more than a storefront.

The advice for the fledgling theater critic is pretty consistent with that offered in other chapters: Go with your gut. But do your research.

Selection 5.1

A close comparison of these two reviews reveals crucial differences in the renown of Beckett and his theatrical masterwork over 60 years' time. Long the chief theater critic for The Times, Brooks Atkinson recognizes the play's provocative quality, yet suggests that audiences might find the production a puzzlement—though he assures in the kicker that Beckett is "a valid writer."

BOOKS
Beckett's 'Waiting for Godot'
By BROOKS ATKINSON

Don't expect this column to explain Samuel Beckett's "Waiting for Godot," which was acted at the John Golden last evening. It is a mystery wrapped in an enigma.

But you can expect witness to the strange power this drama has to convey the impression of some melancholy truths about the hopeless destiny of the human race. Mr. Beckett is an Irish writer who has lived in Paris for years, and once served as secretary to James Joyce.

Since "Waiting for Godot" has no simple meaning, one seizes on Mr. Beckett's experience of two worlds to account for his style and point of view. The point of view suggests Sartre—bleak, dark, disgusted. The style suggests Joyce—pungent and fabulous. Put the two together and you have some notion of Mr. Beckett's acrid cartoon of the story of mankind.

Literally, the play consists of four raffish characters, an innocent boy who twice arrives with a message from Godot, a naked tree, a mound or two of earth and a sky. Two of the characters are waiting for Godot, who never arrives. Two of them consist of a flamboyant lord of the earth and a broken slave whimpering and staggering at the end of a rope.

Since "Waiting for Godot" is an allegory written in a heartless modern tone, a theatregoer naturally rummages through the performance in search of a meaning. It seems fairly certain that Godot stands for God. Those who are loitering by the withered tree are waiting for salvation, which never comes.

The rest of the symbolism is more elusive. But it is not a pose. For Mr. Beckett's drama adumbrates—rather than expresses—an attitude toward man's experience on earth; the pathos, cruelty, comradeship, hope, corruption, filthiness and wonder of human existence. Faith in God has almost vanished. But there is still an illusion of faith flickering around the edges of the drama. It is as though Mr. Beckett sees very little reason for clutching at faith, but is unable to relinquish it entirely.

Although the drama is puzzling, the director and the actors play it as though they understand every line of it. The performance Herbert Berghof has staged against Louis Kennel's spare setting is triumphant in every respect. And Bert Lahr has never given a performance as glorious as his tatterdemalión Gogo, who seems to stand for all the stumbling, bewildered people of the earth who go on living without knowing why.

Published: April 20, 1956.

Although "Waiting for Godot" is an uneventful, maundering, loquacious drama, Mr. Lahr is an actor in the pantomime tradition who has a thousand ways to move and a hundred ways to grimace in order to make the story interesting and theatrical, and touching, too. His long experience as a bawling mountebank has equipped Mr. Lahr to represent eloquently the tragic comedy of one of the lost souls of the earth.

The other actors are excellent, also E. G. Marshall as a fellow vagrant with a mind that is a bit more coherent; Kurt Kasznar as a masterful egotist reeking of power and success; Alvin Epstein as the battered slave who has one bitterly satirical polemic to deliver by rote; Luchino Solito de Solis as a disarming shepherd boy—complete the cast that gives this diffuse drama a glowing performance.

Although "Waiting for Godot" is a "puzzlement," as the King of Siam would express it, Mr. Beckett is no charlatan. He has strong feelings about the degradation of mankind, and he has given vent to them copiously. "Waiting for Godot" is all feeling. Perhaps that is why it is puzzling and convincing at the same time. Theatregoers can rail at it, but they cannot ignore it. For Mr. Beckett is a valid writer.

Selection 5.2

By the time of the revival, Brantley can take Beckett's place in the pantheon for granted, while assuring readers that this work of genius is also "entertainment of a high order." Note also the comparative lengths of the reviews, and how the "theatregoer" of Atkinson's era (when The Times stylebook preferred the British spelling) now goes to the theater.

THEATER REVIEW | 'WAITING FOR GODOT'
Tramps for Eternity
By BEN BRANTLEY

Half a century after he first appeared on Broadway, which is also how long it's been since he last appeared on Broadway, the old tramp still can't deliver a simple song. Heck, Vladimir can't even get the tune right as he wanders through the graveyard ditty that begins the second act of Samuel Beckett's "Waiting for Godot," which opened on Thursday night at Studio 54.

Yet by the time he's finished struggling through his number— and moods that dance between defeat and defiance—Vladimir the hobo (played by Bill Irwin) is more inspirational than a dozen

Published: May 1, 2009.

Susan Boyles belting beat-the-odds renditions of dream-dreaming anthems.

Ms. Boyle's closely watched performance in a British talent contest may capture show-biz fantasies of the ordinary transfigured. Vladimir's clumsy musical stylings follow how ordinary life really plays out. His making it through his song, step by faltering step, is like anybody making it through a single day. And the next day, and the next day, and all the next days to come. If he isn't some sort of hero, then none of us are.

That's entertainment? A grotty, half-senescent guy wrestling a song to a draw? When "Waiting for Godot" first arrived in New York 53 years ago, critics and theatergoers were divided on that question. (It ran for 59 performances, with a revival the following year that lasted less than a week.)

But in 2009, Anthony Page's smart, engaging production for the Roundabout Theater Company makes it clear that this greatest of 20th-century plays is also entertainment of a high order. It seems fitting that "Godot"—which also stars Nathan Lane, John Glover and John Goodman—returns to Broadway in an interpretation that emphasizes the irresistible rhythms achieved by Beckett's radical literary surgery, that of cutting basic theatrical diversions off at the knees.

Listen, for example, to Estragon (Mr. Lane), Vladimir's vagabond companion of many decades, starting to tell a joke about an Englishman in a brothel and then forgetting all about it after the first line.

Or the lordly, arrogant Pozzo (Mr. Goodman), his booming authority fading as he finishes a lush pastoral description and says: "I weakened a little toward the end. Did you notice?" Or the cadaverous Lucky (Mr. Glover), Pozzo's ill-used slave, trying to dance on collapsing legs.

At first glance, Vladimir and Estragon (or Didi and Gogo), side by side, resemble Judy Garland and Fred Astaire, slumming it in Irving Berlin's larky hobo duet, "A Couple of Swells." Look closer, though: these tramps' faces are encrusted with what look like syphilitic chancres and fresh cuts, as well as stage dirt.

All the classic music-hall routines have been crippled and in the process acquire their own compelling grace and energy. "Waiting for Godot" may well be the ultimate statement in world drama on existential futility in the wake of the atom bomb and all that. But it's also a brilliant piece of craftsmanship, which exactly matches its form to its content, while holding a mirror to its audience.

As Kenneth Tynan wrote of Beckett's tramps after the infamous London premiere of "Godot" in 1955: "Were we not in the theater, we should, like them, be clowning and quarreling, aimlessly bickering and aimlessly making up—all, as one of them says, 'to give the impression that we exist.' "

The high-concept reframing of this play over the years, the versions that have set it in assorted slums and postnuclear wastelands, have overdressed a work that needs no accessories. Mr. Page is a strong, naturalistic director who works from within the text rather than layering over it. (His previous Broadway productions include the excellent revivals of "A Doll's House" in 1997 and "Who's Afraid of Virginia Woolf?" in 2005.)

His approach to "Godot" (here pronounced GOD-oh) is respectful without being reverent, and it scales up the stark minimalism indicated by Beckett's script into the sort of good-looking production that most Broadway theatergoers (and particularly Roundabout subscribers) seem to demand without sacrificing the play's complex simplicity.

So rather than the usual basic mound of dirt and lone tree, we have a complete rocky landscape (designed by Santo Loquasto and exquisitely lighted by Peter Kaczorowski) and, in Mr. Lane (king of the Broadway musicals) and Mr. Goodman (who starred in the long-running sitcom "Roseanne") two performers with marquee appeal who are not generally associated with classical drama. (Such casting has famous precedents: the comedian Bert Lahr played Estragon in the 1956 version, and Robin Williams and Steve Martin starred in the much debated 1988 Lincoln Center production, in which Mr. Irwin appeared as Lucky.)

As it turns out, these actors serve the purposes of Beckett's bleak comedy admirably (and in Mr. Goodman's case, spectacularly). I can't recall another "Godot" that passed so quickly or that felt so assured in its comic timing. Such confidence doesn't come easy in depicting a world in which, as Vladimir says anxiously, "time has stopped."

The play's narrative is defined, as its title promises, by the intransitive act of waiting for someone who is unlikely ever to show up. (Cameron Clifford and Matthew Schechter alternate in the role of the child who announces Godot's nonarrival.) Yet Mr. Page and his cast generate brisk comic liveliness throughout the show with tasty variety of style and pacing enforced by the paradoxical grace of fine actors artfully being inept.

As a profound comedy, this "Godot" is deeply satisfying. As an emotionally moving work, it is less so, except when Mr. Goodman and Mr. Glover are onstage. That's because while Mr. Irwin and Mr. Lane have each mapped credible paths to their roles, mostly the paths are parallel and rarely intersect.

Mr. Irwin, famous as an inventively original mime before wowing audiences with his Tony-winning turn in Mr. Page's "Virginia Woolf," takes a cerebral approach. He applies to his verbal comedy the same careful imbalance that he brings to his physical comedy. His Vladimir, the talkier of the tramps, is suspicious of every word he speaks. His sentences are a study in fragmentation, sometimes to brilliant effect.

Mr. Lane is a classic Broadway baby, a master of the one-liner with topspin. As Estragon, he's in a subdued mode, which gives an extra piquancy to his trademark wryness. But his clarion voice and ringing delivery are that of a comic in command. This is a bit confusing, since Vladimir, in the reading of "Godot," is more the take-charge guy.

But more pertinently, this Estragon and Vladimir don't feel like a real couple except in their moments of synchronized vaudeville. I was glad to have contrasting actors up there. (Two of either would have been too much.) But I only rarely felt the poignancy of these longtime fellow travelers' interdependence.

I should note that Mr. Lane and Mr. Irwin are never more convincingly allied, like people bonding in an earthquake, than when Mr. Goodman is onstage. As well they should be. Mr. Goodman's blusteringly genteel Pozzo explodes with the nonsensical tyranny of the autocrats in Lewis Carroll's "Alice" books. In his relationship with Mr. Glover's superb Lucky, who suggests a broken-down horse trying to avoid the glue factory, his Pozzo embodies centuries of aristocratic entitlement and subjugation. (This is a performance that any student of class systems needs to see.) But Mr. Goodman lets us glimpse the tickling uncertainty within the stolidness. He is human, after all, which means his very foundation is doubt.

"I've been better entertained," says Vladimir dismissively, when asked his opinion of one of Pozzo's perorations. But if, as this play contends, all life is nothing but passing time that would have passed anyway, I can think of few more invigorating ways of both doing and acknowledging exactly that.

Selection 5.3

Here's a review of the original production of another classic, recently revived, that recognizes the power of the material, yet is more equivocal about the nature of it. "Admirable" seems like faint praise considering the position this work would hold in the development of the modern musical.

THEATER REVIEW
West Side Story
By BROOKS ATKINSON

Although the material is horrifying, the workmanship is admirable.

Published: September 27, 1957.

Gang warfare is the material of West Side Story, which opened at the Winter Garden last evening, and very little of the hideousness has been left out. But the author, composer and ballet designer are creative artists. Pooling imagination and virtuosity, they have written a profoundly moving show that is as ugly as the city jungles and also pathetic, tender and forgiving.

Arthur Laurents has written the story of two hostile teen-age gangs fighting for supremacy amid the tenement houses, corner stores and bridges of the West Side. The story is a powerful one, partly, no doubt, because Mr. Laurents has deliberately given it the shape of Romeo and Juliet. In the design of West Side Story he has powerful allies. Leonard Bernstein has composed another one of his nervous, flaring scores that capture the shrill beat of life in the streets. And Jerome Robbins, who has directed the production, is also its choreographer.

Since the characters are kids of the streets, their speech is curt and jeering. Mr. Laurents has provided the raw material of a tragedy that occurs because none of the young people involved understands what is happening to them. And his contribution is the essential one. But it is Mr. Bernstein and Mr. Robbins who orchestrate it. Using music and movement they have given Mr. Laurents' story passion and depth and some glimpses of unattainable glory. They have pitched into it with personal conviction as well as the skill of accomplished craftsmen.

In its early scenes of gang skirmishes, West Side Story is facile and a little forbidding—the shrill music and the taut dancing movement being harsh and sinister. But once Tony of the Jets gang sees Maria of the Sharks gang, the magic of an immortal story takes hold. As Tony, Larry Kert is perfectly cast, plain in speech and manner; and as Maria, Carol Lawrence, maidenly soft and glowing, is perfectly cast also. Their balcony scene on the firescape of a dreary tenement is tender and affecting. From that moment on, West Side Story is an incandescent piece of work that finds odd bits of beauty amid the rubbish of the streets.

Everything in West Side Story is of a piece. Everything contributes to the total impression of wildness, ecstasy and anguish. The astringent score has moments of tranquillity and rapture, and occasionally a touch of sardonic humor. And the ballets convey the things that Mr. Laurents is inhibited from saying because the characters are so inarticulate. The hostility and suspicion between the gangs, the glory of the nuptials, the terror of the rumble, the devastating climax—Mr. Robbins has found the patterns of movement that express these parts of the story.

Most of the characters, in fact, are dancers with some images of personality lifted out of the whirlwind—characters sketched on the wing. Like everything also in West Side Story, they are admirable. Chita Rivera in a part equivalent to the Nurse in the Shakespeare play; Ken Le Roy as leader of The Sharks; Mickey Calin as leader of The Jets; Lee Becker as a hobble-dehoy girl in one gang—give terse and vigorous performances.

Everything in West Side Story blends—the scenery by Oliver Smith, the costumes by Irene Sharaff, the lighting by Jean Rosenthal. For this is one of those occasions when theatre people, engrossed in an original project, are all in top form. The subject is not beautiful. But what West Side Story draws out of it is beautiful. For it has a searching point of view.

Selection 5.4

Among contemporary playwrights, Tom Stoppard also enjoys almost unanimous acclaim. "Almost," because this gut response by Charles Isherwood is a classic example of the "Emperor has no clothes" assessment. Such a piece is as much a response to the critical response to the play as it is to the play itself. This reflection acknowledges that other critics have already hailed "Coast of Utopia" as a magnum opus. But he suggests that such "coercive" critical plaudits bully the theatergoer into thinking she should like it (or at least understand it), when plainly she doesn't. And Isherwood doesn't either.

Sara Krulwich/The New York Times

'Utopia' Is a Bore. There, I Said It

By CHARLES ISHERWOOD

The question was straightforward, but it was voiced in a tone fraught with frustration, even desperation. It sounded more like a cry for help: "Are you understanding it?"

It emerged from a woman in her 60s, or perhaps a little older, who was slowly making her way across the Lincoln Center plaza, leaning heavily on a walker, as evening fell after a matinee performance of the second installment of Tom Stoppard's "Coast of Utopia" at the Vivian Beaumont Theater.

She called it out, apparently to me and my companion as we moved past her, but perhaps more generally to the world at large. With a friendly laugh I allowed that I thought I was getting most of it. This seemed only to darken her mood.

Clearly Mr. Stoppard's expansive panorama of 19th-century Russian philosophy and history has left at least one customer unsatisfied, or at least bewildered. This might come as a surprise if you've read the almost unalloyed praise that has been heaped upon this ambitious three-part opus, which has become a sort of cultural juggernaut and the season's indispensable ticket for those who consider themselves serious theatergoers. But if that bewildered woman had asked me one or two corollary questions, namely "Are you enjoying it?" or "Do you think it's a great play?," my answers would have been "not so much" and "no."

Coming from someone who earns his living writing about theater, this may sound like madness, heresy or facile provocation. Even nonprofessional critics—which is to say any member of the audience—may hesitate to register a negative opinion about a play so widely regarded as evincing all the virtues serious theatergoers look for: intelligence, eloquence, sophistication, ambition and, of course, a good dose of medicinal seriousness alongside a balm of wit. Mr. Stoppard's plays have long been celebrated for all of these qualities, and rightly so.

Some may fear, as my new acquaintance from the plaza did, that to admit dissatisfaction or outright dislike is to advertise one's intellectual obtuseness or philistinism. The coercive reasoning goes something like this: Everyone says it's brilliant; I am bored; therefore I am not smart enough to appreciate its brilliance. The play isn't a failure: I am. I am rushing home to read Isaiah Berlin's "Russian Thinkers" right now. I mean reread it.

But I would argue that Mr. Stoppard's brilliance, while on obvious display in this densely woven portrait of the growing pains of the Russian intelligentsia, is in this instance simply not serving

Published: February 4, 2007.

the playwright's ostensible goal of creating a satisfactory work of dramatic art.

In my view much of "The Coast of Utopia" consists of great chunks of erudition and history untransformed by the playwright's imagination and craft into a compelling play. Checking my notes after a dispiriting afternoon at Part 1, "Voyage," I came across the scribbled phrase: "CliffsNotes," followed by an exasperated exclamation point, or maybe two. (Later a fellow critic used the same words to describe the play.) That impulsive reaction, glib though it may seem, has stuck with me since, even as the second act of Part 2, "Shipwreck," finally began to display some of the hallmarks of real drama: the artful exploration of fully felt human experience.

Obviously plenty of theatergoers are finding much to enjoy in "The Coast of Utopia," and in a generally vacuous Broadway environment it may seem churlish to complain that a play is too darn edifying for its own good. The Lincoln Center Theater production is far livelier and more inventively staged than the play's stodgy world premiere in 2002 at London's National Theater, where it was directed by Trevor Nunn as a series of talking tableaux vivants set against a backdrop of digital video projections. The director of the Broadway staging, Jack O'Brien, could probably bring sweep and vitality to a staged reading of The Congressional Record. Here he displays a canny sense of how to animate Mr. Stoppard's dense streams of conversation with action, color, humor and warmth.

The ghostly columns of wretched-looking serfs (some played by mannequins) that serve as a backdrop to Part 1 gives important context to arguments over the backwardness of Russia that might otherwise seem arid and theoretical. And the handsome, evocative sets by Bob Crowley and Scott Pask move us briskly through the laborious narrative with a compelling sense of motion; it's as if we're on a moving walkway, looking at brightly lighted dioramas sweeping past.

But the fluid staging—and the largely fine acting of a smartly assembled cast—can ultimately only provide the appearance of momentum and aesthetic cohesion, not these important qualities themselves. The play itself strikes me as a stubbornly diffuse, inert and intractable slab of oral history, one that lacks either the driving force of a strong narrative or the emotional appeal of life drawn in sensitive, truthful detail.

Sheer volume is an important part of the problem. A play needs to possess a dramatic cohesion, a "unity in the mind," to borrow a phrase from the critic Richard Gilman. But it is hard to discover a harmonious order if the mind is preoccupied with the simple task of registering the details of plot, character and incident, of giving the play literal coherence, or understandability, as my friend from the plaza might put it. Clearly her mind had been taxed to the point of exhaustion in trying to keep the play's narrative in order. Any larger points Mr. Stoppard means to transmit—about the conflict between philosophy and experience, historical processes and the shape of individual lives, ideals and realities—were not going to register very strongly, if indeed they did at all.

Mr. Stoppard has always written plays dense with intelligent talk and big ideas, but he has generally limited himself to single evenings. The exhilaration of his best plays—"Arcadia," "The Real Thing," "The Invention of Love"—derives from the tension between the richness of their subject matter and the artful economy required to communicate it in a single play. Giving himself a wider canvas here, he has allowed his strengths to slacken into weaknesses. That glorious eloquence becomes oppressive, as his characters flatten into talking heads espousing their philosophies in elegant paragraphs of dialogue. By the midpoint of Part 2 I was ready to cringe every time Alexander Herzen, the aristocrat-intellectual played by Brian F. O'Byrne, opened his mouth. "The Coast of Utopia" doesn't seem to build or deepen, to gain in emotional density; it just keeps going.

It has so many characters that halfway through the second part none has gotten much of a purchase on our hearts. Some are dead before they've finished a thought, it seems, while others pontificate at such length that their humanity is obscured by their loquacity. Mr. Stoppard has so much history to relate that the usual fermenting process that takes place in his imagination, turning arcana into entertainment, never seems to have occurred.

It may seem, on the surface, to be packed with morsels of meaning, but "The Coast of Utopia" is Stoppard diluted to a big bowl of thin soup. (A single-day immersion in the whole play—the marathons begin Feb. 24—may be more conducive to appreciation of its episodic narrative and its ideological underpinnings, but my experience in London suggests that it ain't necessarily so.)

I do hold out hope that the stirrings of feeling that engaged me in the second act of Part 2, "Shipwreck," will be sustained in the final installment. When the play finally stands still to train its focus more strongly on the tragedies that beset the exiled Herzen and his wife (played by Jennifer Ehle), it lets us enter at last more fully into the fates of characters who have mostly been kept at a distance. Of course by this point four hours of stage time have elapsed.

Yet I cannot say I look forward to Part 3 with absolute excitement. A measure of anxiety is involved too. It would not entirely surprise me if, after the lights have dimmed at the final curtain, ushers swarmed the aisles handing out final exams. (Which of the following characters does not die of consumption? Which German philosopher argued for the primacy of sensory experience? What is the significance of the Ginger Cat?)

I must remember to bring a No. 2 pencil.

Selection 5.5

Before leaving his position as the chief theater critic at The Times to cover the theater of politics as a Sunday columnist, Frank Rich had earned a reputation as a demanding critic who pulled no punches when theater failed to meet his standards, or, conversely, praised a work that did. Whether or not Rich's verdict alone was enough to determine whether a production would live or die, he argued (correctly) that many productions he disliked had long runs despite his opinion. And his prominence within a newspaper that covers theater more thoroughly than any other in the country made him a must-read. Here is a full review of a populist favorite that Rich loved far more than other critics at the time, followed by opening paragraphs of two other reviews that show how swiftly, and entertainingly, he could render judgment of another sort.

THEATER REVIEW
Stage: 'Dreamgirls,' Michael Bennett's New Musical, Opens
By FRANK RICH

When Broadway history is being made, you can feel it. What you feel is a seismic emotional jolt that sends the audience, as one, right out of its wits. While such moments are uncommonly rare these days, I'm here to report that one popped up at the Imperial last night. Broadway history was made at the end of the first act of Michael Bennett's beautiful and heartbreaking new musical, "Dreamgirls."

"Dreamgirls" is the story of a black singing group that rises from the ghetto to national fame and fortune during the 1960's. Like the Supremes, to which they bear more than a passing resemblance, the Dreams have their share of obstacles to overcome on the way up. At the end of Act I, the heroines are beginning to make it in Las Vegas, but there's some nasty business to be dealt with backstage. The act's hard-driving manager, Curtis (Ben Harney), has come into the Dreams' dressing room to inform Effie, who is both his lover and the group's best singer, that she is through.

Effie is through because the Dreams are at last escaping the showbiz ghetto of rhythm and blues to cross over into the promised and lucrative land of white pop. To take the final leap, the Dreams must change their image—to a new, more glamorous look and a "lighter" sound. Effie no longer fits: she's fat, and her singing is anything but light. And Curtis's bad news does not end there. Not only does he have a brand-new, svelte Dream in costume, ready to replace Effie on stage, but he also has chosen another Dream to replace Effie in his bed.

It's at this point that Jennifer Holliday, the actress who plays Effie, begs Curtis to let her stay, in a song titled "And I Am Telling

Published: December 21, 1981.

You I'm Not Going." Miss Holliday is a young woman with a broad face and an ample body. Somewhere in that body—or everywhere—is a voice that, like Effie herself, won't take no for an answer. As Miss Holliday physically tries to restrain her lover from leaving, her heart pours out in a dark and gutsy blues; then, without pause, her voice rises into a strangled cry.

Shortly after that, Curtis departs, and Miss Holliday just keeps riding wave after wave of painful music—clutching her stomach, keeling over, insisting that the scoundrel who has dumped her is "the best man I'll ever know." The song can end only when Mr. Bennett matches the performer's brilliance with a masterstroke of his own— and it's a good thing that Act I of "Dreamgirls" ends soon thereafter. If the curtain didn't fall, the audience would probably cheer Jennifer Holliday until dawn.

And, with all due respect to our new star, there's plenty more to cheer. If Miss Holliday's Act I solo is one of the most powerful theatrical coups to be found in a Broadway musical since Ethel Merman sang "Everything's Coming Up Roses" at the end of Act I of "Gypsy," so "Dreamgirls" is the same kind of breakthrough for musical stagecraft that "Gypsy" was.

In "Gypsy," the director-choreographer Jerome Robbins and his collaborators made the most persuasive case to date (1959) that a musical could be an organic entity—in which book, score and staging merged into a single, unflagging dramatic force. Mr. Bennett has long been Mr. Robbins's Broadway heir apparent, as he has demonstrated in two previous "Gypsy"-like backstage musicals, "Follies" (which he staged with Harold Prince) and "A Chorus Line." But last night the torch was passed, firmly, unquestionably, once and for all. Working with an unusually gifted new composer, Henry Krieger, and a clever librettist, the playwright Tom Eyen—as well as with a wholly powerhouse cast and design team—Mr. Bennett has fashioned a show that strikes with the speed and heat of lightning.

He has done so in a most imaginative way. "Dreamgirls" is full of plot, and yet it has virtually no spoken scenes. It takes place in roughly 20 locations, from Harlem to Hollywood, but it has not one realistic set. It is a show that seems to dance from beginning to end, yet in fact has next to no dance numbers.

How is this magic wrought? "Dreamgirls" is a musical with almost 40 numbers, and virtually everything, from record-contract negotiations to lovers' quarrels, is sung. More crucially, Mr. Krieger has created an individual musical voice for every major player and interweaves them all at will: in one cathartic backstage confrontation ("It's All Over"), the clashing of seven characters is realized entirely in musical terms.

What's more, the score's method is reinforced visually by Robin Wagner's set. Mr. Wagner has designed a few mobile, abstract scenic elements—aluminum towers and bridges—and keeps them moving to form an almost infinite number of configurations. Like the show's voices, the set pieces—gloriously abetted by Tharon Musser's lighting and Theoni V. Aldredge's costumes—keep coming together and falling apart to create explosive variations on a theme.

Linking everything together is Mr. Bennett. He keeps "Dreamgirls" in constant motion—in every conceivable direction—to perfect his special brand of cinematic stage effects (montage, dissolve, wipe). As if to acknowledge his historical debt to Mr. Robbins, he almost pointedly recreates moments from "Gypsy" before soaring onward in his own original way.

Some of his images are chilling. In Act I, an exchange of payola money between two men blossoms into a surreal panorama of mass corruption that finally rises, like a vision out of hell, clear to the roof of the theater. Throughout the show, Mr. Bennett uses shadows and klieg lights, background and foreground action, spotlighted figures and eerie silhouettes, to maintain the constant tension between the dark and bright sides of his dreamgirls' glittery dreams.

And in that tension is the emotional clout of the show. Like its predecessors among backstage musicals, "Dreamgirls" is about the price of success. Some of that price is familiar: broken love affairs, broken families, broken lives. But by telling the story of black entertainers who make it in white America, this musical's creators have dug into a bigger, more resonant drama of cultural assimilation. As the Dreams blunt the raw anger of their music to meet the homogenizing demands of the marketplace, we see the high toll of guilt and self-hatred that is inflicted on those who sell their artistic souls to the highest bidder. If "dreams" is the most recurrent word in the show, then "freedom" is the second, for the Dreams escape their ghetto roots only to discover that they are far from free.

This upsetting theme is woven into the evening's very fabric. Mr. Krieger gives the Dreams songs that perfectly capture the rhythm-and-blues music of the 50's, and then replays them throughout the evening to dramatize (and satirize) the ever-changing, ever-more-emasculated refining of the Motown sound. (Indeed, the Dreams' signature number is used to clock their personal and esthetic progression much as "Let Me Entertain You" was used in "Gypsy.") Mr. Eyen has supplied ironic, double-edge lyrics (notably in a song called "Cadillac Car"), and Harold Wheeler's subtle, understated orchestrations are sensitive to every delicate nuance of the Dreams' advance through recent pop-music history.

Perhaps inevitably the cast's two standouts are those who play characters who do not sell out and who suffer a more redemptive form of anguish: Miss Holliday's Effie and Cleavant Derricks, as a James Brown–like star whose career collapses as new musical fashions pass him by. Like Miss Holliday, Mr. Derricks is a charismatic singer, who conveys wounding, heartfelt innocence. When, in Act II, he rebels against his slick new Johnny Mathis–esque image by reverting to his old, untamed Apollo shenanigans during a fancy engagement, he gives "Dreamgirls" one of its most crushing and yet heroic solo turns. But everyone is superb: Mr. Harney's Machiavellian manager, Sheryl Lee Ralph's Diana Ross–like lead Dream, Loretta Devine and Deborah Burrell as her backups, Obba Babatunde as a conflicted songwriter and Vondie Curtis-Hall as a too-honest agent.

Is "Dreamgirls" a great musical? Well, one could quarrel with a few lapses of clarity, some minor sags, the overpat and frantic plot resolutions of Act II. But Mr. Bennett and Miss Holliday have staked their claim to greatness. And if the rest of "Dreamgirls" isn't always quite up to their incredible level, I'm willing to suspend judgment until I've sampled the evidence another four or five times.

Selection 5.6

The opening of the following suggests that the critic is taking revenge for having to endure the production.

Theater Review
Stage: 'Moose Murders,' A Brand of Whodunit
By FRANK RICH

From now on, there will always be two groups of theatergoers in this world: those who have seen "Moose Murders," and those who have not. Those of us who have witnessed the play that opened at the Eugene O'Neill Theater last night will undoubtedly hold periodic reunions, in the noble tradition of survivors of the Titanic. Tears and booze will flow in equal measure, and there will be a prize awarded to the bearer of the most outstanding antlers. As for those theatergoers who miss "Moose Murders"—well, they just don't rate. A visit to "Moose Murders" is what will separate the connoisseurs of Broadway disaster from mere dilettantes for many moons to come.

***

Published: February 23, 1983. Full text available at: http://theater.nytimes.com/mem/theater/treview. html?_r=1&res=9400E3DF133BF930A157751C0A965948260.

Selection 5.7

And here he's plainly having more fun than he had at the theater.

THEATER
'Private Lives,' Burton and Miss Taylor
By FRANK RICH

The tone of the Richard Burton–Elizabeth Taylor "Private Lives" is established right off. When Mr. Burton makes his first entrance on to the attractive Deauville hotel terrace designed by David Mitchell, he looks anything but happy. His face is a taut mask, frozen in an expression of less-than-exquisite pain, and there's no bounce as he walks about on his stacked boots. He's not Noel Coward's flippant hero Elyot Chase—he doesn't even seem to be an actor. In his immaculate Savile Row business suit, Mr. Burton mostly resembles a retired millionaire steeling himself for an obligatory annual visit to the accountant. He's bored out of his mind but grimly determined to clip the coupons and sign the papers that will allow him to maintain his cash flow for the next year.

Miss Taylor, soon to follow, is scarcely more buoyant. She enters in the first of several Theoni V. Aldredge costumes that fail to further the illusion of what Coward described as his "quite exquisite" heroine. Her curly mop of hair is meant to suggest the fashion of the 1920's but instead recalls the matronly Toni permanents that were in vogue during the 1950's. Not that it matters—Miss Taylor isn't trying to play Amanda Prynne. When she looks at her co-star, her glances betray neither rapture nor revulsion; she looks past him, not at him. It's only when she stares out into the vast reaches of the Lunt-Fontanne that her eyes reveal a hint of sparkle: what she sees then is a full house.

And so you have the complete picture. While this "Private Lives" does plod on—and on and on—for another two and a half hours (despite substantial pruning of the script), the first impression it leaves is the last. From the start, the production never even pretends to be anything other than a calculated business venture. Though the irresistible plot mechanics keep Act I sporadically afloat, the two acts to come have all the vitality of a Madame Tussaud's exhibit and all the gaiety of a tax audit. Nothing that happens at any time has any bearing on Coward's classic 1930 comedy.

***

Published: May 9, 1983. Full text available at: www.nytimes.com/1983/05/09/theater/theater-private-lives-burton-and-miss-taylor.html.

The New York Times

Selection 5.8

Now occupying the role chief theater critic at The Times that Rich once held, Ben Brantley uses the revival of three musicals (a genre that Broadway so often revives) to provide context, analysis and critical argument. Though plainly an incisive, intelligent critic, here he responds with his heart as well as his head, as expressed through his appreciation of "the sensual appeal that comes from feeling the quickening warmth of real life given stirring artistic form."

Again, for the First Time
By BEN BRANTLEY

When your high school English teachers talked about the rewards of revisiting the classics, they probably didn't mean musicals. Most likely they were referring to fat, dense novels ("Middlemarch," "Anna Karenina") and long, lofty plays ("Hamlet," "Long Day's Journey Into Night"): works of weight, they liked to tell us, dragging out a favorite dog-eared phrase, with "universal human truth."

Weighty is not an adjective commonly attached to musicals, which were born to divert, to tickle. They came into existence as the paler, thinner cousins of light operas, for heaven's sake. Yet after

Published: June 1, 2008.

experiencing, in recent weeks, the Tony-nominated Broadway revivals of "Rodgers & Hammerstein's South Pacific," "Gypsy" and "Sunday in the Park With George," I'm carving out new space for these shows on my list of all-time favorite literary masterpieces, right near the top.

Granted, on the page the lyrics and librettos may not parse neatly enough to satisfy Miss Kapp, the woman who taught me to diagram sentences. But as seen in the remarkable productions that opened this year, these shows from different decades of the last half-century easily meet my checklist for great narrative art: complex and constantly evolving characters, a sense that what happens is both spontaneous and inevitable, and a sustained perspective that finds poetic patterns in our daily muddles.

Heck, I'll even throw in those Aristotelian prerequisites about self-knowledge and catharsis. These beauties have it all. Not to mention the sensual appeal that comes from feeling the quickening warmth of real life given stirring artistic form.

It's rare that the race for best revival of a musical is the sexiest category at the Tony Awards, which will be bestowed this year on June 15 at Radio City Music Hall. But what's most striking about "South Pacific" (first staged on Broadway in 1949), "Gypsy" (1959) and "Sunday in the Park With George" (1984) is how much fuller and juicier they feel than any of the newer musical fare this season. (Yes, there is a fourth contender for best revival of a musical: "Grease," which cast its leads via reality television. Enough said.)

I much enjoyed three of the nominees for best new musical: "In the Heights," "Passing Strange" and "Xanadu." (The fourth is "Cry-Baby." Enough said.) But it was on the diverting level that my parents might have enjoyed, say, "Wonderful Town" or a "New Faces" revue in the 1950s, or "The Fantasticks" a few years later.

Though they embrace musical forms unknown to Comden and Green (like hip-hop and rap) and a Latino and African-American perspective rarely evident in Broadway musicals until the 1960s, "In the Heights" and "Passing Strange" are also throwbacks to a more overtly sentimental era of entertainment, with hymns to Mother (and Grandmother) of which George M. Cohan might have approved.

Their characters—even the self-portraits of the talented Stew, the creator and star of "Passing Strange"—are largely drawn in bright comic shorthand. "Xanadu," a droll reworking of a notorious cinematic flop from the disco era, doesn't have a thought in its fluffy head beyond wanting us to feel good.

That's fine. Broadway needs its fluff, especially the kind that doesn't go limp under a tonnage of special effects. (I'll take "Mamma Mia!" over "The Little Mermaid" any day.) What makes you want to keep going back to the most recent versions of "South Pacific," "Gypsy" and "Sunday," though, isn't the need for a cotton-candy fix. It's that you sense there's always something more to be gleaned from them. And that—and this is the special dividend of live theater—the shows might have grown even more since you last saw them.

What sets these productions apart from other fine revivals of recent years is how true they remain to the spirit of the originals while exuding a new-born freshness. The hit reincarnations of "Carousel" (1994), "Cabaret" (1998) and "Sweeney Todd" (2005) were all, in different ways, dazzlers. But each was shaped, first and foremost, by an intellectual concept imposed by a director (each, coincidentally, a Briton). The implicit message, at least with "Carousel" and "Cabaret," was that in the late 20th century it was possible to be perfectly frank, to make dark subtext the main text.

The difference with "Gypsy," "Sunday" and "South Pacific" is that they work entirely from within. There's no postmodern distance about them, no we-know-better-now wink. The directors Arthur Laurents ("Gypsy"), Sam Buntrock ("Sunday") and Bartlett Sher ("South Pacific") instead have demanded that their performers dig like archaeologists into the existing libretto, lyrics and music. And what treasures they have found.

With "South Pacific," adapted from James Michener's stories of American military men and women far from home during World War II—which, like the musical, won a Pulitzer Prize—Mr. Sher doesn't apologize for such potentially dated elements as yesteryear's progressive political conscience or an unconditional belief in love at first sight. He scales up, though, the always implicit elements of wartime disorientation and of cultures in collision.

Michael Yeargan's beautiful beachscape of a set appropriately suggests a dreamlike isolation from conventions, a sense of a world in which old rules no longer apply, and only military discipline keeps people from sliding into anomie. But most important is the fear and uncertainty with which the cast members invest their characters, even in their most frivolous moments.

Kelli O'Hara's plucky ensign from Little Rock, Ark.; Paulo Szot's self-exiled French plantation owner; Matthew Morrison's battle-rattled Ivy League lieutenant: they're all trying to make sense of reactions they never expected to have.

Mr. Sher stages breakout songs, including the love duet "Some Enchanted Evening" and "Bali Ha'i" (performed by Loretta Ables Sayre as the survival-conscious island entrepreneur Bloody Mary), as double-edged studies in seduction, shot through with menace as well as allure. His performers seep emotional anxiety, the awareness that all bets are off in war, from their pores. And the show acquires a timeless visceral charge.

The same commitment to character is what brings such eye-opening vitality to Mr. Buntrock's interpretation of "Sunday in the Park With George," Stephen Sondheim and James Lapine's meditation on art according to the pointillist George Seurat. Certainly the digital projections of Seurat's art coming into being are wonderful.

But they wouldn't count for nearly as much if they weren't backed up with the ensemble's ability to convey the different visions with which different people shape the world. Chief among these, of course, are Daniel Evans's magnificent double portrait of the obsessive Seurat (in the first act) and his American descendant, a conceptual artist, in the second; and Jenna Russell as Seurat's pragmatic model and lover (and, in the second act, her daughter).

But every performance in the show is blessed with thought-through detail that defines each character as an individual of conflicting needs and perspectives. When the ensemble sings "Sunday," one of Mr. Sondheim's most diversely inflected songs, it's like hearing a storm of separate thoughts. The harmony—spatial, visual, musical—achieved by the Georges at the end of both acts is thus all the more moving in its transcendence.

If the performances are broader in "Gypsy," adapted from the memoirs of the stripper Gypsy Rose Lee and featuring a crackerjack score by Jule Styne (with lyrics by Mr. Sondheim), well, these characters belong to show business, a world in which success is built on the ability to make yourself seen.

This production's director also happens to be the man who wrote the original book, the 90-year-old Mr. Laurents. And though I saw and admired two earlier Broadway revivals by Mr. Laurents (with Angela Lansbury and Tyne Daly), this one has a singular fierceness and clarity of vision.

It's not just that Patti LuPone is so commandingly intense in the central role of Momma Rose, the stage mother to end all stage mothers. It's that every character onstage is so obviously driven by an aching hunger to be noticed. That includes Rose's daughters, June (Leigh Ann Larkin) and Louise (Laura Benanti), and her lover, Herbie (Boyd Gaines). And for once, none of them easily yields the stage to Rose.

Everyone is fighting for love here. And the genius of this production is how astutely it blends garden-variety inter-family struggles for attention into the look-at-me competitiveness of the theater. Of course these folks sing their thoughts. That's show biz. And show biz, in this instance, becomes a magnifying mirror for your basic parent-child relationship.

Definitive is a dangerous word in criticism. And I hesitate to call these productions that, even though they're the best interpretations of these three musicals that I've ever seen. Definitive suggests set in stone. These shows all have a fluid, organic life that honors the mutability of great art.

Every time I reread "Anna Karenina" or "King Lear," they seem different to me, because I keep seeing new things in them. What this season's triumvirate of great revivals demonstrates is that these shows have the innate richness and substance to sustain repeated interpretations in the years to come. Meanwhile they're as close to, well, definitive as you're likely to see in this lifetime.

A Conversation with . . . **Ben Brantley**

CHIEF THEATER CRITIC

© The New York Times

Ben Brantley became chief theater critic in 1996, three years after joining The Times. He had previously done reporting and reviewing for other publications. With a varied journalistic background, he now has the job he's always wanted. This is an edited transcript of an e-mail interview.

What sort of experience or training prepared you to become chief theater critic at The New York Times?

My road to the job I now have was neither straight nor typical. Before becoming a theater critic at The Times, I had worked as a news reporter, a fashion critic and a European bureau chief, out of Paris, for Women's Wear Daily; a staff writer at Vanity Fair and The New Yorker; and a film critic for Elle magazine. My editor at Elle was Alex Witchel, who was soon to marry Frank Rich, then the chief theater critic of The New York Times. When The Times was looking for a new second-string critic, Alex suggested me. After a series of interviews and audition pieces (I reviewed six plays, not for publication), I was given the job.

That said, I should also note that in my first job interview out of college—with John Fairchild, the publisher of Women's Wear Daily—I was asked if I could have any job in the world, what it would be. I answered without hesitation: "Theater critic for The New York Times." It didn't seem likely that this would ever happen. But in truth, I'd been preparing for it all my life. Theater was my first and most abiding passion, something I fell in love with as a child. I acted in productions from kindergarten through college, read plays the way other kids read comic books and went to the theater—in New York and later in London (when I was living in Paris)—as often as I could.

How does reviewing theater for The Times differ from doing so for another publication, or in another city?

The Times has a singular position in relationship to the theater. It's the most nationally prominent paper in a city that remains the capital of theater in America. And its verdict on plays counts disproportionately. (In London, another theater hub, no single paper is similarly dominant.) Awareness of this position could be paralyzing if you let it be. So it's an awareness that you store only in the back of your mind, where it casts a sense of responsibility on what you write without suffocating it.

Does a theater review in The Times have more commercial impact than a movie or book review?
For the reasons mentioned above, I suppose a Times theater review does have a greater impact than a book or movie review would, although I think in all three fields, The Times still has the greatest power to boost works that might slip away unnoticed otherwise. There are certain types of Broadway productions—big musical behemoths, in particular—that are critic-proof in the way that literary or movie blockbusters are.

Does The Times review all theatrical productions that open in New York? Who decides who reviews what?
Dearly though we would like to review every production that opens in New York, that would be impossible. This, in a way, is a good thing, since it means that New York continues to be a fertile breeding ground for theater of many forms. I am given first choice on what I want to review, and then my colleague Charles Isherwood, makes his choices.

Do you apply different critical standards to a big-budget Broadway production than to a bare-bones off-Broadway play?
I try to apply the same critical standards to everything I see, though I do think there's wisdom to the adage that you don't shoot a mouse with an elephant gun. Basically, I try to evaluate a show according to what standards it sets for itself and how successfully it realizes its own ambitions. So in that sense, I wouldn't ask a tiny Off-Broadway revue to perform on the scale of a Broadway extravaganza.

How much research and what kind do you do before seeing a play? Or do you prefer to experience it fresh, like much of the audience will?
When I was first at The Times, I researched every play I was seeing to the teeth. I'd look at tapes (at the New York Public Library's Theater on Film and Tape Archives) of previous work by the director and performers I would be seeing, and if the play was a revival, earlier productions. I'd read as much as I could of a writer's work, as well as reviews and biographical material.

The longer I've been in this job, the less necessary this kind of research is, partly because being a critic for many years automatically broadens your frame of reference. I still tend to at least eyeball texts of classics—especially Shakespeare and the ancient Greeks—before I see revivals of them, so I'll know how much they've been tampered with or rearranged. But no matter what kind of background work I've done, I try to turn myself into a blank slate when I sit down with the audience, before the curtain goes up. It's good to have a sense of context, but whether a show works or not has little to do with what you know about it and everything to do with your immediate feelings as you watch it, in the present tense.

Does an audience's response influence your review? Are there plays that a paying audience loves, and you can't share that enthusiasm? (Or vice versa?)

I am definitely not always on the same page as the audience with which I see a show. Theater, like all art, is such a subjective experience, and you can't expect everyone to respond in the same way. How often do you leave a movie with, say, two friends and realize you've all seen different shows? I should also add that the critics' previews I attend—performances set aside for reviewers just before official openings—usually do not have representative audiences. Those houses are often "papered" with friends, relations, industry people, press agents and eager volunteers, so you take the reactions that emerge from this pre-fab crowd with a certain skepticism.

Do you ever discover some dimensions to your response to the work through the process of writing about it? Or do you pretty much know what you think before starting?

I know the overall frame and tenor of what I'm going to write when I sit down at the computer. I try to re-create as closely as I can what I felt as I was watching the production. But the distance of even a few hours allows you to see how aspects of the play fit (or don't fit) together. You're more conscious of details then that might have escaped you in your first response.

Are you writing for the avid theatergoer or the general reader? Or both?

If you write for only the avid theatergoer, you're cutting off a large part of your potential readership. Part of my job is to seduce people who might not go to the theater ordinarily into taking a chance on it. So you try to impart as much of the enthusiasm you feel without sounding like an insider in sealed world.

How is theater different from the other art forms?

Theater is a very personal art form. I mean, personal for those watching it, in that the audience is complicit in what's happening on stage. Subliminally, you're feeding the performers and shaping what they do. Which means that no performance is ever going to be exactly the same. It's a wonderful hybrid of "finished" and evolving art.

Has the shift from newsprint to the Web changed anything about your job or your relationship with your readers?

For the past several years, I've been blogging my trips to London—theater-going marathons of several weeks to a month—with new entries each day. And this, of course, creates an immediate dialogue with readers that more formal reviews don't allow. And I find that because of e-mail—with Times Web readers being able to click onto my byline to send me a message—I hear from readers much more quickly than I did in the past. This is all to the good. What worries me a bit about blogging is that instant writing doesn't allow for the kind of digestive process (not to mention editorial vetting and fact checking) that is essential to sober criticism. Still, I admit I enjoy the rush of instant journalism.

MAKING**CONNECTIONS**

1 What are the analytical and evaluative differences between the two reviews of "Waiting for Godot"? How does the context provided in the second review reflect the content of the first review?

How does the response by Charles Isherwood to "Coast of Utopia" differ from the way he summarizes the responses of other critics? Where does he agree with the critical consensus on Stoppard, and where does he disagree? **2**

3 Compare the writing style in the very positive review by Frank Rich and the very negative reviews. What does the writing have in common?

4

What argument does Ben Brantley make about ranking the best musicals with the greatest literary classics? Write a short response in which you agree or disagree with him.

film

IN THE ESSAY THAT'S THE LAST PIECE IN THIS CHAP-
TER, A. O. Scott asks the question, "Why do we [critics] go sniffing after art
where everyone else is looking for fun?" An uncommonly insightful and entertaining journalist, as you'll see in the interview with him that concludes this
chapter, Scott knows he is oversimplifying about both critics and audiences.

The reality is that critics also like to have fun at the movies, and they
respond with positive reviews when they do. And audiences ("everyone else")
are often looking for art—at least some audiences, with some movies. But
blanket generalizations about popular and critical responses to movies are
impossible, because the moviegoing experience is so varied, and so is the audience, and so are the critics who cover the beat.

Depending on the day, our mood, perhaps the company that we are with,
some of us go to some movies for roller-coaster thrills, for heart-stopping terror, for comedy so raucous (and perhaps even crude) that the whole theater
explodes in laughter, for romantic fantasies, even for sexual titillation. We may
respond to small movies—ones that impress with the subtleties of character
and dialogue—far differently from the way we respond to the action-driven,
spectacle-filled, star-studded larger ones.

Movie critics, like audiences and like critics in other fields, generally
respond first with their gut. They like or they don't like, and then they attempt
to analyze why. What distinguishes the movie beat from others is that the offerings each week are comparatively few, and thus the coverage is comparatively
comprehensive.

A book critic with no affinity for mysteries or a pop critic with no appreciation for jazz might avoid reviewing those for years, decades, forever. But
reviewers at The Times cover every movie that opens in New York. Even
when studios try to discourage reviews by not offering advance screenings
(so that bad reviews won't diminish opening-weekend receipts), a reviewer
will buy a ticket on the opening Friday and file a review for Saturday. Most
news organizations that review films have more than one reviewer (some of
them freelance), but the fact remains that if you are a professional film critic,
you will inevitably review chick flicks, slasher movies, art films and gross-out
comedies, along with foreign, independent and art films.

Movies and music are the two most common beats to which fledgling critics aspire, with an appreciation that typically begins as a fan. One difference
between music and movie reviewers is that the latter typically have more to
consider—or more they *can* consider. If a movie really works, is it because of

the directing? (What constitutes good directing?) The acting? (Are the actors responsible or is the director?) The cinematography? The writing? The costumes or set design? The music? The special effects? One of the reasons there are so many categories at the Academy Awards is that all of these specialties can contribute to the impact of a movie.

Where plays, as discussed in the previous chapter, are typically considered an "actor's medium"—because the audience appreciates the actor's artistry live, unmediated—movies are a "director's medium." For the finished film, a director may choose from dozens of takes, in which actors tried different approaches. The director might leave entire scenes, even an actor's whole performance, on the cutting room floor. The director might allow the actors to take great liberties with the script, or insist that they strictly adhere to it. The vision of how the film looks may well be the cinematographer's, but typically at the behest of or in collaboration with the director.

Even though you're going with your gut as an aspiring reviewer, contextual research will enrich your work. If the director has specialized in a particular type of film, is the new work a progression or departure? Does the director work with many of the same actors in different films? Does he coax different types of performances out of them from the ones they're known for in other movies? Do this director and cinematographer often work as a team?

Source material often provides rewarding context as well. If the movie is based on a book, analyze how well it works as a movie, rather than how faithful it is to the book (which most moviegoers won't have read, unless we're dealing with a Harry Potter–scale phenomenon, as Elvis Mitchell is in one of the following reviews). Much of the writing in novels describes what's going on inside a character's head, which is difficult to convey on the screen except through voice-overs. Plus a faithful adaptation of most novels would require many more hours than movies typically last; a lot inevitably has to be cut.

Similarly, films based on real life or historical incident must often heighten drama, compress or eliminate key figures, or employ other measures that make for a better movie at the expense of factual record. Unless the results are egregiously misleading, judge the film not by how faithful it is to the events that inspired it, but by how well it works as a film.

Sometimes plays, particularly very successful ones, inspire movies. A chief consideration will be how well the movie has "opened up" the scenes, so that what was once comparatively static, with sets on a single stage, now takes place beyond the four walls of the theater. Increasingly, some movies are based on graphic novels, others on old TV series, some even on video games. At least some familiarity with the source material will be helpful in relating how—and how well—it has been transformed into film.

DVD reviews constitute a category of their own (not covered here), but the reviewer must assess them not only in terms of the quality of the film but in terms of additional material (commentary, "director's cut" expansion outtakes). And if the film was widely reviewed and seen upon theatrical release, the reviewer can assume some familiarity with the material (if only name recognition) on the part of the reader, while still making the review engaging and intelligible for those who come to it without that contextual background.

Whoever the director might be, whatever the source material—and some projects, of course, have been written specifically for the screen—the biggest driving force in ticket sales, and frequently audience response, is star power. Movie stars receive the biggest salaries because they sell tickets. Some of us will pay repeatedly to see Jack Nicholson be Jack, Julia Roberts be Julia, Bruce Willis be Bruce. Some of us will applaud George Clooney for stretching himself and playing against type; some of us will resent Jim Carrey for the same.

Increasingly, big-budget studios have hedged their bets with franchises: sequels or prequels that constitute a brand-name series. Often a law of diminishing returns prevails, though occasionally (as with the Batman franchise) a renewal brings even greater critical plaudits along with commercial success.

One of the challenges of writing about movies is that there is so much you could possibly write about. And that richness of possibility is also one of the rewards. The following selections invite you to compare approaches from different decades, and by different critics, as you explore the myriad methods to share insightful, provocative responses with a movie-loving readership.

Selection 6.1

Let's begin with a populist defense of the sort of blockbuster that critics often disdain, written in a style that befits the subject. ("Just because a movie blows stuff up doesn't mean it automatically stinks.") As co-chief film critic of The Times, Manohla Dargis recognizes the art of movies but also appreciates the fun. Examine how she provides critical context—in terms of range, history, audience response—or the kind of movies typically maligned.

Defending Goliath: Hollywood and the Art of the Blockbuster

By MANOHLA DARGIS

Summertime and the viewing is lousy and noisy and deedle-dee dumb, or so the received wisdom has it. It is our season of stupidity, summertime, that interminable stretch when adults surrender the nation's theaters to hordes of popcorn-chugging, sugar-jonesing, under-age nose-pickers for whom the cinematic experience means nothing more than recycled big, bigger, biggest bangs. It is the season of mass distraction, of the tent pole, the event movie, the blockbuster.

Blockbuster is really just descriptive, but it often carries with it a down-market whiff, as do many pop-cultural products that come with eye-catching price tags and seem precision-tooled for young

Published: May 6, 2007.

audiences. Critics, including, yes, yours truly, often use blockbuster as easy (too easy) shorthand for overinflated productions that rely more on special effects than words and characters, and that distract rather than engage the audience. At its most reductive the negative spin on blockbusters is that they signal the death of cinema art and mark the triumph of the corporate bottom line, of marketing strategies, product placements and opening-weekend returns. And here you thought you were just watching Tobey Maguire run around in a unitard.

But just because a movie blows stuff up doesn't mean it automatically stinks. A good blockbuster, like the recent Bond flick "Casino Royale," takes you places you might never otherwise go and shows you things you could never do. It brings you into new worlds, offers you new attractions. It takes hold of your body, making you quiver with anxiety, joy, laughter, relief. When great blockbusters sweep you up and away—I'm thinking about watching "The Matrix" for the first time with a few hundred other enraptured souls—they usher you into a realm of communal pleasure. In a culture of entertainment niches, they remind you of what going to the movies can still be like.

They also remind you that without the human factor a blockbuster is nothing but a big empty box. Blockbusters that endure strike a balance between the spectacular and the ineffably human, whether it's Peter O'Toole framed against the never-ending desert in "Lawrence of Arabia" or Keanu Reeves coming down to earth in "The Matrix" as he realizes that he knows kung fu. It's the epic story of America refracted through one family in the "Godfather" films. It's a mechanical shark and Robert Shaw remembering the U.S.S. Indianapolis in "Jaws." It's Tom Cruise hanging by a thread in "Mission: Impossible" and Christian Bale standing amid a cloud of bats in "Batman Begins." It's Leonardo DiCaprio's wild eyes in "Titanic" and Kirsten Dunst's sad ones in "Spider-Man."

Blockbuster usually describes products sold in enormous quantities, like movies, but also theater productions, museum shows, hit songs, books and even pharmaceuticals. The word probably originated with the powerful bombs that the British Royal Air Force used to decimate German cities during World War II, the so-called blockbusters. It soon entered the vernacular, appearing in advertisements before the end of the war, and as a clue in a 1950 crossword puzzle in this newspaper (46 across). In the early 1950s the heavyweight champion Rocky Marciano was known as the Brockton Blockbuster, after the city where he was born, and the word blockbuster routinely appeared in articles about the Hollywood vogue for super-size entertainments.

These days highbrows dismiss movie blockbusters because they are often based in fantasy rather than reality, which is generally a bad thing unless the fantasy comes with a literary pedigree like "The Lord of the Rings." Blockbusters tend to be made for adolescents instead of adults, which is also a bad thing because youngsters are untrustworthy cultural consumers. (One exception: blockbusters based on children's books that also appeal to adults, like the Harry Potter cycle.) Blockbusters based on comics are invariably questionable unless they are called graphic novels and then not always. Blockbusters that open on thousands of screens are also considered dubious because anything that appeals to a wide audience is inherently suspect. I'm joking, but not really.

In recent years it has become axiomatic that the 1970s special-effects-laden blockbusters "Jaws" and "Star Wars" helped bring an end to New Hollywood's flirtation with creative freedom (think of "Nashville"), ushering in the era of juvenile diversions like "Raiders of the Lost Ark." Never mind that "Jaws" is a good movie, far better at least for some than "Nashville." As Martin Scorsese says in "Easy Riders, Raging Bulls," Peter Biskind's history of 1970s American cinema: " 'Star Wars' was in. Spielberg was in. We were finished." Well, not exactly, as suggested by the little gold statue presented to Mr. Scorsese in February by Steven Spielberg, George Lucas and Francis Ford Coppola, whose 1972 blockbuster, "The Godfather," also happens to be a masterpiece.

The movie industry has been in the business of big—big stars, big stories, big productions, big screens and big returns—about as long as it's been a business. And as long as the movies have told stories, they have used spectacle to sell those stories. In the silent era motion-picture producers employed spectacle to help distinguish the new medium from that of the theater, creating what were essentially protoblockbusters. In the 1950s the faltering movie industry went into the business of the supercolossus, delivering epic-size stories on ever-widening big screens in part to distinguish itself from that small-screen menace called television. Much has changed about the movies in the decades since, but not so the uses of pyrotechnics, sweeping landscapes and all manner of cinematic awesomeness.

Nowadays the armies of sword-brandishing soldiers may be largely computer generated, as in "300," but film spectacle works more or less the same now as it did in 1912 when the Italian epic "Quo Vadis?" hit screens with a cast of literally thousands and extreme action in the form of a chariot race. That film's pageantry, its gladiators and sacrificed Christians earned an enthusiastic thumb's up from the sculptor Auguste Rodin, who declared it "a masterpiece." (Everyone really is a critic.) The Italians were among the first in the film-spectacle business, but the Americans soon jumped in with costly productions like D. W. Griffith's benighted masterpiece, "The Birth of a Nation," which dramatically advanced the art.

Spectacle didn't just enthrall audiences; it was instrumental to the very development of feature filmmaking, as directors learned how to make longer-running entertainments. Not that spectacle and narrative always mesh, then or now. In 1923 an anonymous critic for The New York Times wrote that Cecil B. DeMille's "Ten Commandments" was divided into two sections, "the spectacle and the melodrama," that might as well have been directed by two different men. The critic's admiration for the spectacle ("done with meticulous precision") tempered the larger criticism. ("It would have needed an unusually perfect modern drama to stand up in comparison.") Somewhere the producer Jerry Bruckheimer is shaking his head, wondering why he can't catch a similar break with today's reviewers.

Yet if audiences dig spectacle, critics often view it with suspicion, as sneers about the modern blockbuster suggest. The negative rap on blockbusters is partly due to the literary bent of a lot of critics, who privilege words over images and tend to review screenplays, or what's left of them, rather than the amalgamation of sights and sounds in front of them. But the sneers also suggest an underlying and familiar contamination anxiety. In the 1980s "Top Gun" wasn't just a glib divertissement; it was evidence that MTV had infected the movies like a deadly virus. In the same grim light "300" isn't just a shell of a movie; it's proof that the movies have been infiltrated by an outside force, namely video games.

The threats have changed over the years—from television to music videos, comic books, digital technologies and so on—yet what has remained constant is the idea that the movies are under siege. But if the movies have taught us anything it is that they are brilliant adapters. They mutate and shift, stretch and adjust, and they neutralize those threats the way an organism absorbs nutrients, by assimilating them. We call some of these movie mutations comic-book flicks and compare still others to music videos, sometimes with a sigh, sometimes with a smile. We complain about car chases and forget that D. W. Griffith was among the first to put pedal to the metal on screen. And we condemn blockbusters for, if we're lucky, doing the very thing we say we want from the movies: giving us a reason to watch.

Selection 6.2

Where Dargis praises the type of movie not made for critics, Elvis Mitchell turns a critical eye on a movie for which he is obviously not the target audience. A more timid critic could write more ambivalently about the pleasures a child (or Harry Potter fan) will receive from the transfer of the best-selling book to the big screen. What others might praise as faithfulness to the text strikes this critic as "a dreary, literal-minded competence," an evaluation that comes early and pulls no punches. Also, consider how much cultural context he brings; Mitchell plainly doesn't see movies in a vacuum.

FILM REVIEW
The Sorcerer's Apprentice
By ELVIS MITCHELL

The world may not be ready yet for the film equivalent of books on tape, but this peculiar phenomenon has arrived in the form of the film adaptation of J. K. Rowling's "Harry Potter and the Sorcerer's Stone." The most highly awaited movie of the year has a dreary, literal-minded competence, following the letter of the law as laid down by the author. But it's all muted flourish, with momentary pleasures, like Gringott's, the bank staffed by trolls that looks like a Gaudí throwaway. The picture is so careful that even the tape wrapped around the bridge of Harry's glasses seems to have come out of the set design. (It never occurred to anyone to show him taping the frame together.)

The movie comes across as a covers act by an extremely competent tribute band—not the real thing but an incredible simulation—and there's an audience for this sort of thing. But watching "Harry Potter" is like seeing "Beatlemania" staged in the Hollywood Bowl, where the cheers and screams will drown out whatever's unfolding onstage.

To call this movie shameless is beside the point. It would probably be just as misguided to complain about the film's unoriginality because (a) it has assumed that the target audience doesn't want anything new and (b) Ms. Rowling's books cannibalize and synthesize pop culture mythology, proof of the nothing-will-ever-go-away ethic. She has come up with something like "Star Wars" for a generation that never had a chance to thrill to its grandeur, but this is "Young Sherlock Holmes" as written by C. S. Lewis from a story by Roald Dahl.

The director, Chris Columbus, is as adept as Ms. Rowling at cobbling free-floating cultural myths into a wobbly whole. The first film from a Columbus script, "Gremlins," had the cheeky cheesiness of an urban legend written for Marvel Comics. Mr. Columbus probably felt like the right choice for "Harry Potter" because he has often used the same circuit boards as Ms. Rowling to design his fables. His "Home Alone" movies, "Mrs. Doubtfire" and "Stepmom" employ the theme of abandonment by parents as if it were a brand name. And like Mr. Columbus's films, Ms. Rowling's novels pull together archetypes that others have long exploited. This movie begins with a shot of a street sign that will cause happy young audiences to erupt in recognition, as the dry-witted giant Hagrid (Robbie Coltrane) and Professor McGonagall (Maggie Smith) drop a baby at the Doorstep of Destiny.

Years later Harry (Daniel Radcliffe), sporting the jagged thunderbolt scar across his forehead, is living there with his terrors of an aunt (Fiona Shaw) and uncle (Richard Griffiths).

Published: November 16, 2001.

Harry is the kid all kids dream they are. His special abilities are recognized by people other than the ones who have raised him. Hagrid returns to rescue him from his tiny room under the stairs and clues Harry in about the boy's inner force, which is why he doesn't fit into the world of Muggles, the nonmagical and nonbelievers.

Harry is shown the way to Hogwarts, an English boarding school for wizards run by Professor Dumbledore (Richard Harris), where Harry pals up with the gawky but decent Ron (Rupert Grint) and the bossy, precocious Hermione (Emma Watson). The instructors, who rule the classrooms with varying degrees of imperiousness, include the acid Snape (Alan Rickman) and the mousy stutterer Quirrell (Ian Hart).

The casting is the standout, from the smaller roles up; it seems that every working British actor of the last 20 years makes an appearance. John Hurt blows through as an overly intense dealer in magic equipment, schooling Harry on selecting his tools. While shopping for his magic equipment, Harry comes across the Sorcerer's Stone, a bedeviled jewel whose power affects his first year at the enchanted school.

Mr. Radcliffe has an unthinkably difficult role for a child actor; all he gets to do is look sheepish when everyone turns to him and intones that he may be the greatest wizard ever. He could have been hobbled by being cast because he resembles the Harry of the book cover illustrations. It's a horrible burden to place on a kid, but it helps that Mr. Radcliffe does have the long-faced mournfulness of a 60's pop star. He also possesses a watchful gravity and, shockingly, the large, authoritative hands of a real wizard.

The other child actors shine, too. Ms. Watson has the sass and smarts to suggest she might cast a spell of her own on Harry in the coming years and, one supposes, sequels. Mr. Grint has a surprising everyman quality, but the showstopper is Tom Felton as Draco Malfoy. This drolly menacing blond with a widow's peak is Harry's plotting foe, and he has the rotted self-confidence of one of the upperclassmen from Lindsay Anderson's "If." There has never been a kid who got so much joy from speaking his oddball name.

Ms. Shaw and Mr. Griffiths are enjoyably swinish, the most resolute of Muggles. Mr. Rickman, whose licorice-black pageboy has the bounce of a coiffure from a hair products ad, is a threatening schoolroom don who delivers his monologues with a hint of mint; his nostrils flare so athletically that he seems to be doing tantric yoga with his sinuses. The mountainously lovable Mr. Coltrane really is a fairy-tale figure that kids dream about.

The movie's most consistently entertaining scene features a talking hat, and that's not meant as an insult. The Sorting Hat, which has more personality than anything else in the movie, assigns the students to the various dormitories; it puts Harry, Ron and Hermione together.

But the other big set pieces are a letdown. The Quidditch match—the school sport that's part polo, part cricket and part Rollerball, played on flying brooms—has all the second-rate sloppiness of the race in "Stars Wars—Episode 1: The Phantom Menace." It's a blur of mortifyingly ordinary computer-generated effects.

Given that movies can now show us everything, the manifestations that Ms. Rowling described could be less magical only if they were delivered at a news conference. And the entrance that may be as eagerly awaited as Harry's appearance—the arrival of Voldemort (Richard Bremmer), the archvillain—is a disappointment, a special effect that serves as a reminder of how much he stands in Darth Vader's shadow.

This overly familiar movie is like a theme park that's a few years past its prime; the rides clatter and groan with metal fatigue every time they take a curve. The picture's very raggedness makes it spooky, which is not the same thing as saying the movie is intentionally unsettling.

No one has given Harry a pair of Hogwarts-edition Nikes, nor do he, Hermione and Ron stop off to super-size it at the campus McDonald's: exclusions that seem like integrity these days. (There's no need for product placement. The Internet is likely to have a systems crash from all the kids going online to order maroon-and-gold scarves, which Harry and his dorm mates wear.)

Another kind of exclusion seems bothersome, though. At a time when London is filled with faces of color, the fleeting appearances by minority kids is scarier than Voldemort. (Harry's gorgeous owl, snow white with sunken dark eyes and feather tails dappled with black, gets more screen time than they do.)

Mr. Columbus does go out of his way to give a couple of lines to a little boy with a well-groomed head of dreadlocks. This movie may not be whiter than most, but the peering-from-the-sidelines status accorded to minorities seems particularly offensive in a picture aimed at kids. It's no different in the books, really, but young imaginations automatically correct for this paucity.

A lack of imagination pervades the movie because it so slavishly follows the book. The filmmakers, the producers and the studio seem panicked by anything that might feel like a departure from the book— which already feels film-ready—so "Harry Potter and the Sorcerer's Stone" never takes on a life of its own.

Someone has cast a sleepwalker's spell over the proceedings, and at nearly two and a half hours you may go under, too. Its literal-mindedness makes the film seem cowed by the chilling omnipresence of its own Voldemort, Ms. Rowling, who hovered around the production.

The movie is so timid it's like someone who flinches when you extend a hand to shake. This film is capable of a certain brand of magic: it may turn the faithful into Muggles.

Selection 6.3

As the chief film critic at The Times during an era that many would consider a golden age for the American cinema, Vincent Canby showed his appreciation for the wide range of experiences offered the moviegoer. Here he praises, early and strongly, a special-effects blockbuster that (as his kicker suggests) might best be viewed in a state of childlike innocence.

'Star Wars': A Trip to a Far Galaxy That's Fun and Funny
By VINCENT CANBY

"Star Wars," George Lucas's first film since his terrifically successful "American Graffiti," is the movie that the teen-agers in "American Graffiti" would have broken their necks to see. It's also the movie that's going to entertain a lot of contemporary folk who have a soft spot for the virtually ritualized manners of comic-book adventure.

"Star Wars," which opened yesterday at the Astor Plaza, Orpheum and other theaters, is the most elaborate, most expensive, most beautiful movie serial ever made.

It's both an apotheosis of "Flash Gordon" serials and a witty critique that makes associations with a variety of literature that is nothing if not eclectic: "Quo Vadis?", "Buck Rogers," "Ivanhoe," "Superman," "The Wizard of Oz," "The Gospel According to St. Matthew," the legend of King Arthur and the knights of the Round Table.

All of these works, of course, had earlier left their marks on the kind of science-fiction comic strips that Mr. Lucas, the writer as well as director of "Star Wars," here remembers with affection of such cheerfulness that he avoids facetiousness. The way definitely not to approach "Star Wars," though, is to expect a film of cosmic implications or to footnote it with so many references that one anticipates it as if it were a literary duty. It's fun and funny.

The time, according to the opening credit card, is "a long time ago" and the setting "a galaxy far far away," which gives Mr. Lucas and his associates total freedom to come up with their own landscapes, housing, vehicles, weapons, religion, politics—all of which are variations on the familiar.

When the film opens, dark times have fallen upon the galactal empire once ruled, we are given to believe, from a kind of space-age Camelot. Against these evil tyrants there is, in progress, a rebellion led by a certain Princess Leia Organa, a pretty round-faced young woman of old-fashioned pluck who, before you can catch your breath, has been captured by the guardians of the empire. Their object is to retrieve some secret plans that can be the empire's undoing.

Published: May 26, 1977.

That's about all the plot that anyone of voting age should be required to keep track of. The story of "Star Wars" could be written on the head of a pin and still leave room for the Bible. It is, rather, a breathless succession of escapes, pursuits, dangerous missions, unexpected encounters, with each one ending in some kind of defeat until the final one.

These adventures involve, among others, an ever-optimistic young man named Luke Skywalker (Mark Hamill), who is innocent without being naive; Han Solo (Harrison Ford), a free-booting freelance space-ship captain who goes where he can make the most money; and an old mystic named Ben Kenobi (Alec Guinness), one of the last of the Old Guard, a fellow in possession of what's called "the force," a mixture of what appears to be ESP and early Christian faith.

Accompanying these three as they set out to liberate the princess and restore justice to the empire are a pair of Laurel-and-Hardyish robots. The thin one, who looks like a sort of brass woodman, talks in the polished phrases of a valet ("I'm adroit but I'm not very knowledgeable"), while the squat one, shaped like a portable washing machine, who is the one with the knowledge, simply squeaks and blinks his lights. They are the year's best new comedy team.

In opposition to these good guys are the imperial forces led by someone called the Grand Moff Tarkin (Peter Cushing) and his executive assistant, Lord Darth Vader (David Prowse), a former student of Ben Kenobi who elected to leave heaven sometime before to join the evil ones.

The true stars of "Star Wars" are John Barry, who was responsible for the production design, and the people who were responsible for the incredible special effects—space ships, explosions of stars, space battles, hand-to-hand combat with what appear to be lethal neon swords. I have a particular fondness for the look of the interior of a gigantic satellite called the Death Star, a place full of the kind of waste space one finds today only in old Fifth Avenue mansions and public libraries.

There's also a very funny sequence in a low-life bar on a remote planet, a frontierlike establishment where they serve customers who look like turtles, apes, pythons and various amalgams of same, but draw the line at robots. Says the bartender piously: "We don't serve *their* kind here."

It's difficult to judge the performances in a film like this. I suspect that much of the time the actors had to perform with special effects that were later added in the laboratory. Yet everyone treats his material with the proper combination of solemnity and good humor that avoids condescension. One of Mr. Lucas's particular achievements is the manner in which he is able to recall the tackiness of the old comic strips and serials he loves without making a movie that is, itself, tacky. "Star Wars" is good enough to convince the most skeptical 8-year-old sci-fi buff, who is the toughest critic.

Selection 6.4

Here is a very different sort of classic hailed by Canby, who recognized from the outset the implications of the film and the impact it would enjoy. Note in both this review and the previous one that Canby uses less than half the space that today's reviews of major movies typically receive.

MOVIE REVIEW
The Godfather
By VINCENT CANBY

Taking a best-selling novel of more drive than genius (Mario Puzo's "The Godfather"), about a subject of something less than common experience (the Mafia), involving an isolated portion of one very particular ethnic group (first-generation and second-generation Italian-Americans), Francis Ford Coppola has made one of the most brutal and moving chronicles of American life ever designed within the limits of popular entertainment.

"The Godfather," which opened at five theaters here yesterday, is a superb Hollywood movie that was photographed mostly in New York (with locations in Las Vegas, Sicily and Hollywood). It's the gangster melodrama come of age, truly sorrowful and truly exciting, without the false piety of the films that flourished forty years ago, scaring the delighted hell out of us while cautioning that crime doesn't (or, at least, shouldn't) pay.

It still doesn't, but the punishments suffered by the members of the Corleone Family aren't limited to sudden ambushes on street corners or to the more elaborately choreographed assassinations on thruways. They also include lifelong sentences of ostracism in terrible, bourgeois confinement, of

Overview

New York Times Review

Cast, Credits & Awards

Readers' Reviews

Trailers & Clips

▶ View Clip...

🛒 | Buy From Amazon

⊘ | Add to Netflix Queue

The New York Times

Published: March 16, 1972.

money and power, but of not much more glory than can be obtained by the ability to purchase expensive bedroom suites, the kind that include everything from the rug on the floor to the pictures on the wall with, perhaps, a horrible satin bedspread thrown in.

Yet "The Godfather" is not quite that simple. It was Mr. Puzo's point, which has been made somehow more ambiguous and more interesting in the film, that the experience of the Corleone Family, as particular as it is, may be the mid-twentieth-century equivalent of the oil and lumber and railroad barons of nineteenth-century America. In the course of the ten years of intra-Mafia gang wars (1945–1955) dramatized by the film, the Corleones are, in fact, inching toward social and financial respectability.

For the Corleones, the land of opportunity is America the Ugly, in which almost everyone who is not Sicilian or, more narrowly, not a Corleone, is a potential enemy. Mr. Coppola captures this feeling of remoteness through the physical look of place and period, and through the narrative's point of view. "The Godfather" seems to take place entirely inside a huge, smoky, plastic dome, through which the Corleones see our real world only dimly.

Thus, at the crucial meeting of Mafia families, when the decision is made to take over the hard drug market, one old don argues in favor, saying he would keep the trade confined to blacks—"they are animals anyway."

This is all the more terrifying because, within their isolation, there is such a sense of love and honor, no matter how bizarre.

The film is affecting for many reasons, including the return of Marlon Brando, who has been away only in spirit, as Don Vito Corleone, the magnificent, shrewd old Corleone patriarch. It's not a large role, but he is the key to the film, and to the contributions of all of the other performers, so many actors that it is impossible to give everyone his due.

Some, however, must be cited, especially Al Pacino, as the college-educated son who takes over the family business and becomes, in the process, an actor worthy to have Brando as his father; as well as James Caan, Richard Castellano, Robert Duvall, Al Lettieri, Abe Vigoda, Gianni Russo, Al Martino and Morgana King. Mr. Coppola has not denied the characters' Italian heritage (as can be gathered by a quick reading of the cast), and by emphasizing it, he has made a movie that transcends its immediate milieu and genre.

"The Godfather" plays havoc with the emotions as the sweet things of life—marriages, baptisms, family feasts—become an inextricable part of the background for explicitly depicted murders by shotgun, garrote, machine gun, and booby-trapped automobile. The film is about an empire run from a dark, suburban Tudor palace where people, in siege, eat out of cardboard containers while babies cry and get underfoot. It is also more than a little disturbing to realize that characters, who are so moving one minute, are likely, in the next scene, to be blowing out the brains of a competitor over a white tablecloth. It's nothing personal, just their way of doing business as usual.

Selection 6.5

Canby's predecessor appears prescient in his praise of a film often hailed as the greatest ever, celebrating it upon release as the "most sensational film ever made in Hollywood." Bosley Crowther also provides plenty of context from the start about the pre-release controversy surrounding the film, which might be new to today's reader. If this wasn't new to readers then, why spend so much of the lead on considerations other than the quality of the film? The vitality of Crowther's style brings an immediacy to a film that we now regard as historic.

MOVIE REVIEW
Orson Welles's Controversial 'Citizen Kane' Proves a Sensational Film at Palace
By BOSLEY CROWTHER

Within the withering spotlight as no other film has ever seen before, Orson Welles's "Citizen Kane" had its world première at the Palace last evening. And now that the wraps are off, the mystery has been exposed and Mr. Welles and the RKO directors have taken the much-debated leap, it can be safely stated that suppression of this film would have been a crime. For, in spite of some disconcerting lapses and strange ambiguities in the creation of the principal character, "Citizen Kane" is far and away the most surprising and cinematically exciting motion picture to be seen here in many a moon. As a matter of fact, it comes close to being the most sensational film ever made in Hollywood.

Count on Mr. Welles; he doesn't do things by halves. Being a mercurial fellow, with a frightening theatrical flair, he moved right into the movies, grabbed the medium by the ears and began to toss it around with the dexterity of a seasoned veteran. Fact is, he handled it with more verve and inspired ingenuity than any of the elder crafts-men have exhibited in years. With the able assistance of Gregg Toland, whose services should not be overlooked, he found in the camera the perfect instrument to encompass his dramatic energies and absorb his prolific ideas. Upon the screen he discovered an area large enough

Published: May 2, 1941.

for his expansive whims to have free play. And the consequence is that he has made a picture of tremendous and overpowering scope, not in physical extent so much as in its rapid and graphic rotation of thoughts. Mr. Welles has put upon the screen a motion picture that really moves.

As for the story which he tells—and which has provoked such an uncommon fuss—this corner frankly holds considerable reservation. Naturally we wouldn't know how closely—if at all—it parallels the life of an eminent publisher, as has been somewhat cryptically alleged. But that is beside the point in a rigidly critical appraisal. The blamable circumstance is that it fails to provide a clear picture of the character and motives behind the man about whom the whole thing revolves.

As the picture opens, Charles Kane lies dying in the fabulous castle he has built—the castle called Xanadu, in which he has surrounded himself with vast treasures. And as death closes his eyes his heavy lips murmur one word, "Rosebud." Suddenly the death scene is broken; the screen becomes alive with a staccato March-of-Time-like news feature recounting the career of the dead man—how, as a poor boy, he came into great wealth, how he became a newspaper publisher as a young man, how he aspired to political office, was defeated because of a personal scandal, devoted himself to material acquisition and finally died.

But the editor of the news feature is not satisfied; he wants to know the secret of Kane's strange nature and especially what he meant by "Rosebud." So a reporter is dispatched to find out, and the remainder of the picture is devoted to an absorbing visualization of Kane's phenomenal career as told by his boyhood guardian, two of his closest newspaper associates and his mistress. Each is agreed on one thing—that Kane was a titanic egomaniac. It is also clearly revealed that the man was in some way consumed by his own terrifying selfishness. But just exactly what it is that eats upon him, why it is there and, for that matter, whether Kane is really a villain, a social parasite, is never clearly revealed. And the final, poignant identification of "Rosebud" sheds little more than a vague, sentimental light upon his character. At the end Kubla Kane is still an enigma—a very confusing one.

But check that off to the absorption of Mr. Welles in more visible details. Like the novelist Thomas Wolfe, his abundance of imagery is so great that it sometimes gets in the way of his logic. And the less critical will probably be content with an undefined Kane, anyhow. After all, nobody understood him. Why should Mr. Welles? Isn't it enough that he presents a theatrical character with consummate theatricality?

We would, indeed, like to say as many nice things as possible about everything else in this film—about the excellent direction of Mr. Welles, about the sure and penetrating performances of literally every member of the cast and about the stunning manner in which the music of Bernard Herrmann has been used. Space, unfortunately, is short. All we can say, in conclusion, is that you shouldn't miss this film. It is cynical, ironic, sometimes oppressive and as realistic as a slap. But it has more vitality than fifteen other films we could name. And, although it may not give a thoroughly clear answer, at least it brings to mind one deeply moral thought: For what shall it profit a man if he shall gain the whole world and lose his own soul? See "Citizen Kane" for further details.

Selection 6.6

More than 25 years after his review of "Citizen Kane," Crowther savages another movie that has since been almost unanimously hailed as an American classic. Did his standards change, did the times change or both? At little more than 400 words (and not one them positive), this review is half the length of the previous one—and about a quarter of the length of the lead review in The Times today.

MOVIE REVIEW
Bonnie and Clyde
By BOSLEY CROWTHER

A raw and unmitigated campaign of sheer press-agentry has been trying to put across the notion that Warner Brothers' "Bonnie and Clyde" is a faithful representation of the desperado careers of Clyde Barrow and Bonnie Parker, a notorious team of bank robbers and killers who roamed Texas and Oklahoma in the post-Depression years.

It is nothing of the sort. It is a cheap piece of bald-faced slapstick comedy that treats the hideous depredations of that sleazy, moronic pair as though they were as full of fun and frolic as the jazz-age cutups in "Thoroughly Modern Millie." And it puts forth Warren Beatty and Faye Dunaway in the leading roles, and Michael J. Pollard as their sidekick, a simpering, nose-picking rube, as though they were striving mightily to be the Beverly Hillbillies of next year.

It has Mr. Beatty clowning broadly as the killer who fondles various types of guns with as much nonchalance and dispassion as he airily twirls a big cigar, and it has Miss Dunaway squirming grossly as his thrill-seeking, sex-starved moll. It is loaded with farcical holdups, screaming chases in stolen getaway cars that have the antique appearance and speeded-up movement of the clumsy vehicles of the Keystone Kops, and indications of the impotence of Barrow, until Bonnie writes a poem about him to extol his prowess, that are as ludicrous as they are crude.

Published: April 14, 1967.

Such ridiculous, camp-tinctured travesties of the kind of people these desperados were and of the way people lived in the dusty Southwest back in those barren years might be passed off as candidly commercial movie comedy, nothing more, if the film weren't reddened with blotches of violence of the most grisly sort.

Arthur Penn, the aggressive director, has evidently gone out of his way to splash the comedy holdups with smears of vivid blood as astonished people are machine-gunned. And he has staged the terminal scene of the ambuscading and killing of Barrow and Bonnie by a posse of policemen with as much noise and gore as is in the climax of "The St. Valentine's Day Massacre."

This blending of farce with brutal killings is as pointless as it is lacking in taste, since it makes no valid commentary upon the already travestied truth. And it leaves an astonished critic wondering just what purpose Mr. Penn and Mr. Beatty think they serve with this strangely antique, sentimental claptrap, which opened yesterday at the Forum and the Murray Hill.

This is the film that opened the Montreal International Festival!

Selection 6.7

Here is a typically provocative piece from Mitchell, one that reflects the relationship between movies and real life and offers a perspective (of an African-American critic raised in the Rust Belt) different from that of other film critics at The Times and most of their readers. Examine how Mitchell weaves his responses to a variety of movies into an argument that transcends a review of any one.

FILM
You Won't See My Detroit in the Movies
By ELVIS MITCHELL

Whenever I tell someone from another country that I grew up in Detroit, I'm asked about one of three things—cars, crime or Motown. Invariably, these strangers have gotten their less-than-complicated views of the city from movies, like the 1973 urban heist film "Detroit 9000" or the grisly sci-fi "RoboCop" series.

As it happens, this has been a boom year for movies based in Detroit. Just this fall, we've had "Standing in the Shadows of Motown," "Bowling for Columbine" and "8 Mile"; and Joe Carnahan's crime thriller "Narc" is to open in New York on Dec. 20. Unfortunately, these pictures aren't going to broaden the associations

Published: December 8, 2002.

that outsiders have with Detroit. But at least they take the city seriously enough to actually use it. Often, films that take place in Detroit don't actually spend much time in the city.

The three "RoboCop" movies were filmed in Houston. I'm not sure if Eddie Murphy ever set foot in the Motor City, which is his character's home, for any of the "Beverly Hills Cop" pictures; Jay Leno probably spent more time in Detroit for the making of "Collision Course," the damaged 1987 culture-clash comedy in which he and Pat Morita played warring cops. "Detroit Rock City" (1999) seemed to suggest that Detroit itself was a small enclave in suburban Toronto. Tony Scott's "True Romance" (1993) actually used a movie theater in Los Angeles to represent downtown Detroit; its makers couldn't even be bothered to buy stock film of the city. Such films have made Detroit seem like some vast, featureless stretch of nameless peril; it's impossible to get a sense of it as a real place when Houston is standing in for it.

So it's something of a relief when a director manages to capture some of Detroit's personality on film, as Steven Soderbergh did in "Out of Sight," his 1998 version of a crime story by the city's own Elmore Leonard. For many Detroiters, the logo for "8 Mile" provokes a little smile. A more rounded, slightly neon-bright version of the street signs that line the real 8 Mile Road, which divides Detroit from its affluent northern suburbs, the film logo suggests that the sign itself has gone Hollywood. But the Detroit of the movie is, frankly, exactly what you might see if you drove down certain sections of 8 Mile Road—struggling businesses and abandoned buildings.

The acres of city blocks riddled with grand and empty decaying homes are an undeniable source of shame for Detroiters, and some "8 Mile" viewers there have voiced their anger over what they feel is an unfair exaggeration of that aspect of their city. But it would have been dishonest for the director, Curtis Hanson, to have glossed over that part of Detroit; it's too integral to his protagonist's story.

What the movie's detractors miss is Mr. Hanson's affection for the city's gone-to-seed curves, and the magnificence of its huge, nearly haunted buildings. He's the filmmaker as anthropologist, and he invests the movie with a deft, understated sadness about what Detroit once was. That quality is especially evident in a scene in which a squatter is burned out of the derelict house he's taken over. As the house goes up in flames, Eminem's Jimmy is absorbed by a dirty, beat-up picture he's found there—of a serene, middle-class black family. (At its best, family is what the picture is really about.)

Detroit is essential to the main character of "8 Mile" because it's as a day laborer in one of its car factories that he tries to put together enough cheddar to finance his dream. In this, he's also part of what is apparently becoming a sad movie tradition: music stars who get punishing jobs in metalworking. (Think of Bjork in "Dancer in the Dark.") Pop music and the United Auto Workers, it seems, don't mix. Of course, there are more non-union laborers in the auto industry than there used to be. Still, why is it so difficult for filmmakers to understand that in the old days, the factories that spit out cars for the Big Three automakers created a thriving middle class in Detroit?

The lure that drew people from all over to work at G.M., Ford and Chrysler is very much a part of "Standing in the Shadows of Motown," the documentary about the anonymous musicians who played on the records that defined the Motown sound. Sweating in those foundries is how several of the Funk Brothers, as they were known, made an honest wage until Berry Gordy plucked them from the obscurity of the factory to offer them more obscurity in the recording studio.

With rare exceptions—Paul Schrader's "Blue Collar" is one—Detroit movies tend to ignore the motors in the Motor City. (Let's not even mention "The Betsy," the 1978 picture about a debased auto tycoon—it's so cynical that you can practically see Sir Laurence Olivier cashing his check on the set.) But in Michael Moore's new documentary, "Bowling for Columbine," he evokes the honorable existence his family eked out in Michigan's motor industry before G.M. cut and ran; Mr. Moore invests that legacy with the same emotional power he displays in portraying America's lethal gun culture. No other filmmaker has his sentimental attachment to autoworkers, and he understands better than anyone the causes of the desolation that has made Detroit the butt of movie jokes for decades. His justifiable outrage motivates his best pictures, and accounts for the link between "Columbine," "Shadows" and "8 Mile"—a link that other moviemakers would do well to investigate.

Selection 6.8

These two responses by a single critic to "Thelma and Louise," three weeks apart, illustrate the concept of criticism as an ongoing dialogue with readers. The second and longer piece (not printed here in its entirety) reflects the reaction not only to Maslin's original review but to the larger cultural response to the film. Much of this dialogue now takes place on the Web, where readers approach movie criticism as an interactive debate. A rock critic before joining The Times, Maslin became a staff book critic after her long stint on the film beat.

FILM REVIEW
On the Run With 2 Buddies and a Gun
By JANET MASLIN

"I don't remember ever feeling this awake!" exclaims one of the
two freewheeling runaways of Ridley Scott's hugely appealing new
road movie, as they race ecstatically across the American Southwest.
Funny, sexy and quick-witted, these two desperadoes have fled the
monotony of their old lives and are making up new ones on a minute-
by-minute basis. Their adventures, while tinged with the fatalism that
attends any crime spree, have the thrilling, life-affirming energy for
which the best road movies are remembered. This time there's a difference: This story's daring anti-heroes are beautiful, interesting women.

Mr. Scott's "Thelma and Louise," with a sparkling screenplay
by the first-time writer Callie Khouri, is a surprise on this and many
other scores. It reveals the previously untapped talent of Mr. Scott
(best known for majestically moody action films like "Alien," "Blade
Runner" and "Black Rain") for exuberant comedy, and for vibrant
American imagery, notwithstanding his English roots. It reimagines
the buddy film with such freshness and vigor that the genre seems
positively new. It discovers unexpected resources in both its stars,
Susan Sarandon and Geena Davis, who are perfectly teamed as the
spirited and original title characters. Ms. Sarandon, whose Louise
starts out as a waitress, seems to have walked right out of her "White
Palace" incarnation into something much more fulfilling. Ms. Davis
may have already won an Oscar (for "The Accidental Tourist"), but
for her the gorgeous, dizzy, mutable Thelma still amounts to a career-
making role.

"Thelma and Louise," with a haunting dawn-to-nightfall title
image that anticipates the story's trajectory, is immediately engaging.
Even its relatively inauspicious opening scenes, which show the wise-
cracking Louise planning a weekend getaway with Thelma, a desper-
ately bored housewife who hates her husband, Darryl (Christopher
McDonald), have self-evident flair.

"Are you at work?" Thelma asks when Louise telephones her
from the coffee shop where she is employed, somewhere in Arkansas. "No, I'm callin' from the Playboy Mansion," snaps Louise, who
goes on to propose a fishing trip to a friend's cabin. "I still don't
know how to fish," Thelma muses, nibbling on a frozen candy bar.
"Neither do I, sweetie, but Darryl does it," Louise answers. "How
hard could it be?"

Soon the two of them have taken off in Louise's turquoise Thun-
derbird convertible, with Thelma dressed for the occasion in ruffles,
denim and pearls. Eager to escape her stifling home life, she has left

Published: May 24, 1991.

behind a note for Darryl and borrowed a little something in return: his gun. Later that same evening, when Thelma insists on stopping at a honky-tonk bar despite Louise's protestations, the gun comes in handy. It is used, by Louise, to settle a dispute between Thelma and a would-be rapist (Timothy Carhart) in the parking lot, and it forever changes the complexion of Thelma and Louise's innocent little jaunt. From this point on, they are killers on the run.

Ms. Khouri's screenplay never begins to provide the moral justification for Louise's violent act. But it does a remarkably smooth job of making this and other outlaw gestures at least as understandable as they would be in a traditional western. It also invests them with a certain flair. When detectives investigate the slaying of this inveterate ladies' man, a local waitress says: "Has anyone asked his wife? She's the one I *hope* did it!" Later on, when cornering a truck driver who has pestered them on the highway, Louise furiously asks, "Where do you get off behavin' like that with women you don't know?"

That "Thelma and Louise" is able to coax a colorful, character-building escapade out of such relatively innocuous beginnings is a tribute to the grace of all concerned, particularly the film's two stars, whose flawless teamwork makes the story gripping and believable from start to finish. On the run, Louise evolves from her former fast-talking self into a much more moving and thoughtful figure, while Thelma outgrows her initial giddy hedonism and develops real grit. Their transformation, particularly in its final stages, gives the film its rich sense of openness and possibility even as the net around Thelma and Louise closes more tightly.

Some of what Thelma learns en route comes by way of a foxy young hitchhiker named J. D. (Brad Pitt), who eradicates the memory of Darryl and also gives a memorable lesson, with the help of a hair dryer, in how to rob a convenience store. "My goodness, you're so gentlemanly about it!" exclaims Thelma. "Well now, I've always believed that if done properly, armed robbery doesn't have to be a totally unpleasant experience," J. D. says.

Like any good road movie, "Thelma and Louise" includes a number of colorful characters who wander entertainingly in and out of the principals' lives. Among them, in this film's fine cast, are Mr. Pitt, who so convincingly wows Thelma; Michael Madsen, bringing shades of Elvis Presley to the role of Louise's once foot-loose and now devoted beau; and Harvey Keitel and Stephen Tobolowsky, as two of the detectives on Thelma and Louise's trail. Mr. Keitel, in a role resembling the one he has in "Mortal Thoughts," has this time learned to say "mo-tel" in the spirit of the region, and conveys a great and touching concern for the renegades' well-being. His character alone, in a role that could have been perfunctory but is instead so full, gives an indication of how well developed this story is.

Among the film's especially memorable touches are those that establish its feminine side: the way Thelma insists on drinking her liquor from tiny bottles, or the way a weary Louise considers using lipstick after a few days in the desert but then disgustedly throws the thing away. "He's putting on his hat!" Louise confides to Thelma when a police officer stops them, which is surely not the kind of thing two male outlaws would notice. But the film's sense of freedom and excitement, as when the women exult in feeling the wind in their hair, goes well beyond sexual distinctions.

"Thelma and Louise" is greatly enhanced by a tough, galvanizing country-tinged score, and by Adrian Biddle's glorious cinematography, which gives a physical dimension to the film's underlying thought that life can be richer than one may have previously realized. At the story's end, as Thelma and Louise make their way through Monument Valley and to the Grand Canyon, the film truly lives up to its scenery.

"I guess I've always been a little crazy, huh?" Thelma muses in this majestic setting.

"You've always been crazy," Louise acknowledges. "This is just the first chance you've ever had to really express yourself."

Selection 6.9

And here's her response to the response to the movie, an invitation to further dialogue.

FILM REVIEW
Lay Off 'Thelma and Louise'
By JANET MASLIN

Because he didn't smile when he said it. Because he stole, cheated or lied. Because he wasn't lucky. Because it was a good day to die.

Those are traditional reasons for which characters in outlaw movies are disposed of, sometimes only in the wink of an eye. It's a list to which a new one can now be added: because he tried to rape and beat a woman whose best friend had once been the victim of a sex crime, and the best friend went berserk while watching history repeat itself. And because he was smug instead of sorry.

"Thelma and Louise," the film in which this new pretext for killing turns an Arkansas waitress and an Arkansas housewife into ebullient runaways, is obviously a crime story of a different stripe. Though

Published: June 16, 1991. Full text available at: www.nytimes.com/1991/06/16/movies/film-view-lay-off-thelma-and-louise.html.

it takes much of its inspiration from the road movies of 20 years ago, its style and attitudes are thoroughly up to date. Though it tells a tale of violence, its spirit could not be more benign. Though it employs certain conventions of the buddy-film genre, it feels unfamiliar in the best possible way. In viewing the desperado's life through the eyes of two suddenly adventurous women, it sees something other movies have not seen.

It also raises new hackles, having been tarred as a kind of she-"Rambo" by those who deem it mindlessly violent and uncharitable to men. The charge that this is "toxic feminism" has been leveled by sources as diverse as John Leo of U.S. News & World Report and the columnist Liz Smith. "Nobody in 'Thelma and Louise' worries about AIDS, using condoms or encountering a serial killer," Ms. Smith noted, and that's true; nobody worries about the greenhouse effect or wears seat belts, either. But what is it that really rankles about "Thelma and Louise"?

Not the violence: the amount of violence seen here is remarkably small, especially in view of the casual flare-ups with which male-oriented road movies are often loaded. Out for a weekend's fishing trip, mischievously stealing away from Thelma's husband and Louise's boyfriend, the two heroines first get into trouble in an Arkansas honky-tonk, where a man who makes a pass at Thelma mistakes her high spirits and alcoholic haze for sexual availability. This leads to the shooting incident that turns Thelma and Louise into outlaws and also gives the story its momentum. It's a legal and moral lapse, but also a plot necessity. Without events like this, the heroes of most road movies would have to pack up and go back home.

Later on, Thelma and Louise have their run-ins with a truck driver, a police officer and a storeful of customers at a grocery, none of whom is injured by their behavior. The truck driver does incur property damage, the grocery store customers are robbed, and the policeman becomes the victim of a potentially dangerous prank; but these events deserve to be seen in some kind of perspective. Last summer was the season of the sky-high body count, with Arnold Schwarzenegger blasting his way across Mars in "Total Recall," all of whose female characters were prostitutes. In "Another 48 Hours," a buddy film tailored to more conventional tastes, Eddie Murphy and Nick Nolte killed enemy after enemy without batting an eye. So, once again, what's so egregious about "Thelma and Louise"?

The heroines of this story happen to look quite innocent by comparison with the road movie characters of the late 1960's and early 1970's, when the genre was in full bloom. Compared with the stoned, messianic drug dealers of "Easy Rider," who traveled the highways fueled by condescension and paranoia and took it as their sexual due to visit a whorehouse in New Orleans, Thelma (Geena Davis) and Louise (Susan Sarandon) seem infinitely more level-headed and kind. (Anyone who remembers "Easy Rider" fondly but has not watched it since its 1969 release should be reminded that Billy and Captain America visit a commune that has its own resident mime troupe, complete with stage. Timeless it's not.)

And compared with Bonnie Parker, who got a sexual thrill out of the way Clyde Barrow announced, "We rob banks" in Arthur Penn's "Bonnie and Clyde" in 1967, Thelma and Louise have no real taste for crime. Furthermore, compared with the wandering sex offenders of Bertrand Blier's "Going Places" in 1974, their feelings about the opposite sex are positively friendly. They are mobilized not by hostility or anomie but by a sudden, unexpected glimpse of what life might have been like for them without a bad marriage (Thelma's) and a dead-end job (Louise's). Their dissatisfaction with their everyday lives is something anyone in the audience will understand.

While it's true that criminal behavior plays a role in this story, it requires extraordinary blinders to regard "Thelma and Louise" solely as an account of antisocial depravity. Besides, criminal behavior on screen can be as well used in the service of virtue as in glorification of crime. "The Silence of the Lambs," for example, can be seen as a grisly film, but it is much more persuasively a film in which the saving of a single life becomes all-important, in which a fundamental decency prevails. The heroism of its central character, Clarice Starling, emerges in stark relief against the horrors she has battled.

In the case of "Thelma and Louise," a violent and tragic mistake becomes the crucible in which character is formed. One of the most invigorating things about this film is the way its heroines, during the course of a few brief but wildly eventful days, crystallize their thoughts and arrive at a philosophical clarity that would have been unavailable to them in their prior lives. By the end of the film, the director Ridley Scott and the screenwriter Callie Khouri are ready to allow Thelma and Louise the opportunity to take full charge of their lives and full responsibility for their missteps, too. The film's bracing ending has a welcome toughness.

In fact, throughout the course of the story, Thelma and Louise have been seen learning to take charge of their own lives. And there may lie the problem: it's something that goes beyond Thelma and Louise's aggressiveness, their politics, their cavalierness about condoms (a matter not remotely addressed by the movie, by the way) or any other aspect of the film that strikes some small segment of the audience as hotheaded. It's something as simple as it is powerful: the fact that the men in this story don't really matter.

--*

 STORY**SCAN**

Selection 6.10

As co-chief film critic for The Times, Scott is a master of rendering complications of art and response in an incisive, engaging manner. Here he explores how a movie that is "bleak, scary and relentlessly violent" can also be "pure heaven." He thus provides an effective consumer guide as well as inspired criticism, letting the reader compare her evaluative yardstick to his. This Oscar-winning movie was not for everyone, but Scott revels in the riches that await those who submit to it. (This sort of review might better be skimmed for its evaluation before seeing the movie and then read for its analysis to deepen the viewer's appreciation after seeing it.)

Movie Review | 'No Country for Old Men'
He Found a Bundle of Money, and
Now There's Hell to Pay

By A. O. SCOTT

This is the sort of description that some readers will find evaluative—whether positive or negative. Either way, it lets readers know whether this is a film for them.

Evaluation—this is a rave review of the sort of movie that will bother some.

The evaluative yardstick is purely aesthetic, not moral.

"No Country for Old Men," adapted by Joel and Ethan Coen from Cormac McCarthy's novel, is bleak, scary and relentlessly violent. At its center is a figure of evil so calm, so extreme, so implacable that to hear his voice is to feel the temperature in the theater drop.

But while that chilly sensation is a sign of terror, it may equally be a symptom of delight. The specter of Anton Chigurh (Javier Bardem), a deadpan sociopath with a funny haircut, will feed many a nightmare, but the most lasting impression left by this film is likely to be the deep satisfaction that comes from witnessing the nearly perfect execution of a difficult task. "No Country for Old Men" is purgatory for the squeamish and the easily spooked. For formalists—those moviegoers sent into raptures by tight editing, nimble camera work and faultless sound design—it's pure heaven.

Published: November 9, 2007.

So before I go any further, allow me my moment of bliss at the sheer brilliance of the Coens' technique. And it is mostly theirs. The editor, Roderick Jaynes, is their longstanding pseudonym. The cinematographer, Roger Deakins, and the composer, Carter Burwell, are collaborators of such long standing that they surely count as part of the nonbiological Coen fraternity. At their best, and for that matter at their less than best, Joel and Ethan Coen, who share writing and directing credit here, combine virtuosic dexterity with mischievous high spirits, as if they were playing Franz Liszt's most treacherous compositions on dueling banjos. Sometimes their appetite for pastiche overwhelms their more sober storytelling instincts, so it is something of a relief to find nothing especially showy or gimmicky in "No Country." In the Coen canon it belongs with "Blood Simple," "Miller's Crossing" and "Fargo" as a densely woven crime story made more effective by a certain controlled stylistic perversity.

Could he love it any more?

The remainder of this graf provides context, compressing all sort of information about the Coens' previous films, their collaborator and working processes.

The script follows Mr. McCarthy's novel almost scene for scene, and what the camera discloses is pretty much what the book describes: a parched, empty landscape; pickup trucks and taciturn men; and lots of killing. But the pacing, the mood and the attention to detail are breathtaking, sometimes literally.

In one scene a man sits in a dark hotel room as his pursuer walks down the corridor outside. You hear the creak of floorboards and the beeping of a transponder, and see the shadows of the hunter's feet in the sliver of light under the door. The footsteps move away, and the next sound is the faint squeak of the light bulb in the hall being unscrewed. The silence and the slowness awaken your senses and quiet your breathing, as by the simplest cinematic means—Look! Listen! Hush!—your attention is completely and ecstatically absorbed. You won't believe what happens next, even though you know it's coming.

Two grafs of description, until that final sentence of analysis. Addressing the reader as "you" adds intimacy, while he doesn't spoil anything essential about the plot.

By now, Scott is speaking for all—or at least all serious—filmgoers.

evaluation

Context, both literary and cinematic.

By the time this moment arrives, though, you have already been pulled into a seamlessly imagined and self-sufficient reality. The Coens have always used familiar elements of American pop culture and features of particular American landscapes to create elaborate and hermetic worlds. Mr. McCarthy, especially in the western phase of his career, has frequently done the same. The surprise of "No Country for Old Men," the first literary adaptation these filmmakers have attempted, is how well matched their methods turn out to be with the novelist's.

Mr. McCarthy's book, for all its usual high-literary trappings (many philosophical digressions, no quotation marks), is one of his pulpier efforts, as well as one of his funniest. The Coens, seizing on the novel's genre elements, lower the metaphysical temperature and amplify the material's dark, rueful humor. It helps that the three lead actors—Tommy Lee Jones and Josh Brolin along with Mr. Bardem—are adept at displaying their natural wit even when their characters find themselves in serious trouble.

Evaluation shifts from the movie and its makers to the actors.

A graf of analysis.

The three are locked in a swerving, round-robin chase that takes them through the empty ranges and lonely motels of the West Texas border country in 1980. The three men occupy the screen one at a time, almost never appearing in the frame together, even as their fates become ever more intimately entwined.

Mr. Jones plays Ed Tom Bell, a world weary third-generation sheriff whose stoicism can barely mask his dismay at the tide of evil seeping into the world. Whether Chigurh is a magnetic force moving that tide or just a particularly nasty specimen carried in on it is one of the questions the film occasionally poses. The man who knows him best, a dandyish bounty-hunter played by Woody Harrelson, describes Chigurh as lacking a sense of humor. But the smile that rides up one side of Chigurh's mouth as he speaks suggests a diabolical kind of mirth—just as the haircut suggests a lost Beatle from hell—and his conversation has

ha ha

Interweaving of description and analysis.

a teasing, riddling quality. The punch line comes when he blows a hole in your head with the pneumatic device he prefers to a conventional firearm.

And the butt of his longest joke is Llewelyn Moss (Mr. Brolin), a welder who lives in a trailer with his wife, Carla Jean (Kelly MacDonald) and is dumb enough to think he's smart enough to get away with taking the $2 million he finds at the scene of a drug deal gone bad. Chigurh is charged with recovering the cash (by whom is neither clear nor especially relevant), and poor Sheriff Bell trails behind, surveying scenes of mayhem and trying to figure out where the next one will be.

Taken together, these three hombres are not quite the Good, the Bad and the Ugly, but each man does carry some allegorical baggage. Mr. Jones's craggy, vinegary warmth is well suited to the kind of righteous, decent lawman he has lately taken to portraying. Ed Tom Bell is almost continuous with the retired M.P. Mr. Jones played in Paul Haggis's "In the Valley of Elah." It is hard to do wisdom without pomposity, or probity without preening, but Mr. Jones manages with an aplomb that is downright thrilling.

Still, if "No Country for Old Men" were a simple face-off between the sheriff's goodness and Chigurh's undiluted evil, it would be a far stiffer, less entertaining picture. Llewelyn is the wild card—a good old boy who lives on the borderline between good luck and bad, between outlaw and solid citizen—and Mr. Brolin is the human center of the movie, the guy you root for and identify with even as the odds against him grow steeper by the minute.

And the minutes fly by, leaving behind some unsettling notions about the bloody, absurd intransigence of fate and the noble futility of human efforts to master it. Mostly, though, "No Country for Old Men" leaves behind the jangled, stunned sensation of having witnessed a ruthless application of craft.

Great turn of phrase from a writer who's smart enough to keep it simple.

Plot description.

Context and analysis that proceed to evaluation.

Evaluation, though he's already made plain that you have to have an affinity for the dark depths of human nature to find entertainment here.

analysis

Philosophy aside, craft is justification enough, bringing his evaluation and review back to the opening invocation of formalistic heaven.

Selection 6.11

This essay addresses a question that lies at the heart of this book and one that by no means is confined to film: Why do critics and the public respond differently? Writes Scott, "the discrepancy between what critics think and how the public behaves is of perennial interest because it throws into relief some basic questions about taste, economics and the nature of popular entertainment, as well as the more vexing issue of what, exactly, critics are for." Daringly, he attempts to answer many of those questions.

CRITIC'S NOTEBOOK
Avast, Me Critics! Ye Kill the Fun: Critics and the Masses Disagree About Film Choices
By A. O. SCOTT

Let's start with a few numbers. At Rottentomatoes.com, a Web site that quantifies movie reviews on a 100-point scale, the aggregate score for "Pirates of the Caribbean: Dead Man's Chest" stands at a sodden 54. Metacritic.com, a similar site, crunches the critical prose of the nation's reviewers and comes up with a numerical grade of 52 out of 100. Even in an era of rampant grade inflation, that's a solid F.

Meanwhile, over at boxofficemojo.com, where the daily grosses are tabulated, the second installment in the "Pirates" series, which opened on July 7, plunders onward, trailing broken records in its wake. Its $136 million first-weekend take was the highest three-day tally in history, building on a best-ever $55 million on that Friday, and it is cruising into blockbuster territory at a furious clip. As of this writing, a mere 10 days into its run, the movie has brought in $258.2 million, a hit by any measure.

All of which makes "Dead Man's Chest" a fascinating sequel—not to "Curse of the Black Pearl," which inaugurated the franchise three years ago, but to "The Da Vinci Code." Way back in the early days of the Hollywood summer—the third week in May, to be precise—America's finest critics trooped into screening rooms in Cannes, Los Angeles, New York and points between, saw Ron Howard's adaptation of Dan Brown's best seller, and emerged in a fit of collective grouchiness. The movie promptly pocketed some of the biggest opening-weekend grosses in the history of its studio, Sony.

For the second time this summer, then, my colleagues and I must face a frequently—and not always politely—asked question: What is wrong with you people? I will, for now, suppress the impulse to turn the question on the moviegoing public, which persists in paying good

Published: July 18, 2006.

money to see bad movies that I see free. I don't for a minute believe that financial success contradicts negative critical judgment; $500 million from now, "Dead Man's Chest" will still be, in my estimation, occasionally amusing, frequently tedious and entirely too long. But the discrepancy between what critics think and how the public behaves is of perennial interest because it throws into relief some basic questions about taste, economics and the nature of popular entertainment, as well as the more vexing issue of what, exactly, critics are for.

Are we out of touch with the audience? Why do we go sniffing after art where everyone else is looking for fun, and spoiling everybody's fun when it doesn't live up to our notion or art? What gives us the right to yell "bomb" outside a crowded theater? Variations on these questions arrive regularly in our e-mail in-boxes, and also constitute a major theme in the comments sections of film blogs and Web sites. Online, everyone is a critic, which is as it should be: professional prerogatives aside, a critic is really just anyone who thinks out loud about something he or she cares about, and gets into arguments with fellow enthusiasts. But it would be silly to pretend that those professional prerogatives don't exist, and that they don't foster a degree of resentment. Entitled elites, self-regarding experts, bearers of intellectual or institutional authority, misfits who get to see a movie before anybody else and then take it upon themselves to give away the ending: such people are easy targets of populist anger. Just who do we think we are?

There is no easy answer to this question. Film criticism—at least as practiced in the general-interest daily and weekly press—has never been a specialist pursuit. Movies, more than any other art form, are understood to be common cultural property, something everyone can enjoy, which makes any claim of expertise suspect. Therefore, a certain estrangement between us and them—or me and you, to put it plainly—has been built into the enterprise from the start.

The current schism is in some ways nothing new: go back and read reviews in The New York Times of "Top Gun," "Crocodile Dundee" and "The Karate Kid Part II" to see how some of my predecessors dealt with three of the top-earning movies 20 years ago. (The Australian with the big knife was treated more kindly than the flyboy or the high-kicker, by the way.) And the divide between critic and public may also be temporary. Last year, during the Great Box-Office Slump of 2005, we all seemed happy to shrug together at the mediocrity of the big studio offerings.

No more. Whatever the slump might have portended for the movie industry, it appears to be over for the moment, and the critics have resumed their customary role of scapegoat. The modern blockbuster—the movie that millions of people line up to see more or less simultaneously, on the first convenient showing on the opening weekend—can be seen as the fulfillment of the democratic ideal the movies were born to fulfill. To stand outside that happy communal experience and, worse, to regard it with skepticism or with scorn, is to be a crank, a malcontent, a snob.

So we're damned if we don't. And sometimes, also, if we do. When our breathless praise garlands advertisements for movies the public greets with a shrug, we look like suckers or shills. But these accusations would stick only if the job of the critic were to reflect, predict or influence the public taste.

That, however, is the job of the Hollywood studios, in particular of their marketing and publicity departments, and it is the professional duty of critics to be out of touch with—to be independent of—their concerns. These companies spend tens of millions of dollars to persuade you that the opening of a movie is a public event, a cultural experience you will want to be part of. The campaign of persuasion starts weeks or months—or, in the case of multisequel cash cows, years—before the tickets go on sale, with the goal of making their purchase a foregone conclusion by the time the first reviews appear. Sometimes it works and sometimes it doesn't, but the judgment of critics almost never makes the difference between failure and success, at least for mass-release, big-budget movies like "Dead Man's Chest" or "The Da Vinci Code."

So why review them? Why not let the market do its work, let the audience have its fun and occupy ourselves with the arcana—the art—we critics ostensibly prefer? The obvious answer is that art, or at least the kind of pleasure, wonder and surprise we associate with art, often pops out of commerce, and we want to be around to celebrate when it does and to complain when it doesn't. But the deeper answer is that our love of movies is sometimes expressed as a mistrust of the people who make and sell them, and even of the people who see them. We take entertainment very seriously, which is to say that we don't go to the movies for fun. Or for money. We do it for you.

A Conversation with . . . **A. O. Scott**

CO-CHIEF FILM CRITIC

Courtesy of Matt Septimus

As he explains, the co-chief film critic came to The Times in 2000 with minimal experience reviewing movies, but had impressed with his criticism on books (for Newsday and others) and had served on the editorial staffs of The New York Review of Books and Lingua Franca. This is an edited transcript of an e-mail interview.

What sort of experience or expertise qualified you to become co-chief film critic at The Times? How did you prepare for this job?

I had no formal preparation or training at all. I'd been a book critic and a freelance opinionator on various topics in culture and the arts for a while, and though I'd always had a passionate interest in movies and film criticism, I'd never practiced it on a regular basis until The Times' editors hired me. What possessed them to do so remains a mystery, but I'm grateful that they gave me the opportunity to educate myself in public and to share my evolving sense of what a critic should do with a wide readership.

How do you envision your readership? Is it a general readership or a readership that knows a lot about movies?

I make no assumptions, other than that my readers are smart, curious and thoughtful. Every week I receive dozens of letters and e-mails that confirm this hunch, and one or two that challenge it.

If you're not the target audience for a type of movie (a chick flick or a teen comedy), do you adjust your critical standards?

I'm a strong believer in the (at least potential) universality of movies, and also that open-mindedness is an important aspect of criticism. I'm actually a longtime devotee of romantic comedies and teen movies, though there are genres (horror, for instance) that I have less affinity for. In those cases, it's still possible and important to evaluate originality, skill of execution and overall quality—there are better and worse examples of every kind of movie. I also have no problem in acknowledging that a particular movie might not be meant for someone like me. A critic is a person, after all, and can only write from his or her own perspective and experience.

Film reviews at The Times tend to be much longer—perhaps twice as long—as they once were, as recently as the 1970s or '80s. How come?

I'm not sure. There is—or has been until recently—more space to fill, and also, since the 1990s, more of an interest in allowing writers to develop their voices at greater length.

How does the impact of a film review at The Times compare with that of a book review or a theater review at The Times?

There are a few salient differences. The Times reviews every movie released for at least a week in New York—about 600 a year nowadays—a kind of comprehensiveness that isn't possible with books. So in that case, the selection of a book for review has an impact all by itself. Film has a wider reach and a more highly developed hype machine than the theater, so the movie studios are able to dilute the impact of movie critics. Large-scale commercial movies looking to make most of their money from teenagers in the first weekend of release are designed to be critic-proof, and mostly are. Our impact is greatest on small and medium-sized films aimed at audiences that read reviews, and in some cases it can be profound. Other times, though, we will champion a worthy little movie and it will still flop.

Do you see yourself as providing a consumer guide—letting people know what movies are worth their time and money?
To some extent, yes. Though I also see myself as beginning a conversation about movies.

You've addressed this in your writing, but what accounts for the difference between critical consensus and popular taste?
I don't think there's such a thing as critical consensus, and I think popular taste is more mysterious than box officer numbers would suggest. People like what they like, and some of us have the curious job of explaining and analyzing our own likes and dislikes.

How does your experience of watching a movie differ from that of an avid film buff? Do you enjoy yourself? Take notes?
I do enjoy myself, and I do take notes. What I don't do, entirely, is surrender to the experience. Or, rather, I watch the movie just as anyone else would—laughing, crying, yawning, etc.—and at the same time try to watch myself watching, so I can better understand and have some perspective on the sources of my experience.

You've written about literature, about books on popular music and likely about other arts, as well. Do you consider yourself primarily a film critic? Or are you a critic whose beat at The Times happens to be film?
Criticism is the kind of writing I do. Film is what I mostly write about, but I'm always the same critic.

Has the shift from newsprint to the Web changed anything about your job and/ or your relationship with your readers?
People who have seen my Web videos recognize me on the street, which is odd but mostly pleasant. And I hear from readers more quickly, and also from readers in a wider variety of places. *[As co-host of "At the Movies," Scott likely finds himself recognized more often.]*

Do you ever change your mind about a movie after you've written about it?
If I ever do, I never admit it.

MAKING CONNECTIONS 🤝

1. The more recent film reviews in this section are considerably longer than the earlier ones. Are the longer ones too long? Are the shorter ones too short? Take one of the longer reviews and analyze what could be cut. And take one of the shorter ones and analyze what could be expanded.

2. Compare and contrast Elvis Mitchell's Harry Potter review with Vincent Canby's one on "Star Wars." Is Canby's response as personal as Mitchell's? How much responsibility does a critic have in helping the target audience predict whether it will enjoy a movie?

3. Does Janet Maslin respond differently to "Thelma and Louise" than a man might? Analyze how your own gender influences your response to Maslin's pieces.

4. Is there an essential difference between critical taste and popular taste? If so, why?

television

AS A CONSUMER GUIDE, television reviewing differs from the reviewing discussed in other chapters. For readers, the commitment to follow a critic's advice is a different form of investment—perhaps even a greater investment. Instead of advising whether a movie is worth nine dollars or a book 25, the television critic helps potential viewers decide whether a series is worth the commitment of hours a year, for perhaps years on end. Which is the greater investment—a few bucks for a CD or the countless hours spent with "Friends," "Seinfeld" or the various permutations of "CSI"?

Since different viewers make that commitment at different points, the television critic must also face the challenge of engaging the interest of those who are already following the series (as in this chapter's review of "The Sopranos"), while providing enough context for those who haven't watched but might be interested in starting to do so. When a series review focuses on an episode or two, it employs these as microcosms for the program's dynamic as a whole, rather than treating them as discrete entities deserving reviews of their own.

Technology has transformed the medium for both critic and viewer. Where television into the 1980s typically meant a choice of three national networks, an educational channel and perhaps a local station or two, cable has both multiplied the choices and diminished the percentage of viewership that all but the biggest blockbusters are likely to achieve. The advent of digital video recorders (such as TiVo) and online viewing means that viewers can watch what they want, when they want to watch it, rather than the old "appointment television" model of sitting down at the same time each week. They can even watch competing programs at their convenience.

As we can see from the reviews that follow, more choices have led to greater extremes in terms of quality. Where the "vast wasteland" of television in general rarely aspired to the quality of great films or literature, premium cable offerings in particular have raised the standards, attracting a viewership that is willing to pay for those commercial-free offerings. (Paying for television programs was once considered as unthinkable as paying for drinking water.)

At the same time, mindless television has become even more mindless, sexy has become sexier, violent has become more violent and dumb has become dumber. Still, an intelligent critic can engage an intelligent readership even when writing about television programming that doesn't brim with intelligence. In fact, the astute critic must do so, particularly when the programming has become a popular phenomenon, because the success of a program says something about the culture that might be more significant than the critic's elitist view toward the viewing masses.

In the pieces that follow, you will see how both television and the attitudes toward it have changed, from the horror that greeted Elvis Presley's early TV appearances, to the counterintuitive perspective on the action-packed "24," to the reality behind so-called "reality TV." Television has been such an integral art of politics since the 1960 Nixon vs. Kennedy debates that a TV critic's beat inevitably covers political campaigning, as well as televised coverage of disasters, triumphs, sports and whatever else constitutes special-events programming.

There's a lot of humor in the best television reviewing, a lot of conversational phrasing and a lot more women among recent TV reviewers at The Times than in some of the other arts. TV is the most populist of media; culture snobs don't make good television critics.

Selection 7.1

This counterintuitive review shows the critic having a change of heart, and we get to follow her thought processes as she alters her perspective, approaching the series more as an engrossing drama about family dynamics than as an increasingly preposterous program. She lets us see the series through fresh eyes, her eyes, whether we agree with her evaluation or not.

In the '24' World, Family Is the Main Casualty
By GINIA BELLAFANTE

The frenetic, labyrinthine, exhausting counterterrorism drama "24" concludes its sixth year on Monday night with its ratings slipping and its fans in revolt. With each season of the series transpiring over a single day, this one, detractors lament, has felt like 70. The producers themselves have acknowledged the challenges of maintaining the story line's intensity and focus. Recently in his blog on "24," the humorist Dave Barry expressed a wish for Congressional hearings into the show's crimes against narrative cohesiveness.

Until two weeks ago I had included myself among the dissenters, complaining that digressions and strange forays into cold war nostalgia had subsumed the larger plot and proclaiming, to the walls in my living room, that "24" ought to become "12"—or "8" or "6." But during Hour 21, Agent Jack Bauer's father, Phillip (played by the gifted James Cromwell), re-emerged to subject members of his family to renewed acts of twisted venality. And the effect was intense and chilling, a reminder that "24" has always sustained its tension

Published: May 20, 2007.

by operating in two genres, not one, deploying the conventions of domestic horror in the language of an apocalyptic thriller.

Since it first appeared in 2001, "24" has successfully woven the terrors of intimate life through its narrative of an America facing potential annihilation. Parents kill children. Husbands abuse wives. Sisters try to kill sisters. Wives fire husbands—or stab them, as Martha Logan, ex-wife of Charles Logan, the former president, did earlier this year, plunging a knife into his shoulder as recompense for his treacheries, both personal and civic.

Discussions of "24" have long concentrated on its depiction of torture—elaborate to the point of parody this season—as the source of its controversy. But it is the show's treatment of family as an impossible and even dangerous illusion that truly challenges our complacency. The anxious gloom of watching "24" comes not from wondering whether the world will blow up (obviously it won't; Jack Bauer—played by Kiefer Sutherland—is protection against all that) but from knowing that the bonds that hold people together will eventually be imperiled or destroyed, perfidy and neglect so often the forces.

The introduction of Phillip Bauer early in the season quickly established that Jack did not inherit his rectitude from his father. Shortly after he appeared, Phillip suffocated his son Graem, forced his daughter-in-law to endanger the lives of federal agents and threatened Jack. When he reappeared, weeks later, Phillip was kidnapping his grandson, Josh, for the second time in a single day.

Parenthood, untouchably sacrosanct in so much of our culture, is on "24" a grotesquely compromised institution. During Season 4 we witnessed the show's defense secretary subject his son to torture for refusing to divulge information that might help track down a terrorist. At the same time we observed the director of the Counter Terrorist Unit labor to thwart a nuclear attack despite the deterioration of her mentally disturbed daughter in a nearby room.

That each child was portrayed as a petulant nuisance made it easier to see that the country's security imperatives had to come first. The perverse brilliance of "24" lies, at least in some part, in its capacity to elicit our sympathies for heinous miscalculations of judgment. In the end we feel less for the troubled girl than we do for her beleaguered mother, who after all has been making sound decisions every step of the way.

The most enduring relationships on "24" are not between parents and children, boyfriends and girlfriends, spouses or siblings, but between individuals and their governments and causes. And in this way the show seems committed not to the politics of the left or right, but to a kind of quasi-totalitarianism in which patriotism takes precedence over everything else and private life is eroded, undermined, demeaned. Privacy isn't even a viable concept in a world in which there is no taco stand, phone booth, laptop or S.U.V. that isn't immediately accessible to the advanced surveillance systems of the ever-vigilant Counter Terrorist Unit.

Human connection is forever suffocated. Totalitarianism, Hannah Arendt wrote, "bases itself on loneliness, on the experience of not belonging to the world at all." And above and beyond everything else, the universe of "24" is a very lonely place.

Friendship can barely be said to exist beyond the parameters of bureaucracy: the offices of the Los Angeles division of the unit and the halls of the White House. And when men and women become involved, it is not only with each other but also with the greater American purpose. Ordinary social intercourse simply doesn't exist. The idea that two people might sit down for a cup of coffee is as contrary to the show's internal logic as the idea that polar bears might someday learn to sing.

On "24" the choice to forfeit all that and respond to your country's call is never the wrong choice, no matter how regrettable the personal consequences. Five seasons ago Jack was a married man who played chess with his teenage daughter. Since then he has lost his wife (at the hands of a unit mole), his daughter (to his own emotional inattention) and various girlfriends to his unfailing devotion to eradicating the state's enemies, whatever the cost. He has killed colleagues who have impeded his pursuit of justice, lost his identity and acquired a heroin addiction combating drug lords. The price of a safe world is considerable, "24" tells us: love and the rest of it mortgaged for some other lifetime.

Selection 7.2

Though the television critic's beat has frequently been characterized as escapism, this review shows not only how television reflects real life (in a manner different from so-called "reality TV"), but how news often packages itself for television. In an analysis that appeared in the news section, this column analyzes a different sort of real-time TV drama from "24," but TV drama nonetheless.

THE TV WATCH
Not Speaking for Obama, Pastor Speaks for Himself, at Length
By ALESSANDRA STANLEY

The Rev. Jeremiah A. Wright Jr. has wriggled out from under sound bites and screen-grab loops to put himself into context in that most American of ways: on television.

Published: April 29, 2008.

And he went deep into context—a rich, stem-winding brew of black history, Scripture, hallelujahs and hermeneutics. Mr. Wright, Senator Barack Obama's former pastor, was cocky, defiant, declamatory, inflammatory and mischievous, but most of all, he was all over the place, performing a television triathlon of interview, lecture and live news conference that pushed Mr. Obama aside and placed himself front and center in the presidential election campaign.

His rehabilitation tour has done no favors to the Obama campaign, which has expressed distress over Mr. Wright's timing and intemperance. "He does not speak for me; he does not speak for the campaign," Mr. Obama said Monday.

But Mr. Wright's monomania over the last three days has helped prove the point Mr. Obama made about his former pastor last month in his speech on race, in which he described Mr. Wright as "imperfect" but having also been "like family to me." Mr. Wright revealed himself to be the compelling but slightly wacky uncle who unsettles strangers but really just craves attention.

Viewers who had seen the Chicago preacher only in brief cable news clips or campaign attack ads finally saw the unexpurgated version, and it was an illuminating display.

Followers of Fox News may have been appalled by the sound bites, but so were members of Mr. Wright's congregation, including Mr. Obama, who complained that the inflammatory snippets were reductive and unfair.

Now it turns out that Mr. Wright doesn't hate America, he loves the sound of his own voice. He is not out of touch with the American culture, he is the avatar of the American celebrity principle: he grabbed his 30-second spots of infamy and turned them into 15 minutes of fame.

Cable news commentators have focused on the damage the spectacle inflicted on the embattled Obama campaign. And while Mr. Wright's behavior may not have been politic for Mr. Obama, it was politics as usual for the television age. In at least one way, Mr. Wright's star turn may have helped defuse his importance in the long run. The pastor who was thrust upon the public consciousness as a caricature of the angry black man emerged after an exhaustive series of performances as a more familiar television persona: a voluble, vain and erudite entertainer, a born televangelist who quotes Ralph Ellison as well as the Bible and mixes highfalutin academic trope with salty street talk.

At a press conference on Monday, Mr. Wright said that his critics were not attacking him, they were attacking African-American culture. "In our community we have something called 'playing the dozens,' " he said with a grin, referring to trash talk competitions that are also known as "yo mama" fights. "If you think I'm going to let you talk about my mama, and her religious tradition," he said, pausing a beat, "you got another thing coming."

Mr. Wright's demystification process began on PBS on Friday. Bill Moyers, the host who knows and obviously admires Mr. Wright, gave the pastor every chance to elaborate on his bona fides, including two years in the Marine Corps and four as a Navy cardiopulmonary technician. Mr. Moyers showed old footage of Mr. Wright in surgical scrubs monitoring President Lyndon B. Johnson's heart after his gall bladder surgery at Bethesda Naval Hospital in 1965. (Mr. Moyers, who was then the White House press secretary, stood behind Mr. Wright.)

He showed Mr. Wright's service to his community throughout the years—tutoring programs, women's groups, H.I.V. ministries. And he also gave Mr. Wright a chance to deconstruct the fiery sermon that seemed to blame America for the Sept. 11 attacks and clarify that he was quoting a former ambassador and intended to condemn the American government, not the nation itself. Mostly, he gave his guest a chance to show his softer side: in a dark suit and gray tie, Mr. Wright was courtly, genial, and something of an egghead, tossing out academic citations, literary references and words like "hermeneutics."

He pumped up the volume on Sunday in his keynote address to the N.A.A.C.P. in Detroit, delivering a thundering lecture about cultural differences and historical biases that sought to explain that his more controversial remarks were taken the wrong way by white viewers who are unfamiliar with the traditions of the African-American church.

"I come from a religious tradition where we shout in the sanctuary and march in the picket line," he said. "Different does not mean deficient." He lectured on differences in music, learning styles (left brain vs. right brain), and he mimicked President John F. Kennedy's Boston accent and also mocked Senator Edward M. Kennedy's speech. "Nobody says to a Kennedy, 'You speak bad English,' " he said. "Only to a black child was that said."

By the time he took the stage on Monday at the National Press Club in Washington, Mr. Wright was on a tear, insisting that "this is not an attack on Jeremiah Wright, this has nothing to do with Barack Obama, this is an attack on the black church." He delivered a rambling disquisition on race, African tradition and theology, and he was clearly enjoying himself, frowning in concentration as the moderator read written questions from reporters, then stepping up to the lectern with feisty rejoinders and snappy retorts, looking as pleased with his replies as a contestant in a high school spelling bee who has just correctly spelled the final word.

While MSNBC was waiting to go live to the event, an anchor asked Mr. Obama's chief strategist, David Axelrod, why the campaign had allowed Mr. Wright to refocus attention upon himself. "He is doing his own thing," Mr. Axelrod said wearily by telephone. "There's not a thing we can do about it."

By the time Mr. Wright had finished speaking, he had proved Mr. Axelrod's point. And also one made by Chuck Todd, the NBC political director who summed up Mr. Wright's apologia by paraphrasing a Carly Simon song: "You're so vain, I bet you think this campaign is about you."

Selection 7.3

From the significant to the ludicrous: Even television that is little more than self-parody can inspire an intelligent response, as this review from the same critic responsible for the previous political analysis attests. While you're enjoying the way she plays with language in this piece, notice how much critical context she uses to support her ironic evaluation of the "elegance" of an extreme eating contest.

THE TV WATCH
Gross Out and Knockoff, but Hardly Any Sendup
By ALESSANDRA STANLEY

"Hurl!," an extreme eating contest on the cable channel G4, has a certain elegance, an economy of action and intent that is too often lacking in contemporary ballet or fine dining. Contestants, almost all male, eat as much as they can in one sitting, then exert themselves in a strenuous physical activity. He who eats the most and vomits the least wins $1,000.

As the show's premiere on Tuesday suggested, "Hurl!" will not win any public service awards from the National Eating Disorders Association. It revels in "hurl cams," close-ups of young players power-gobbling tubs of macaroni and cheese, and instant replays of the losers puking. And like so much summer cable fare, it is basically a straight-to-YouTube event, a spectacle that only teenage boys want to watch in full or at any length at all. But just because it is puerile and revolting, doesn't mean it is stupid. "Hurl!" has a disarming "Jackass" knowingness: it is tongue-in-cheek as well as face-in-bucket.

"Athletes have long understood the connection between what they eat and how they perform," a gravel-voiced narrator intones as a supermarket cart careens through well-stocked aisles. "But tonight a new breed of competitor will find that these things are now one and the same."

"Hurl!," like "Reality Bites Back" and "The Gong Show" (back-to-back shows that begin tonight on Comedy Central), are attempts at satire. And at least in that sense they are almost quixotically brave.

Published: July 17, 2008.

It turns out that it is as impossible to parody the fearless, effervescent vulgarity of shows like ABC's "I Survived a Japanese Game Show" or NBC's "America's Got Talent" as it is to outfiddle Yo-Yo Ma or undersell Costco.

Remakes also try for archness, but those that work best don't mess with the original. Last October Drew Carey proved himself a perfect successor to Bob Barker on "The Price Is Right" by not trying to be funny or different. "Celebrity Family Feud," which had its premiere this month, is a drag because guests like Ice-T or Joan Rivers feel obliged to stay true to their onstage personas. (Though it's always entertaining to see Hollywood families that are stretched to include personal assistants.)

"The Gong Show," hosted by the stand-up comic Dave Attell, is a reprise of the 1970s show with Chuck Barris that was itself a parody of variety shows and talent contests. Three comedians act as judges for acts that are too scatological for network television but no more improbable than the average "America's Got Talent" audition: a hugely fat man lies on the floor under 2,000 pounds of human weight: 15 girls in bikinis and stiletto heels. The judges say crude things but not very wittily.

"Reality Bites Back," which follows it on Comedy Central, is a little more successful. It's a deadpan sendup of all the cheesiest reality shows from "The Real World" to "The Mole," and it captures all the usual highlights, from the smarmy host who recaps constantly, to catty cutaways and slow-motion flashbacks. Ten comedians live together and engage in absurd competitions. Before the games begin, one housemate, Jeff, turns out to have already left. "Do we even have enough tape of him to make a slow-motion music montage?" the host Michael Ian Black asks. An elegiac tribute to Jeff follows, only Jeff is never at the center of any frame and has to be pointed out with arrows.

But once again even the most acid mockery cannot match the exquisite cynicism and self-parody of Tuesday's episode of "America's Got Talent."

After a series of eccentric acts that included dueling accordion players and a man who imitates barnyard animal noises came Donald Braswell. This improbably handsome, well-dressed car salesman from San Antonio said that after he damaged his vocal cords in a car accident, he was told he would never sing again. As Mr. Braswell began crooning a Josh Groban hit, "You Raise Me Up," powerfully and in perfect pitch, the audience jeered and gave him the thumbs-down sign, then suddenly and en masse switched to tears, cheers and a standing ovation. It was a heavily choreographed moment borrowed from last year's "Britain's Got Talent" contest, when Paul Potts, a shy, chubby cellphone salesman, sang Puccini's "Nessun Dorma" and brought down the house.

Mr. Braswell's triumph, heavily promoted in advance by NBC, was supersized to fit American tastes: not only did the producers puff up his backstage moment talking to his children by cellphone with the swelling refrain of "You Raise Me Up," but they also kept the mawkish song rolling as David Hasselhoff and the other judges climbed the steps to a private jet, in slow motion, at sunset.

Even "Reality Bites Back" doesn't come close.

Selection 7.4

Another show that many viewers and most critics might dismiss as beneath contempt receives an engagingly poignant response in The Times. This is the sort of program that would not receive a review unless the critic had something provocative to say. Notice in particular her concluding use of the first-person plural ("us"), aligning herself with the program and its viewers rather than the comparative elitism more typical of The Times' readership.

TELEVISION REVIEW
A Morning Show With Sex On The Brain
By VIRGINIA HEFFERNAN

He's smarmy. She's contrived. He leers at girls like an old stage ham. She talks about freezing her eggs and getting her breasts done. Together they're Mike Jerrick and Juliet Huddy, Fox's new morning pair, who use their unholy chemistry to pervert the breakfast hour on "The Morning Show With Mike and Juliet." We owe these two a warm, warm welcome.

We know what morning shows look like on the networks accused by conservatives of liberal bias, but a morning show produced by Fox is more mysterious. Will it just be a last stop for "American Idol" rejects? Can we expect hair-care demos from Hannity and Colmes?

Surprise. In its more than three weeks on the air, "The Morning Show" has opted, above all, for creepy prurience.

There was Ms. Huddy babbling about her father's fixation on the "Idol" singer Katharine McPhee, and Mr. Jerrick implying the obsession was illegal. There was Mr. Jerrick flashing his own deck of 52 illegal desires. Not to be outdone, Ms. Huddy billboarded her lust for under-age men.

Each makes innuendos about the other's sex life and off-camera carousing, and in every episode they come across as teenagers or freshly

Published: February 8, 2007.

divorced 40-somethings after their first Long Island iced teas. In the spirit of Valerie Cherish of "The Comeback," I reflexively thought at first, "I don't want to see that." Especially not in the morning.

But as I watched more and more "Morning Shows," which meant missing Hour 12 or whatever of "Today" and the whole hour of "Live With Regis and Kelly," I began to doubt not my initial conviction but my mental autonomy: Have I been conditioned not to want to hear gruesome double entendres with my toast?

What is it about the hours before 10 a.m. that make a person want nothing but news, traffic, family values and sanctimony? And, really, what has brainwashed us into thinking we need our homeroom teachers married?

The openly single hosts of "The Morning Show" are far and away the program's stand-out feature. Certainly no one will tune in for the brown and off-brown set, brightened by some o'er-the-river-and-through-the-woods Currier and Ives window backdrop, which makes no sense at all. (In summer can we expect to glimpse children at the swimmin' hole?)

The roster of guests is thick with also-rans: punch lines in celebrity divorces, including Chad Lowe and Kimora Lee Simmons, and "Idol" runners-up, including Ms. McPhee and Diane DeGarmo. Experts come on to talk about how old mascara can blind you, Internet dating, clipping coupons and other kill-me-now subjects.

The only happy novelty of "The Morning Show" is the single-ness of the hosts. It's a chintzy novelty, like a Valentine's Day key-chain, but it's the thought that counts. Mr. Jerrick, who looks a little like William H. Macy, is divorced, with two children. He purports to adore women and strenuously advertises his libido, but evidently he has no girlfriend.

And Ms. Huddy—who has a retro look, like an air hostess on a Scandinavian carrier—well, on her Web bio she writes "sniff" when she considers how she lacks a husband, and then goes on to suggest that Mr. Jerrick would make a great boyfriend. Apparently he doesn't like her in that way.

"We're not dating," Ms. Huddy informed audiences yesterday. Again.

No simmering "Moonlighting" romance seems apparent on the set, though producers should keep hoping. That would be a morning show first. And with all the sex talk, the avuncular (or avauntular?) dynamic of Regis Philbin–Kelly Ripa and Meredith Vieira–Matt Lauer is also absent.

So what is the relationship Mr. Jerrick and Ms. Huddy are performing? I argue this: They are playing an older man who, because he loves the ladies too much or not enough, shuns long-term relationships, and an attractive over-30 woman who has pursued her career rather than marrying and regrets it.

This is a kind of marvelous city duo—and a nice breakthrough for morning shows. No giggly hot mom like Kelly Ripa; no model of rectitude and self-sacrifice like Ms. Vieira. And no good old Reege. Or good young Matt.

Instead they're a little sleazy, Mike and Juliet. And a little lonely. Morning shows have long been seen as having two audiences: busy, important people on their way to work, who want to know news, traffic and weather, and stay-at-home mothers and housewives, who like mellower segments about relationships and household economy.

Mike and Juliet suggest that morning shows, at least those that start at 9, might have another audience: single people who have been out late, talking about "American Idol" and drinking, even, only to wake up alone, in no important rush to get anywhere. That's probably a lot of us. And we have mornings too.

Selection 7.5

As the first season of a series immediately proclaimed a classic approaches its end, a review provides enough illumination to engage those who have followed every episode while offering enough context to those who have never seen the series (but will probably feel like they should start). Every review of an ongoing series must find that common denominator for the obsessive expert and the curious newcomer.

Addicted to a Mob Family Potion
By CARYN JAMES

Everyone in therapy talks about mom, but Tony Soprano has a unique family problem. "What do you think?" he asks, outraged at his psychiatrist's suggestion. "My mother tried to have me whacked 'cause I put her in a nursing home?" Well, maybe. In "The Sopranos," HBO's brilliantly nuanced series about a suburban New Jersey mob boss in emotional crisis, the psychiatrist is helping Tony cope with this breakthrough: in the Sopranos' world you truly can't trust your own mother.

When the series began, Mama Livia Soprano was an irascible old woman, addled and comic enough to hit her best friend accidentally with a car. By the time Tony asks that question in the season finale (to be shown on April 4), she has come to resemble a maternal figure with roots in Greek tragedy and even Roman history. Her name should have been a clue from the start. An earlier Livia was the Emperor

Published: March 25, 1999.

Claudius's ruthless, scheming grandmother (embodied by Sian Phil-
lips in the mini-series "I, Claudius"). Both Livias are matriarchs who
know how to play a bloody family power game.

Livia Soprano's darkening character is simply one strand in the
complex web of "The Sopranos," which has become more absorbing
and richer at every turn. The series has pulled off an almost impossible
feat: it is an ambitious artistic success, the best show of this year and
many others; it has also become an addictive audience-pleaser, the rare
show viewers actually talk and get excited about.

Nancy Marchand, who at first seemed unconvincing as the
typical Italian mother, has turned Livia into a singular character.
Tony was always more than the easy joke about a modern mobster
on Prozac, stressed out by the demands of the job. James Gandolfini
plays Tony with a deftness that masks the heft of a tragic hero, with
flaws that might make him hateful and a visible soul that evokes
sympathy.

Such depth helps explain why "The Sopranos" belongs among
the classic miniseries. In its leisurely use of the form, it is strangely like
"Brideshead Revisited," "The Singing Detective" and "I, Claudius"
(whose historical figures have often been compared to a modern Mafia
family). Because the end of this 13-week series was always in sight, it
could develop the self-enclosed dramatic tension of a feature film: in
the end, would his Uncle Junior take out a hit on Tony in a move to
control the family business, or vice versa? Yet it also took the time to
create ambiguous characters and the feel of a world through dozens of
impeccable small touches.

With its flashy characters and human depths, "The Sopranos"
suggests how thoroughly the Mafia wise guy has become ingrained
in American culture, the stuff of both family tragedy and satire.
Physically, Tony displays the trappings of a cliche. Overweight with
a receding hairline, he wears a jogging suit, gold bracelet and pinky
ring. He is a killer. Yet as he frets about his children's education,
about whether to put his mother in a nursing home, or about whether
an old friend has worn a wire for the F.B.I. and has to be killed, his
emotional pain is real. Tony is the mobster as a suburban family man
(with bimbo girlfriends on the side) but also as a sensitive 90's guy
who wasn't loved enough as a child. Emphatically middle-class, he is
like one of your neighbors but with a more dangerous job; that strat-
egy allows viewers to sympathize and experience vicarious danger
at once.

David Chase, its creator, is largely responsible for "The Sopranos," but the series' dual essence has been captured most succinctly in
an unlikely place: a tag line created by an advertising agency. The ad
shows Tony with his mob contacts on one side and his mother, wife
and two children on the other; the line reads, "If one family doesn't
kill him, the other one will." There is no better statement of the way

the two sides of Tony's life converge to give the series its suspense and emotional power.

The earliest episodes only hinted at how rich and tangled its themes would become. The turning point came in Episode 5, when Tony took his daughter, Meadow, to tour New England colleges. Riding in the car, she asks him if he's in the Mafia; at first he denies such a thing exists, then admits that maybe some aspects of his business, ostensibly garbage hauling, are not entirely legal. It is a surprisingly touching conversation, a moment of painful honesty in which the father admits his imperfections and viewers sympathize with his paternal emotions.

Yet while driving Meadow around, he happens to spot a man who once ratted on the mob, then foolishly left the witness protection program. While his daughter is talking to a counselor at Colby College, Tony tracks down the man and garrotes him on camera. Without destroying sympathy for Tony, the series rubs viewers' faces in the fact that he is a murderer.

That on-camera violence, so crucial to the audience's complex, visceral response, is one reason "The Sopranos" could only appear on cable. On network television, his character would surely be sanitized, the violence toned down, the ambiguity cleared up and the entire series diminished. The brilliance of "The Sopranos" depends on the trick of letting us see Tony's worst qualities and getting us to identify with him anyway.

In a later episode, his psychiatrist, Jennifer Melfi (Lorraine Bracco), mentions her patient to her ex-husband, who warns: "Finally, you're going to get beyond psychology with its cheery moral relativism. Finally you're going to get to good and evil, and he's evil." But that voice, from an incidental character, sounds like a disclaimer. It is out of step with the experience of watching "The Sopranos," which is gripping because it is so fraught with moral relativism.

Dr. Melfi remains the weakest link in "The Sopranos," perhaps because she is not truly family. Occasional hints that she will be drawn into Tony's world (he once had a crooked cop tail her on a date) have gone nowhere, and she has remained the ultimate outsider. Viewers, who share Tony's experiences, are more a part of his family than she is.

In fact, feeling inside a Mafia family has become a cultural touchstone. There is some logic behind the coincidence that "The Sopranos" shares a premise with the current hit film "Analyze This," a slight comedy in which Robert De Niro hilariously plays a mobster who, like Tony, suffers panic attacks and ends up at the psychiatrist. Psychiatry is common today, and it is irresistibly funny to imagine a mob boss who is an emotional wreck.

Mafia Movies As Americana

More telling, together these works suggest how deeply Mafia movies have penetrated American culture. In "Analyze This," Mr. De Niro sends up his own classic roles in films like "The Godfather, Part II" and "Goodfellas." In "The Sopranos," Tony's men model themselves on movie mobsters. One man has a car horn that blares out the first bars of "The Godfather" theme; another routinely impersonates Al Pacino as Michael Corleone. Tony's stupidly impulsive nephew, Christopher (Michael Imperioli), tries to write a screenplay about his mob experiences and longs for tabloid fame. Frustrated at his unimportance, Christopher complains that every movie mobster has his own story arc. "Where's my arc?" he says. "I got no identity."

Tony himself is smarter. When he is taken by a neighbor to play golf at a country club, he is bombarded with questions: "How real was 'The Godfather?' " and "Did you ever meet John Gotti?" He may be a killer, but viewers feel for him at that moment; he is wounded at being condescended to and reduced to a cliche.

These 90's mobsters, after all, are a generation removed from the movies that inspired them. "The Sopranos" knowingly hits cultural nerves by responding to the present moment. Meadow reveals the truth about their father's business to her younger brother, Anthony, by showing him a Web site that features pictures of mob bosses. "There's Uncle Jackie!" says Anthony as he spots one of his father's best friends. ("The Sopranos" has its own place on HBO's Web site, which includes a section on the rock-inspired music that is so integral to its realistic feel.)

In the next-to-last episode (this Sunday) Tony becomes so depressed he can't get out of bed. Even in this crisis, the series maintains its focus on the credible details of ordinary life. Tony's wife, Carmela, is perfectly played by Edie Falco with a toughened exterior that suggests how she has had to steel herself to her husband's profession. Carmela says, "If you want me I will be at Paramus Mall getting your son a suit for his first formal." One shrewdly drawn plot involves a situation that is absurdly common in real life but rarely discussed. Carmela has a flirtation with a priest, Father Phil, who comes to the house for ziti and movies before safely fleeing back to the church.

Weighing Guilt And Words

The final episode of "The Sopranos" reaches a crescendo of action and intrigue, guilt and retribution. It sets up the story for the next season, beginning in January. And the cumulative weight of the previous weeks adds a delicious resonance to everything Tony says. When he tells a friend whose restaurant he has ordered set on fire, "I didn't burn down your restaurant, I swear on my mother," what exactly does he mean?

Selection 7.6

As designed by the "Reporter's Notebook" label, this piece includes reportage, by a writer who visited the "American Idol" set and auditions and describes how what he saw differs from what the viewer perceives. But rather than objective journalism, this is commentary—critical analysis—concerning an offshoot of "reality TV" that "is as scripted as a 'reality' show dare be." Examine how the reportage and analysis combine to support an evaluative argument.

REPORTER'S NOTEBOOK
American Idolatry: If Only Reality Were This Well Organized
By EDWARD WYATT

LOS ANGELES—The tens of thousands of hopefuls who lined up last summer to audition for "American Idol" have been trimmed to just six aspiring pop stars, whose fate will be decided by the whims and loyalties of the more than 20 million people who tune in each week to the most-watched show on television.

Determining the winner is about the only part of "American Idol" left to chance. That was made clear during recent visits to Stage 36 in Television City, near Hollywood, where each Tuesday and Wednesday on Fox "American Idol" creates hopes and dashes dreams.

From the placement of local sorority members along camera sight lines to the instructions to the audience members about when to stand and how to wave their hands, "American Idol" is as scripted as a "reality" show dare be.

"At the end of every performance you will stand on your feet." That is one of the commandments offered by Cory Almeida, the indefatigable warm-up man who exhorts and instructs the audience for 15 minutes before each performance and during the numerous commercial breaks.

For the audience members who stand in the "mosh pit," the area immediately in front of the stage, special instructions are required. "When you are applauding after a performance, we need your hands above your head," Mr. Almeida said before a recent Tuesday performance. "Otherwise we can't see that you're clapping." As he spoke other stage technicians offered more individualized guidance to mosh pit enthusiasts, including how to wave their arms from side to side over their heads during slow songs.

Then, three minutes before the live broadcast, the introductions: Ryan Seacrest, the host, who, after the theater is darkened, announces the entrance of the judges as the true stars of the show. First is Randy Jackson, who is followed by a spotlight to his seat at the judges' table, then Simon Cowell. Fifty seconds to air. But where is Paula Abdul?

A Stage-Shrinking Trick

The most striking thing about encountering the sparkling "American Idol" stage set is how much smaller it seems in person than on television. If the camera adds 10 pounds to the average actor, it seems to add acres to a stage set.

Critics have complained this year about the vast, open look of the stage, newly constructed for the final round of 12 contestants. Few of the singers were able quickly to make it their own, opting instead to stay seated in front of a microphone or pace a small area at the front.

The audience too looks expansive on television, but the hall includes only 12 rows of seats, four at floor level and eight in bleachers. The stage, ringed by more flat-screen television monitors than a Best Buy at Christmas, looks like a chrome version of the Emerald City.

Herding Cats on the Set

Performing a live television show is an exercise in exactitude. The broadcast, every Tuesday and Wednesday night, begins regardless of whether Mr. Seacrest is on his mark (he usually is), whether the audience is sufficiently enthused (it usually is) and whether the judges are in their seats. Which, on a recent Tuesday, only two of the three were.

Fifty seconds to air, and Ms. Abdul was missing. Thirty seconds to air, and the lights again went down, and the audience was quieted for the "cold open," the introduction by Mr. Seacrest.

Fifteen seconds to air, as the stage manager, Debbie Williams, began the countdown, Ms. Abdul scurried into the auditorium from the green room, ducking into her seat as Mr. Seacrest began his routine.

That scene is replayed many times each night, and not just by Ms. Abdul. During most commercial breaks the three judges leave their seats, sometimes chatting with the executive producer, Nigel Lythgoe, at other times floating toward the audience to greet guests or sign autographs. Not infrequently they disappear backstage, cellphones pressed to their ears, only to emerge with seconds to spare.

Sometimes they don't quite make it. During a recent broadcast Ms. Abdul ducked behind Mr. Seacrest and a cameraman as the host introduced the next contestant; she sneaked into her chair only as the music rose for the performance.

Herding Sororities

A mystery that has occurred to at least one frequent viewer of "American Idol" is just how the show manages to draw so many homogeneously attractive, well-dressed women to pack the mosh pit, where they produce high-pitched squeals that could probably perk up the ears of dogs in the San Fernando Valley.

The answer: They are recruited.

In early April it was the turn of the women of Alpha Phi, a sorority at the University of California, Los Angeles. About 25 members trekked to the studio one Tuesday, said Rachel Lorack, a member from Half Moon Bay, Calif., and another two dozen were to attend the following week. Last week it was the Delta Gamma and Delta Delta Delta sororities.

The perk is a recruitment tool for some sororities as well. "We sometimes talk about this at rush," said Courtney Lauwereins, a member from Laguna Beach, Calif. "Join Alpha Phi, and you might get to go to 'American Idol.' "

The show, of course, does not just throw a bevy of sorority women in front of the cameras and allow them to cluster as they may. Stage assistants choose specific women and place them where the hand-held cameras will swoop during performances. (Print journalists are generally consigned to the back row of the bleachers, where, thankfully for viewers, they are well out of camera range.)

The 'Secret Service'

If the Wizard of Oz had security guards like these, Toto would never have gotten near that shiny curtain. A veritable platoon of security guards monitors every aspect of the performance, and all judges have bodyguards who follow them from backstage to the judges' table. Mr. Seacrest too is closely tailed when he makes his way into the audience to introduce a segment.

Dressed in casual shirts and jeans, these burly, often crew-cut gentlemen are meant to blend into the audience, at least when the cameras catch them along the edge of the mosh pit. But they often stick out like bikers at a tea party. A few weeks ago the camera panned across a standing group of young fans and seemed nearly to graze the head of an especially tall guard.

The guards apparently spend all week with the contestants as well. Kristy Lee Cook, the Oregon country singer who was eliminated last week, told television interviewers how she and her boyfriend, seeking a few moments of privacy, recently ducked into a nonworking sauna room in the apartment building where the "Idol" contestants live. It was there, she said, that the young man proposed marriage.

'Live' Is a Relative Term

When Mr. Seacrest and others bill "American Idol" as being live, they are slightly fudging the truth. Parts of many shows are recorded, particularly some performances by guests and the segment where callers pose questions to the contestants or judges. "We pretape it because we're afraid somebody might say something bad," Ms. Williams explained to the audience.

On April 1, after the Tuesday broadcast was completed, the producers taped Chris Brown and Jordin Sparks, last year's "Idol" winner, for broadcast a week later. Mariah Carey appeared on last Wednesday's show, but her performance had been taped a half-hour before the live broadcast, then played back during the show. Sometimes "Live From Hollywood" means "Taped in Hollywood, maybe a week ago."

Selection 7.7

A blast from the past shows how much of a threat rock 'n' roll in general—and Elvis Presley in particular—were once considered to polite society, common decency and Western civilization as we know it. Examine the role that one critic expected television to play in the mid-1950s and contrast that with our expectations of television as a moral force today. Early on, critics recognized (for better or worse) what a crucial impact television could have on society. As the suggestive homoeroticism of Adam Lambert's performance on a musical awards show indicates both critics and television continue to wrestle with such issues.

Elvis Presley: Lack of Responsibility Is Shown by TV In Exploiting Teen-Agers
By JACK GOULD

Television broadcasters cannot be asked to solve life's problems. But they can be expected to display adult leadership and responsibility in areas where they do have some significant influence. This they have hardly done in the case of Elvis Presley, entertainer and phenomenon.

Last Sunday on the Ed Sullivan show Mr. Presley made another of his appearances and attracted a record audience. In some ways it was perhaps the most unpleasant of his recent three performances.

Mr. Presley initially disturbed adult viewers—and instantly became a martyr in the eyes of his teen-age following—for his strip-tease behavior on last spring's Milton Berle program. Then with Steve Allen he was much more sedate. On the Sullivan program he injected movements of the tongue and indulged in wordless singing that were singularly distasteful.

At least some parents are puzzled or confused by Presley's almost hypnotic power; others are concerned; perhaps most are a shade disgusted and content to permit the Presley fad to play itself out.

Published: September 16, 1956.

Neither criticism of Presley nor of the teen-agers who admire him is particularly to the point. Presley has fallen into a fortune with a routine that in one form or another has always existed on the fringe of show business; in his gyrating figure and suggestive gestures the teen-agers have found something that for the moment seems exciting or important.

Void

Quite possibly Presley just happened to move in where society has failed the teen-ager. Certainly, modern youngsters have been subjected to a great deal of censure and perhaps too little understanding. Greater in their numbers than ever before, they may have found in Presley a rallying point, a nationally prominent figure who seems to be on their side. And, just as surely, there are limitless teen-agers who cannot put up with the boy, either vocally or calisthenically.

Family counselors have wisely noted that ours is still a culture in a stage of frantic and tense transition. With even 16-year-olds capable of commanding $20 or $30 a week in their spare time, with access to automobiles at an early age, with communications media of all kinds exposing them to new thoughts very early in life, theirs indeed is a high degree of independence. Inevitably it has been accompanied by a lessening of parental control.

Small wonder, therefore, that the teen-ager is susceptible to overstimulation from the outside. He is at the age when an awareness of sex is both thoroughly natural and normal, when latent rebellion is to be expected. But what is new and a little discouraging is the willing-ness and indeed eagerness of reputable business men to exploit those critical factors beyond all reasonable grounds.

Television surely is not the only culprit. Exposé magazines, which once were more or less bootleg items, are now carried openly on the best newsstands. The music-publishing business—as Variety most courageously has pointed out—has all but disgraced itself with some of the "rock 'n' roll" songs it has issued. Some of the finest companies have been willing to go right along with the trend, too.

Distinctive

Of all these businesses, however, television is in a unique position. First and foremost, it has access directly to the home and its wares are free. Second, the broadcasters are not only addressing themselves to the teen-agers but, much more importantly, also to the lower age groups. When Presley executes his bumps and grinds, it must be remembered by the Columbia Broadcasting System that even the 12-year-old's curiosity may be overstimulated. It is on this score that the adult viewer has every right to expect sympathetic understanding and cooperation from a broadcaster.

A perennial weakness in the executive echelons of the networks is their opportunistic rationalization of television's function. The industry lives fundamentally by the code of giving the public what it wants. This is not the place to argue the artistic foolishness of such a standard; in the case of situation comedies and other escapist diversion it is relatively unimportant.

But when this code is applied to teen-agers just becoming conscious of life's processes, not only is it manifestly without validity but it also is perilous. Catering to the interests of the younger generation is one of television's main jobs; because those interests do not always coincide with parental tastes should not deter the broadcasters. But selfish exploitation and commercialized over-stimulation of youth's physical impulses is certainly a gross national disservice.

Sensible

The issue is not one of censorship, which solves nothing; it is one of common sense. It is no impingement on the medium's artistic freedom to ask the broadcaster merely to exercise good sense and display responsibility. It is no blue-nosed suppression of the proper way of depicting life in the theatre to expect stage manners somewhat above the level of the carnival sideshow.

In the long run, perhaps Presley will do everyone a favor by pointing up the need for earlier sex education so that neither his successors nor TV can capitalize on the idea that his type of routine is somehow highly tempting yet forbidden fruit. But that takes time, and meanwhile the broadcasters at least can employ a measure of mature and helpful thoughtfulness in not contributing further to the exploitation of the teen-ager.

With congested schools, early dating, the appeals of the car, military service, acceptance by the right crowd, sex and the normal parental pressures, the teen-ager has all the problems he needs.

Mercenary

To resort to the world's oldest theatrical come-on just to make a fast buck from such sensitive individuals is cheap and tawdry stuff. At least Presley is honest in what he is doing. That the teen-ager sometimes finds it difficult to feel respect for the moralizing older generation may of itself be an encouraging sign of his intelligence. If the profiteering hypocrite is above reproach and Presley isn't, today's youngsters might well ask what God do adults worship.

MAKING**CONNECTIONS**

1

In this chapter's first review, Ginia Bel-lafante employs an early single use of the first person (second paragraph). Why? Would the review be more effective with no "I" in it, or with more? Rewrite that second paragraph without the "I" and compare its effectiveness with the originals.

How did a TV critic cover the contro-versy surrounding the Rev. Jeremiah Wright differently from the way a political columnist might? Look for specific passages in the review that concern television.

In the analysis of "The Sopranos," highlight the passages that will mean the most to those who have followed the series faithfully. In a dif-ferent color, highlight those passages that can engage the interest of those who have never seen the series.

In the concluding piece on Elvis Presley's television appearances with Ed Sullivan, the subhead castigates television's "Lack of Responsibility." What would this reviewer think of "Hurl!" and "A Morning Show With Sex on the Brain," two programs reviewed in this chapter?

books

THE INFLUENCE OF THE TIMES ON BOTH READERS AND PUBLISHERS of books has never been greater, at least partly because of attrition. Though The Times has long been the country's foremost literary authority among dailies (and the paper of record within the New York–centric publishing industry), many other cities once had papers with standalone Sunday books sections, and weekday reviews as well. With advertising (including book ads) and other revenues at newspapers in freefall, books coverage at too many other papers has either diminished or disappeared.

The Washington Post, Los Angeles Times and Atlanta Journal-Constitution are among the papers that have lost long-standing, standalone Sunday book sections. Though book commentary has, like so much commentary, largely shifted to the Web, unpaid blog chatter can't replace the thoughtful, edited literary journalism that was once a newspaper mainstay.

Such journalism continues to flourish at The Times. Three staff critics alternate in generating reviews every Monday through Friday, and the Sunday New York Times Book Review remains a must-read for book buffs across the country and throughout the world. If publishers buy ads in only one publication, that one publication is likely to be The Times. The New York Times Bestseller lists remain the gold standard for commercial achievement, the one most mentioned in promotion and advertising.

At The Times, the daily reviews operate independently of the Sunday Review, with the most significant books receiving reviews (occasionally conflicting ones) in both. Daily reviews are primarily staff-written, though freelancers are typically assigned to review books by other Times staffers and occasionally books in a field that requires a specialist's insight. The New York Times Sunday Book Review primarily assigns freelancers, often noted authors or critics, with occasional contributions from staffers other than the daily book critics.

Book reviewing is the only form of arts criticism where both the art and the review are in the same medium—words written about words. The reviewer thus has greater opportunity to follow the journalistic adage to "show, not tell," by including passages of the actual written work within the review rather than (or in addition to) describing the writing. As you read the reviews in this chapter, pay particular attention to the use of quoted material. How much of it does the reviewer use, and what kind? How early? To serve what argument?

Watch as well for the distinctly different strategies used in reviews of fiction (novels and short stories) and nonfiction (biographies, autobiographies, history, current events, et al.). Though freelancers frequently specialize in one or the other, or in books in a particular subject area, staff critics are generalists who review fiction and nonfiction alike.

Explains staff critic Janet Maslin: "A book reviewer has some very basic work to do. He or she has got to explain what this is, who wrote it, what it's trying to do and whether it succeeds. Starting from scratch. If you can present all that in an interesting way and hold the reader's attention throughout, you're doing it right."

FICTION

While the conventions of novels and the criteria for evaluating them have changed over the decades, some authors have always resisted the trends. And so have some critics. The incisive reviewer has an affinity for both the traditional and the innovative, and understands the interrelationship between the two—how a novel that minimizes character development or narrative momentum offers a critique of those conventions in novelistic tradition. The great literary critic must understand how things change, when things change, why things change.

Just as great paintings teach us how to view them and great pieces of music teach us how to hear them, great fiction teaches us how to read it. Great novels can be very long or very short; they can be hyper-realistic or fantasy or somehow blur the distinction. The narrators of some great novels are omniscient and in others they are unreliable; in some, the reader's trust in the narrative perspective shifts as the novel progresses. Some protagonists of great novels are heroic; others are repugnant. Some great novels sustain a breakneck narrative momentum; in others, not much happens. Some great novels build to a happy ending; others end on a note so sad it might linger with the reader forever.

It's the novel's job (not the novelist's, as we've discussed with "intentional fallacy") to show us what kind of book it is, and the reader's challenge to figure it out. The critic mediates, offering insight and illumination that can enrich the reading experience or warn readers away from a novel that doesn't warrant their time and money. Some readers skim reviews for that consumer-guide evaluation and then read the review again for deeper critical analysis after finishing the book.

Like film reviewers (and occasionally theater critics), reviewers of novels must strike a balance between telling enough and not revealing too much. Writers who are new to reviewing tend to rely too much on plot summary, when actually in many novels the tone and style of the writing, the thematic underpinnings or the progression of character development might be more important. Perhaps the worst sin is to reveal crucial plot twists that will ruin the reader's delight in discovery.

Short story collections present different challenges met by different strategies. If all the stories are by a single author, try to determine an underlying unity (geography, theme, style, etc.). It's less effective to write a little about each story than to go into greater depth on a few stories that reflect the range of the volume (the best and worst ones, the typical and atypical). With an anthology of stories by different authors, again pick representative work rather than trying to cover everything.

NONFICTION

Where reviews of novels must be careful not to give too much away, nonfiction reviews tend to give *everything* away—or at least as much as space permits. Whatever highlights the book—whatever is most revelatory, controversial, newsworthy, noteworthy—will highlight the review as well. For many people, reading a review of a biography or other nonfiction book serves as a shortcut substitute for reading the whole book, whereas a review of fiction never can.

In summarizing whatever makes this person, trend, event or historical period worth writing about, the review summarizes the subject as well as the book. The reviewer might extend the context beyond the author's life and work to a comparison with other books on the same subject. Does this book offer any new information, greater depth, a fresh perspective? Literary considerations can highlight the review, especially if the book is written very gracefully or very poorly. In memoir, style might be as important as it is in fiction—though, as we see in one of the pieces that follows, it's crucial that the author not allow himself the creative license that a novelist does.

Some nonfiction books make arguments, and reviews of those often respond to those arguments, either rebutting or supporting. In the following reviews, pay attention to how the balance of description, context, interpretation and evaluation differs in nonfiction and fiction reviewing.

The chapter does not address reviewing poetry because such analyses might be better left to courses in literary criticism. Unless you write poetry, read a lot of it or otherwise establish yourself as an expert, you're less likely ever to review a book of it.

Selection 8.1

A hallmark of the criticism of Michiko Kakutani, the Pulitzer Prize–winning chief book critic for The Times, is the unflinching strength of her evaluations. From "extraordinary" in her lead sentence to "dazzling" in the kicker, she leaves no doubt how she feels about a book that a survey by The Times of leading literary figures would subsequently proclaim the best American novel of the last 25 years. Consider how much significance she places on the dreamlike mood of the novel rather than plot development.

BOOKS OF THE TIMES
Beloved. By Toni Morrison
By MICHIKO KAKUTANI

At the heart of Toni Morrison's extraordinary new novel, "Beloved," there stands a horrifying event—an event so brutal and

Published: September 2, 1987.

disturbing that it appears to warp time before and after into a single, unwavering line of fate. It will destroy one family's dream of safety and freedom; it will haunt an entire community for generations; and, as related by Ms. Morrison, it will reverberate in readers' minds long after they have finished this book.

What has happened is this: a runaway slave, caught in her attempt to escape, cuts the throat of her baby daughter with a hand-saw, determined to spare the child the fate she herself has suffered.

"Though she and others lived through and got over it," writes Ms. Morrison, "she could never let it happen to her own. The best thing she was, was her children. Whites might dirty her all right, but not her best thing, her beautiful, magical best thing—the part of her that was clean. No undreamable dreams about whether the headless, feetless torso hanging in the tree with a sign on it was her husband or Paul A; whether the bubbling-hot girls in the colored-school fire set by patriots included her daughter; whether a gang of whites invaded her daughter's private parts, soiled her daughter's thighs and threw her daughter out of the wagon. She might have to work the slaughterhouse yard, but not her daughter."

Though this has happened 18 long years ago, time still stops for Sethe on that day she killed her baby. In the years since, she has become the town pariah, living alone with her remaining daughter in a silent house, haunted with ghosts and evil memories and trying in vain to beat "back the past." Then, quite suddenly, everything appears to change: an old friend, Paul D., arrives back in town to offer Sethe the promise of a new beginning, and for a brief moment she's able to envision the possibility of enjoying an ordinary, even happy life.

Just as Paul D. is settling in, however, another visitor materializes—a strange, secretive girl who calls herself Beloved; and in her arrival are contained the seeds of Sethe's redemption and destruction. In time, Beloved will become everything to everyone in the house at 124 Bluestone Road: she will become Paul D.'s mistress, Denver's sister and Sethe's daughter. Indeed, Sethe will come to see Beloved as the reincarnation of the daughter she once killed, and she will attempt, this time around, to make up for all that happened before.

These events unfold before us, like dream images, in a succession of lyrical passages that jump back and forth in time, back and forth in point of view from one character to another. As a result, there is a contemporaneous quality to time past and time present as well as a sense that the lines between reality and fiction, truth and memory, have become inextricably blurred: by the end, we see Beloved as Sethe herself does, as both daughter and ghostly apparition.

Thanks to this narrative method and Ms. Morrison's magisterial yet sensuous prose, "Beloved" possesses the heightened power and resonance of myth—its characters, like those in opera or Greek drama, seem larger than life and their actions, too, tend to strike us as enactments of ancient rituals and passions. To describe "Beloved" only in these terms, however, is to diminish its immediacy, for the novel also remains precisely grounded in an American reality—the reality of black history as experienced in the wake of the Civil War. It's not only possible to recognize the people in "Beloved" as older relatives of the small-town Ohio folks who populated Ms. Morrison's earlier novels "Sula" and "The Bluest Eye"; it's also necessary to understand their story in order to comprehend the loss of innocence that is the legacy of the characters in all her fiction.

In "Sula," the story of two girls coming of age, the reader meets characters so paralyzed by the weight of the past that they desire only survival; and in "Beloved," one sees firsthand the brutalities of slavery that shaped their ancestors' lives. Whites carelessly beat, rape and maim their slaves, sell them for a price and kill them for a lark; and in this world, where a similar violence festers between black men and women, between parents and their children, one begins to see the terrible logic of Sethe's decision to kill her child. In fact, in this frightening world, love becomes a dangerous emotion—dangerous not because it involves emotional vulnerability and the threat of rejection but dangerous because it demands an unaccommodated response.

"For a used-to-be-slave woman to love anything that much was dangerous, especially if it was her children she had settled on to love," Paul D. thinks upon hearing Sethe's story. "The best thing, he knew, was to love just a little bit; everything, just a little bit, so when they broke its back, or shoved it in a croaker sack, well, maybe you'd have a little love left over for the next one."

With Beloved's mysterious arrival, Sethe is given a second chance to reinvent her family, but again she must face up to the possibility of loss. Leaving, of course, is part of the reality of being a slave—having husband and children "moved around like checkers"; but at the same time, Ms. Morrison implies, it's part of life, in which parents die, children grow up and lovers move on. Indeed, the characters in "Beloved" are forced to realize that leaving the past behind may be a necessity, that redemption is to be found not in remembering but in forgetting.

For Sethe's family, her story "is not a story to pass on," but for readers of this novel, it is as magical as it is upsetting. This is a dazzling novel.

Selection 8.2

Decades after Kakutani's review of "Beloved," the novel has achieved widespread critical consensus as the best of the last quarter-century. This opening excerpt from a longer piece by A. O. Scott (moonlighting from his regular beat as co-chief film critic for The Times), suggests just how many considerations must be addressed in such an evaluation, underscoring the challenge of proclaiming anything "the best."

Essay
In Search of the Best
By A. O. SCOTT

More than a century ago, Frank Norris wrote that "the Great American Novel is not extinct like the dodo, but mythical like the hippogriff," an observation that Philip Roth later used as the epigraph for a spoofy 1973 baseball fantasia called, naturally, "The Great American Novel." It pointedly isn't—no one counts it among Roth's best novels, though what books people do place in that category will turn out to be relevant to our purpose here, which has to do with the eternal hunt for Norris's legendary beast. The hippogriff, a monstrous hybrid of griffin and horse, is often taken as the very symbol of fantastical impossibility, a unicorn's unicorn. But the Great American Novel, while also a hybrid (crossbred of romance and reportage, high philosophy and low gossip, wishful thinking and hard-nosed skepticism), may be more like the yeti or the Loch Ness monster—or sasquatch, if we want to keep things homegrown. It is, in other words, a creature that quite a few people—not all of them certifiably crazy, some of them bearing impressive documentation—claim to have seen. The Times Book Review, ever wary of hoaxes but always eager to test the boundary between empirical science and folk superstition, has commissioned a survey of recent sightings.

Or something like that. Early this year, the Book Review's editor, Sam Tanenhaus, sent out a short letter to a couple hundred prominent writers, critics, editors and other literary sages, asking them to please identify "the single best work of American fiction published in the last 25 years." The results—in some respects quite surprising, in others not at all—provide a rich, if partial and unscientific, picture of the state of American literature, a kind of composite self-portrait as interesting perhaps for its blind spots and distortions as for its details.

And as interesting, in some cases, for the reasoning behind the choices as for the choices themselves. Tanenhaus's request, simple and innocuous enough at first glance, turned out in many cases to be downright treacherous. It certainly provoked a lot of other questions in response, both overt and implicit. "What is poetry and if you know what poetry is what is prose?" Gertrude Stein once asked, and the question "what is the single best work of American fiction published in the last 25 years?" invites a similar scrutiny of basic categories and assumptions. Nothing is as simple as it looks. What do we mean, in an era of cultural as well as economic globalization, by "American"? Or, in the age of James Frey, reality television and phantom W.M.D.'s,

Published: May 21, 2006. Full text available at: www.nytimes.com/2006/05/21/books/review/
scott-essay.html.

what do we mean by "fiction"? And if we know what American fiction is, then what do we mean by "best"?

A tough question, and one that a number of potential respondents declined to answer, some silently, others with testy eloquence. There were those who sighed that they could not possibly select one book to place at the summit of an edifice with so many potential building blocks—they hadn't read everything, after all—and also those who railed against the very idea of such a monument. One famous novelist, unwilling to vote for his own books and reluctant to consider anyone else's, asked us to "assume you never heard from me."

More common was the worry that our innocent inquiry, by feeding the deplorable modern mania for ranking, list-making and fabricated competition, would not only distract from the serious business of literature but, worse, subject it to damaging trivialization. To consecrate one work as the best—or even to establish a short list of near-bests—would be to risk the implication that no one need bother with the rest, and thus betray the cause of reading. The determination of literary merit, it was suggested, should properly be a matter of reasoned judgment and persuasive argument, not mass opinionizing. Criticism should not cede its prickly, qualitative prerogatives to the quantifying urges of sociology or market research.

Fair enough. But there would be no point in proposing such a contest unless it would be met with quarrels and complaints. (A few respondents, not content to state their own preferences, pre-emptively attacked what they assumed would be the thinking of the majority. So we received some explanations of why people were not voting for "Beloved," the expected winner, and also one Roth fan's assertion that the presumptive preference for "American Pastoral" over "Operation Shylock" was self-evidently mistaken.) Even in cases—the majority—where the premise of the research was accepted, problems of method and definition buzzed around like persistent mosquitoes. There were writers who, finding themselves unable to isolate just one candidate, chose an alternate, or submitted a list. The historical and ethical parameters turned out to be blurry, since the editor's initial letter had not elaborated on them. Could you vote for yourself? Of course you could: amour-propre is as much an entitlement of the literary class as log-rolling, which means you could also vote for a friend, a lover, a client or a colleague. But could you vote for, say, "A Confederacy of Dunces," which, though published in 1980, was written around 20 years earlier? A tricky issue of what scholars call periodization: is John Kennedy Toole's ragged New Orleans farce a lost classic of the 60's, to be shelved alongside countercultural picaresques like Richard Fariña's "Been Down So Long It Looks Like Up to Me"? Or is it a premonition of the urban-comic 80's zeitgeist in which it finally landed, keeping company with, say, Jay McInerney's "Bright Lights, Big City"? What about story collections—I. B. Singer's,

Donald Barthelme's, Raymond Carver's, for instance—that appeared between 1980 and 2005 but gathered up the work of earlier decades? Do they qualify? And—most consequentially, as it happened—what about John Updike's four "Rabbit" novels? Only the last two were published during the period in question, but all four were bound into a single volume and published, by Everyman's Library, in 1995. Considered separately, "Rabbit Is Rich" (1981) and "Rabbit at Rest" (1990) might have split Updike's vote, which "Rabbit Angstrom" was able to consolidate, placing it in the top five. If Nathan Zuckerman had received a similar omnibus reissue, with "The Counterlife," "The Human Stain," "American Pastoral" and the others squeezed into one fat tome, literary history as we know it—or at least this issue of the Book Review—would be entirely different.

***

ESSAY
Beyond Criticism

By SAM TANENHAUS
Published: February 4, 2007

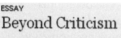
Correction Appended

It may be heretical, or just foolish, for a book review editor to admit it, but there are times when criticism is beside the point. This was brought home to me recently when I read the Library of America's new edition of Saul Bellow's major fiction from the 1950s and '60s, a volume of nearly 800 pages that includes "Seize the Day," "Henderson the Rain King" and "Herzog."

Saul Bellow in 1965.

A Retrospective

Featured Author: Saul

🔍 Enlarge This Image   I've admired Bellow for many years, and plunging again into these middle-period classics seemed a good opportunity to put my stored-up thoughts in order. But I immediately ran into trouble. To begin with, the three works, though they all feature familiar Bellow heroes — disheveled but preening, spiritually hungry, estranged from their wives — are dauntingly dissimilar in form, subject and language.

In the novella "Seize the Day," the action, which unfolds in less than 12 hours, is limited to the fraught interrelations of three inhabitants of an Upper West Side apartment building — Tommy Wilhelm, an unemployed salesman on the skids; and the two elders, his disapproving father and a huckster neighbor, who compete for control over his life.

Selection 8.3

In this appreciation of Nobel Prize–winning novelist Saul Bellow, a critic and editor of the Sunday Times Book Review ventures to suggest that some art is so transcendent that it is, as the headline suggests, "beyond criticism." If so, why? If not, why not? And if critics take this position too often, won't they argue their way out of a job? The headline notwithstanding, this is obviously a piece of criticism, one that looks thoughtfully not just at Bellow's work but at the role of criticism itself.

Essay
Beyond Criticism
By SAM TANENHAUS

It may be heretical, or just foolish, for a book review editor to admit it, but there are times when criticism is beside the point. This was brought home to me recently when I read the Library of America's new edition of Saul Bellow's major fiction from the 1950s and '60s, a volume of nearly 800 pages that includes "Seize the Day," "Henderson the Rain King" and "Herzog."

I've admired Bellow for many years, and plunging again into these middle-period classics seemed a good opportunity to put my stored-up thoughts in order. But I immediately ran into trouble. To begin with, the three works, though they all feature familiar Bellow heroes—disheveled but preening, spiritually hungry, estranged from their wives—are dauntingly dissimilar in form, subject and language.

In the novella "Seize the Day," the action, which unfolds in less than 12 hours, is limited to the fraught interrelations of three inhabitants of an Upper West Side apartment building—Tommy Wilhelm, an unemployed salesman on the skids; and the two elders, his disapproving father and a huckster neighbor, who compete for control over his life.

A chasm separates this spare little work from the exuberant, fantastical "Henderson the Rain King," a travel narrative, situated in an imagined Africa (Bellow did in fact eventually take a trip to the continent, in 1970), that stretches the boundaries of the picaresque Bellow had already tested in "The Adventures of Augie March"; Henderson's adventures lampoon the chest-thumping exploits of Hemingway even as they parody Bellow's firsthand investigations of the "orgone experiments" of the psychologist Wilhelm Reich.

Finally, there is "Herzog," a comic-philosophical meditation on cultural disorder centered on the mishaps of a cuckolded scholar whose famous first words—"If I am out of my mind, it's all right with me"—propel him on a five-day flight from his disintegrating life and

Published: February 4, 2007.

on a letter-writing spree "to the newspapers, to people in public life, to friends and relatives and at last to the dead, his own obscure dead, and finally the famous dead."

Impossible to impose a single line of argument on these books, so I approached them separately, taking notes and jotting little eurekas! in the margins. For instance, "Seize the Day" owed an unexpected debt—actually two debts—to James Joyce, to the short story "The Dead" and to "Ulysses," each set on a single day, the first a fine-tuned study in failure, the second an epic of father-son reconciliation.

In "Henderson," I detected ominous foreshadowings of the elderly Bellow's mischievous joke about multiculturalism—"Who is the Tolstoy of the Zulus? The Proust of the Papuans? I'd be glad to read him"—that had cost him much grief in his last years.

And it occurred to me that Moses Herzog's high-flown communications to Nietzsche and Adlai Stevenson resembled, tonally, the letter Bellow himself, in a fit of magnificent outrage, had sent to William Faulkner in 1956, after Faulkner had fatuously championed Ezra Pound despite Pound's loathsome anti-Semitic tirades.

These insights, such as they were, seemed plausible, but inconsequential, for they ignored the one essential truth about Bellow's novels: they collectively yield a vision of the human universe as apprehended by a being of higher intelligence who is touched also with a rare depth of feeling.

But what, then, of the many defects—the longueurs and digressions, the lectures on anthroposophy and religion, the arcane reading lists? What of the characters who don't change or grow but simply bristle onto the page, even the colorful lowlifes pontificating like fevered students in the seminars Bellow taught at the University of Chicago? And what of the punitively caricatured ex-wives drawn from the teeming annals of the novelist's own marital discord?

Shortcomings, to be sure. But so what? Nature doesn't owe us perfection. Novelists don't either. Who among us would even recognize perfection if we saw it? In any event, applying critical methods, of whatever sort, seemed futile in the case of an author who, as Randall Jarrell once wrote of Walt Whitman, "is a world, a waste with, here and there, systems blazing at random out of the darkness"— those systems "as beautifully and astonishingly organized as the rings and satellites of Saturn."

Thus, the overdetermination in "Seize the Day" ("the first of the cancer novels," Norman Mailer once called it) suddenly cracks open to provide a surreally detailed portrait of the demiurge Tamkin, who has tricked the gullible Wilhelm out of his last $700: "His figure was stocky, rigid, short in the neck, so that the large ball of the occiput touched his collar. His bones were peculiarly formed, as though twisted twice where the ordinary bone was turned only once, and his shoulders rose in two pagoda-like points." And on it goes, down to Tamkin's eyeballs, underlip, even fingernails: "moonless, concave, clawlike, and they appeared loose."

So, too, the outlandish "Henderson the Rain King"—with its hulking narrator whose declamations ("I want, I want, I want, oh, I want") stream forth in an idiom no actual human has ever spoken, and its cartoon natives enacting rituals cribbed from anthropological literature—mounts toward a climax of uncanny power, as Henderson witnesses the melancholy village chieftain Dahfu in naked combat with a lion: "I looked down from this straw perch—I was on my knees—into the big, angry, hair-framed face of the lion. It was all wrinkled, contracted; within those wrinkles was the darkness of murder."

Not that Bellow's triumphs emerge only from chaos. In "Herzog" he fashions an entire solar system, its space-time continuum shifting fluidly from the present to the past and back again, as the milieus (the Berkshires, Manhattan, Chicago) multiply, often within the confines of a few paragraphs—the intricate structure held together by Bellow's free-form ponderings, his vast world-historical knowledge honed to the task of dissecting the ideology of sexual narcissism in the "swinging '60s."

And the prose! Here is Herzog, the most fully realized intellectual in all of American fiction, aflame with lofty ideas and petty grievances, aboard a train hurtling along the Connecticut shore: "The wheels of the cars stormed underneath. Woods and pastures ran up and receded, the rails of sidings sheathed in rust, the dripping racing wires, and on the right the blue of the Sound, deeper, stronger than before. Then the enameled shells of the commuters' cars, and the heaped bodies of junk cars, the shapes of old New England mills with narrow, austere windows; villages, convents; tugboats moving in the swelling fabric-like water; and then plantations of pine, the needles on the ground of a life-giving russet color. So, thought Herzog, acknowledging that his imagination of the universe was elementary, the novae bursting and the worlds coming into being, the invisible magnetic spokes by means of which bodies kept one another in orbit. Astronomers made it all sound as though the gases were shaken up inside a flask. Then after many billions of years, light-years, this childlike but far from innocent creature, a straw hat on his head, and a heart in his breast, part pure, part wicked, who would try to form his own shaky picture of this magnificent web."

It is tempting to conclude that "Herzog" represents an advance over the previous two novels. But the verdict imposes factitious standards of growth or development on Bellow and at the same time diminishes the act of reading him, the almost physical sensation one has that each book is a fresh attempt to grab hold of knowable reality, in its many pulsating forms, and to fathom its latent messages.

Jarrell, again, on Whitman's oeuvre: "We cannot help seeing that there is something absurd about any judgment we make of its whole—for there is no 'point of view' at which we can stand to make the judgment, and the moral categories that mean most to us seem no more to apply to its whole than our spatial or temporal or causal categories seem to apply to its beginning or its end." Ah, the ideal moment to catalog the affinities between Bellow and Whitman—the self-intoxication, the impatience with literary decorum, the ambition to sound the full register of American experience. But why bother? Bellow's books illuminate themselves. And all commentary is only so much background noise.

Selection 8.4

Whether she loves a book or loathes it, Michiko Kakutani never pulls her punches or leaves any doubt about where she stands. In the opening paragraphs of two longer reviews, look at how strong her evaluation is and how early it comes. In her rave review of "Netherland," a single superlative ("stunning") and comparison (to "The Great Gatsby") elevated a novel by an author not known to most of her readers into cultural prominence. (When asked in 2009 what book he'd recently enjoyed, President Barack Obama mentioned only "Netherland.")

BOOKS OF THE TIMES
Post 9/11, a New York of Gatsby-Size Dreams and Loss
By MICHIKO KAKUTANI

Driving a rented car up the Saw Mill River and Taconic State Parkways, Hans, a Dutchman displaced in New York, thinks of the Dutch names—Yonkers, Cortlandt, Verplanck and of course Peekskill—that sprout amid places like Mohegan, Chappaqua and Ossining, and finds himself superimposing on the landscape "regressive images of Netherlanders and Indians, images arising not from mature historical reflection but from a child's irresponsibly cinematic sense of things." He has a similar sense of America's vastness and panoramic possibilities when he travels up the Hudson and glimpses spectacular, unspoiled vistas of forests and mountains "canceling out centuries"— vistas unimaginable, he says, to someone who grew up in the congested, overpopulated landscape of the Low Countries.

Much of New York and America boggles his "newcomer's imagination": the island's "exhilaratory skyward figures" as his taxi

Published: May 16, 2008. Full text available at: www.nytimes.com/2008/05/16/books/16book.html.

from Kennedy Airport crested "the expressway above Long Island City, and Manhattan was squarely revealed"; his observation that making a million bucks in 1990s New York "was essentially a question of walking down the street—of strolling, hands in pockets, in the cheerful expectation that sooner or later a bolt of pecuniary fire would jump out of the atmosphere and knock you flat"; his sense that in New York "selfhood's hill always seemed to lie ahead and to promise a glimpse of further, higher peaks: that you might have no climbing boots to hand was beside the point."

If some of these passages reverberate with echoes of "The Great Gatsby" and its vision of New York—"the old island here that flowered once for Dutch sailors' eyes," the "fresh, green breast of the New World," which nourished its hero's belief "in the green light, the orgiastic future that year by year recedes before us"—the reader can only surmise that they are entirely deliberate, for, like Fitzgerald's masterpiece, Joseph O'Neill's stunning new novel, "Netherland," provides a resonant meditation on the American Dream.

**

Selection 8.5

Literary renown never deters Kakutani, as this dismissal of a Thomas Pynchon novel, in comparison with his earlier "Mason & Dixon," attests. Compare the heavy artillery she aims at this novel with her comparatively understated evaluative praise for "Netherland."

BOOKS OF THE TIMES
A Pynchonesque Turn by Pynchon
By MICHIKO KAKUTANI

Thomas Pynchon's new novel, "Against the Day," reads like the sort of imitation of a Thomas Pynchon novel that a dogged but ungainly fan of this author's might have written on quaaludes. It is a humongous, bloated jigsaw puzzle of a story, pretentious without being provocative, elliptical without being illuminating, complicated without being rewardingly complex.

The novel plays with themes that have animated the whole of Mr. Pynchon's oeuvre: order versus chaos, fate versus freedom, paranoia versus nihilism. It boasts a sprawling, Dickensian cast with distinctly Pynchonian names: Fleetwood Vibe, Lindsay Noseworth, Clive Crouchmas. And it's littered with puns, ditties, vaudevillesque turns and allusions to everything from old sci-fi movies to Kafka to Harry Potter. These authorial trademarks, however, are orchestrated

Published: November 20, 2006. Full text available at: www.nytimes.com/2006/11/20/books/20kaku.html.

in a weary and decidedly mechanical fashion, as the narrative bounces back and forth from America to Europe to Mexico, from Cripple Creek to Constantinople to Chihuahua.

There are some dazzling set pieces evoking the 1893 Chicago World's Fair and a convocation of airship aficionados, but these passages are sandwiched between reams and reams of pointless, self-indulgent vamping that read like Exhibit A in what can only be called a case of the Emperor's New Clothes. Dozens of characters are sent on mysterious (often half-baked) quests that intersect mysteriously with the mysterious quests of people they knew in another context, and dozens of portentous plot lines are portentously twined around even more portentous events: the appearance of a strange figure in the Arctic, a startling "heavenwide blast of light," the hunt for something called a "Time-weapon" that might affect the fate of the globe.

Whereas Mr. Pynchon's last novel, the stunning "Mason & Dixon," demonstrated a new psychological depth, depicting its two heroes as full-fledged human beings, not merely as pawns in the author's philosophical chess game, the people in "Against the Day" are little more than stick figure cartoons.

***

Selection 8.6

Now considered a classic, "Lolita" was reviled in The Times as "dull, dull, dull," "repulsive" and "disgusting" upon publication. Consider why the novel has stood the test of time better than the review has. And compare how the tone of this negative review from the late 1950s compares with the previous one, almost a half-century later.

BOOKS OF THE TIMES
Lolita. By Vladimir Nabokov
By ORVILLE PRESCOTT

Certain books achieve a sort of underground reputation before they are published. Gossip arouses expectations that they are even nastier than the last *succès de scandale*. College students returning from visits to Paris demonstrate their newly acquired sophistication by brandishing paperbound copies. College professors write solemn critical analyses in scholarly publications. And if their authors are really lucky some act of official censorship publicizes their work to the masses. "Lolita" by Vladimir Nabokov is such a book. Mr. Nabokov is particularly lucky because his book was not censored

Published: August 18, 1958.

in the United States, but in France of all places. What more could he hope for? The French ban was eventually removed and now this book written in English in the United States by a White Russian emigré can be bought legally in Paris where it was first published. Its American publication today has been preceded by a fanfare of publicity. Prof. Harry Levin of Harvard says it is a great book and darkly symbolical (Mr. Nabokov explicitly denies any symbolism). Graham Greene says that "Lolita" is a distinguished novel. William Styron says it is "uniquely droll" and "genuinely funny."

Novel Found Dull and Fatuous

"Lolita," then, is undeniably news in the world of books. Unfortunately, it is bad news. There are two equally serious reasons why it isn't worth any adult reader's attention. The first is that it is dull, dull, dull in a pretentious, florid and archly fatuous fashion. The second is that it is repulsive.

"Lolita" is not crudely crammed with Anglo-Saxon nouns and verbs and explicitly described scenes of sexual violence. Its depravity is more refined. Mr. Nabokov, whose English vocabulary would astound the editors of the Oxford Dictionary, does not write cheap pornography. He writes highbrow pornography. Perhaps that is not his intention. Perhaps he thinks of his book as a satirical comedy and as an exploration of abnormal psychology. Nevertheless, "Lolita" is disgusting.

This is a first-person narrative written in prison by a middle-aged European intellectual and pervert called Humbert Humbert. A literary dilettante who had spent considerable time in various sanitariums, Humbert suffered from a mental illness that made him lust for young girls.

"Lolita" is his account of his two-year love affair with a child aged 12 to 14. Part of its theoretical comedy probably lies in the fact that the child, Lolita, turns out to be just as corrupt as Humbert—a notion that does not strike one as notably funny.

The narrative structure of "Lolita" concerns Humbert's marriage to Lolita's mother to be near the object of his passion, the mother's accidental death, the two years spent by Humbert and Lolita roaming the United States by automobile, Lolita's elopement with another middle-aged man, and Humbert's descent into insanity.

All this is described by Humbert with elaborate self-mockery, with much analysis of his distraught emotions and with considerable reportorial attention to the world of the American roadside: hotels, motels, restaurants, filling stations and scenic attractions.

Jocularity Appears Forced

Humbert's prose style is self-consciously ornate and wonderfully tiresome. He tries hard to be witty and once in a long while something clever, but most of his jocularity is forced and flat. This failure to be funny might be an integral part of Humbert's sick mind. But Mr. Nabokov fails to be funny, too, when he supplies material for Humbert's story. Some of his efforts at farce are painfully inept, about on the same level as his "humor" in calling a girls' school "St. Algebra."

"Lolita" is a demonstration of the artistic pitfall that awaits a novelist who invades the clinical field of the case history. Since a large proportion of the human race is emotionally unbalanced and neuroses are so common as almost to be normal, novelists must rightly concern themselves with disturbed minds. But there is a line that is artistically perilous to cross.

When mental illness eliminates the ability to choose, when the patient is no longer responsible for his conduct but only the victim of his mania, there is little left for the novelist to discuss.

A great writer, a genius like Shakespeare, can write superbly of King Lear; but Shakespeare surrounded Lear by other interesting characters and did not write exclusively from within Lear's ruined mind. The writer's subject is human conduct and the motives that inspire it. A madman has no motives, only forces he responds to. His ravaged brain belongs to the psychiatrists and psychoanalysts, not to novelists.

Past the artistic danger line of madness is another even more fatal. It is where the particular mania is a perversion like Humbert's. To describe such a perversion with the pervert's enthusiasm without being disgusting is impossible. If Mr. Nabokov tried to do so he failed.

Selection 8.7

Here is a mixed response in The Times toward a novel that subsequently found both critical and popular favor. What distinguished this review is its parody of the novelist's style, as if it were written in the voice of protagonist Holden Caulfield. Both this review and the previous one are considerably shorter than a book review in The Times typically runs today, particularly in the Sunday books section.

Aw, the World's a Crumby Place

By JAMES STERN

This girl Helga, she kills me. She reads just about everything I bring into the house, and a lot of crumby stuff besides. She's crazy about kids. I mean stories about kids. But Hel, she says there's hardly

Published: July 15, 1951. Book reviewed: "The Catcher in the Rye." By J. D. Salinger.

a writer alive can write about children. Only these English guys
Richard Hughes and Walter de la Mare, she says. The rest is all corny.
It depresses her. That's another thing. She can sniff a corny guy or a
phony book quick as a dog smells a rat. This phoniness, it gives old
Hel a pain if you want to know the truth. That's why she came hol-
lering to me one day, her hair falling over her face and all, and said I
had to read some damn story in The New Yorker. Who's the author?
I said. Salinger, she told me, J. D. Salinger. Who's he? I asked. How
should I know, she said, just you read it.

"For Esme—with Love and Squalor" was this story's crumby
title. But *boy*, was that a story. About a G.I. or something and a couple
of English kids in the last war. Hel, I said when I was through, just
you wait till this guy writes a novel. Novel, my elbow, she said. This
Salinger, he won't write no crumby novel. He's a short story guy.
Girls, they kill me. They really do.

But I was right, if you want to know the truth. You should've
seen old Hel hit the ceiling when I told her this Salinger, he has not
only written a novel, it's a Book-of-the-Month Club selection, too.
For crying out loud, she said, what's it about? About this Holden
Caulfield, I told her, about the time he ran away to New York from
this Pencey Prep School in Agerstown, Pa. Why'd he run away, asked
old Hel. Because it was a terrible school, I told her, no matter how
you looked at it. And there were no girls. What, said old Hel. Well,
only this old Selma Thumer, I said, the headmaster's daughter. But
this Holden, he liked her because "she didn't give you a lot of horse-
manure about what a great guy her father was."

Then Hel asked what this Holden's father was like, so I told her
if she wanted to know the truth Holden didn't want to go into all that
David Copperfield kind of business. It bored him and anyway his
"parents would have [had] about two hemorrhages apiece if [he] told
anything personal about them." You see, this Holden, I said, he just
can't find anybody decent in the lousy world and he's in some sort of
crumby Californian home full of psychiatrists.

That damn near killed Hel. Psychiatrists, she howled. That's
right, I said, this one psychiatrist guy keeps asking Holden if he's
going to apply himself when he goes back to school. (He's already
been kicked out of about six.) And Holden, he says how the hell does
he know. "I *think* I am," he says, "but how do I know. I swear it's a
stupid question."

That's the way it sounds to me, Hel said, and away she went
with this crazy book, "The Catcher in the Rye." What did I tell ya,
she said next day. This Salinger, he's a short story guy. And he knows
how to write about kids. This book though, it's too long. Gets kind of
monotonous. And he should've cut out a lot about these jerks and all
at that crumby school. They depress me. They really do. Salinger, he's
best with real children. I mean young ones like old Phoebe, his kid

sister. She's a personality. Holden and little old Phoeb, Hel said, they kill me. This last part about her and Holden and this Mr. Antolini, the only guy Holden ever thought he could trust, who ever took any interest in him, and who turned out queer—that's terrific. I swear it is.

You needn't swear, Hel, I said. Know what? This Holden, he's just like you. He finds the whole world's full of people say one thing and mean another and he doesn't like it; and he hates movies and phony slobs and snobs and crumby books and war. Boy, how he hates war. Just like you, Hel, I said. But old Hel, she was already reading this crazy "Catcher" book all over again. That's always a good sign with Hel.

Selection 8.8

An equivocal review of a book that inspired generations of students to become journalists finds the former chief book critic at The Times critiquing a competing newspaper. As always with a nonfiction book, consider how much of this review is about the book itself and how much of it is about the events detailed in the book.

BOOKS OF THE TIMES
Story of an Unfinished Story
By CHRISTOPHER LEHMANN-HAUPT

In a way, it's too bad that Carl Bernstein's and Bob Woodward's "All the President's Men" had to appear at the same time that President Nixon decided to publish a book of his own (which is now available in three paperback editions: "Submission of Recorded Presidential Conversations to the Committee on the Judiciary of the House of Representatives by President Richard Nixon," United States Government Printing Office, $12.25; "The White House Transcripts," with an introduction by R. W. Apple Jr. of The New York Times, Bantam, $2.50; and "The Presidential Transcripts," with commentary by the Staff of The Washington Post, Dell, $2.45). It's too bad, because if it had appeared after the Watergate scandal had run its course—a course whose future has only been made more dramatic by the appearance of the Presidential transcripts—Mr. Bernstein's and Mr. Woodward's "All the President's Men" would have been one hell of a book to read.

Rich Drama and Details
Without the distraction of the transcripts and their aftermath, one would have been able to concentrate on what the book really is—a

Published: May 14, 1974. Book reviewed: "All the President's Men." By Carl Bernstein and Bob Woodward.

story of journalistic enterprise recounting how the two young political reporters on The Washington Post dug behind what appeared at first to be a comic-opera spying caper, unearthed what turned out to be a political scandal of unprecedented dimensions, and won a Pulitzer Prize for their paper. One would have been able to immerse oneself in the story's rich drama—to feel one's pulse quicken as the two reporters pick up the scent of the trail (from the moment they began to investigate James W. McCord Jr.'s C.I.A. connections, one thing led logically to the next); to gulp apprehensively when they stumble in their pursuit (their worst moment occurred when they got their sources' signals crossed and reported H. R. Haldeman's putative guilt in the wrong context); and to cheer triumphantly when events finally force Presidential press secretary Ronald L. Ziegler to apologize for castigating The Washington Post (according to the United Press International's report of the apology, "As Ziegler finished he started to say, 'But . . . ' He was cut off by a reporter who said: 'Now don't take it back, Ron.'").

One would have been able to savor the story's colorful details: how Messrs. Bernstein and Woodward began their collaboration feeling skeptical and jealous of each other's skills, and only gradually came to appreciate their merger's synergy (their narrative presents them both in the third-person singular, thus creating a winning impression of objectivity and candor); or how former Attorney General John N. Mitchell reacted when confronted over the telephone with the reporters' information that he had "controlled" the "secret funds" at the Committee to Re-elect the President. ("JEEEEEEEESUS," Mr. Mitchell kept ejaculating, as if giving vent to "some sort of primal scream." "Katie Graham's [Mrs. Katharine Graham, the publisher of The Washington Post] gonna get her [anatomical reference deleted] in a big fat wringer if that's published. Good Christ! That's the most sickening thing I ever heard.")

Most important, one would have read "All the President's Men" as a primer on the techniques of investigative reporting, and studied with the utmost absorption how Messrs. Bernstein and Woodward milked their sources (the most informative and intriguing of whom was someone in the executive branch nicknamed "Deep Throat" because his information was always on "deep background," meaning in newspaper parlance that he could never be quoted either directly of indirectly); how they skirted but never quite crossed over the bounds of ethical decency (for instance, they approached but never asked for information from members of the Watergate grand jury, for which practice they were admonished by Judge John J. Sirica with unexpected mildness); or how they always took pains to ask them-selves whether they were being entirely fair to the people they were investigating.

Looking for Revelations

This is how one would read "All the President's Men" if the
Watergate story were not still unfolding, and this is how one will
doubtless read it when the story is done. But in the meantime,
the story is not done. At the very time that the book appears, the
drama approaches new and unforeseen climaxes. And so willy-nilly
one reads Mr. Bernstein's and Mr. Woodward's report not for the
journalistic story it tells, but for what it reveals behind Watergate.
And as such it is an old story overshadowed by the astonishing
developments that are unfolding daily. And one is left feeling
frustrated and ever-so-slightly disappointed (as I overheard one
bookstore browser muttering, after misguidedly skimming the book
for revelations: "What's the big deal?").

Obviously, all this is not to be blamed on Mr. Bernstein and
Mr. Woodward. When the story passed out of their exclusive control,
they turned to recording their involvement while their impressions
were still fresh. And in compensation for doing so they have been
richly (and with poetic justice) rewarded with lucrative book-club,
paperback and movie contracts. But for the time being at least, the
average reader does lose out. To appreciate "All the President's Men"
properly, one will have to wait until the storm of Watergate has sub-
sided. Then, and only then, will one enjoy it for the classic in the art of
political reportage it will unquestionably turn out to be.

Selection 8.9

An exhaustive cover story in The New York Times Magazine by a former edi-
tor of The Book Review legitimizes the graphic novels that critics for main-
stream news organizations might once have ignored as comic books. This is
a reported piece, one that you're encouraged to read in its entirety, but the
opening paragraphs are pure criticism.

Not Funnies

By CHARLES McGRATH

You can't pinpoint it exactly, but there was a moment when
people more or less stopped reading poetry and turned instead to
novels, which just a few generations earlier had been considered
entertainment suitable only for idle ladies of uncertain morals. The
change had surely taken hold by the heyday of Dickens and Tenny-
son, which was the last time a poet and a novelist went head to head

Published: July 11, 2004. Full text available at: www.nytimes.com/2004/07/11/magazine/11GRAPHIC.html.

on the best-seller list. Someday the novel, too, will go into decline—if it hasn't already—and will become, like poetry, a genre treasured and created by just a relative few. This won't happen in our lifetime, but it's not too soon to wonder what the next new thing, the new literary form, might be.

It might be comic books. Seriously. Comic books are what novels used to be—an accessible, vernacular form with mass appeal—and if the highbrows are right, they're a form perfectly suited to our dumbed-down culture and collective attention deficit. Comics are also enjoying a renaissance and a newfound respectability right now. In fact, the fastest-growing section of your local bookstore these days is apt to be the one devoted to comics and so-called graphic novels. It is the overcrowded space way in the back—next to sci-fi probably, or between New Age and hobbies—and unless your store is staffed by someone unusually devoted, this section is likely to be a mess. "Peanuts" anthologies, and fat, catalog-size collections of "Garfield" and "Broom Hilda." Shelf loads of manga—those Japanese comic books that feature slender, wide-eyed teenage girls who seem to have a special fondness for sailor suits. Superheroes, of course, still churned out in installments by the busy factories at Marvel and D.C. Also, newer sci-fi and fantasy series like "Y: The Last Man," about literally the last man on earth (the rest died in a plague), who is now pursued by a band of killer lesbians.

You can ignore all this stuff—though it's worth noting that manga sells like crazy, especially among women. What you're looking for is shelved upside down and sideways sometimes—comic books of another sort, substantial single volumes (as opposed to the slender series installments), often in hard cover, with titles that sound just like the titles of "real" books: "Palestine," "Persepolis," "Blankets" (this one tips in at 582 pages, which must make it the longest single-volume comic book ever), "David Chelsea in Love," "Summer Blonde," "The Beauty Supply District," "The Boulevard of Broken Dreams." Some of these books have titles that have become familiar from recent movies: "Ghost World," "American Splendor," "Road to Perdition." Others, like Chris Ware's "Jimmy Corrigan: The Smartest Kid on Earth" (unpaged, but a good inch and a quarter thick) and Daniel Clowes's "David Boring," have achieved cult status on many campuses.

These are the graphic novels—the equivalent of "literary novels" in the mainstream publishing world—and they are beginning to be taken seriously by the critical establishment. "Jimmy Corrigan" even won the 2001 Guardian Prize for best first book, a prize that in other years has gone to authors like Zadie Smith, Jonathan Safran Foer and Philip Gourevitch.

***

Selection 8.10

At the height of the controversy about whether memoir plays by different rules than other types of nonfiction, this piece in The Times (about half of which is included here) uses the 2006 James Frey scandal as a springboard for an ambitious piece of criticism that goes well beyond books to explore the realities of truth within the culture at large. The "Critic's Notebook" allows latitude to explore trends and issues beyond a single work.

CRITIC'S NOTEBOOK
Bending the Truth in a Million Little Ways
By MICHIKO KAKUTANI

James Frey's admission last week that he made up details of his life in his best-selling book "A Million Little Pieces"—after the Smoking Gun Web site stated that he "wholly fabricated or wildly embellished details of his purported criminal career, jail terms and status as an outlaw 'wanted in three states' "—created a furor about the decision by the book's publishers, Doubleday, to sell the volume as a memoir instead of a novel.

It is not, however, just a case about truth-in-labeling or the misrepresentations of one author: after all, there have been plenty of charges about phony or inflated memoirs in the past, most notably about Lillian Hellman's 1973 book "Pentimento." It is a case about how much value contemporary culture places on the very idea of truth. Indeed, Mr. Frey's contention that having 5 percent or so of his book in dispute was "comfortably within the realm of what's appropriate for a memoir" and the troubling insistence of his publishers and his cheerleader Oprah Winfrey that it really didn't matter if he'd taken liberties with the facts of his story underscore the waning importance people these days attach to objectivity and veracity.

We live in a relativistic culture where television "reality shows" are staged or stage-managed, where spin sessions and spin doctors are an accepted part of politics, where academics argue that history depends on who is writing the history, where an aide to President Bush, dismissing reporters who live in the "reality-based community," can assert that "we're an empire now, and when we act, we create our own reality." Phrases like "virtual reality" and "creative nonfiction" have become part of our language. Hype and hyperbole are an accepted part of marketing and public relations. And reinvention and repositioning are regarded as useful career moves in the worlds of entertainment and politics. The conspiracy-minded, fact-warping movies of Oliver Stone are regarded by those who don't know

Published: January 17, 2006. Full text available at: www.nytimes.com/2006/01/17/books/17kaku.html.

better as genuine history, as are the most sensationalistic of television docudramas.

Mr. Frey's embellishments of the truth, his cavalier assertion that the "writer of a memoir is retailing a subjective story," his casual attitude about how people remember the past—all stand in shocking contrast to the apprehension of memory as a sacred act that is embodied in Oprah Winfrey's new selection for her book club, announced yesterday: "Night," Elie Wiesel's devastating 1960 account of his experiences in Auschwitz and Buchenwald.

If the memoir form once prized authenticity above all else—regarding testimony as an act of paying witness to history—it has been evolving, in the hands of some writers, into something very different. In fact, Mr. Frey's embellishments and fabrications in many ways represent the logical if absurd culmination of several trends that have been percolating away for years. His distortions serve as an illustration of a depressing remark once made by the literary theorist Stanley Fish—that the death of objectivity "relieves me of the obligation to be right"; it "demands only that I be interesting."

And they remind us that self-dramatization (in Mr. Frey's case, making himself out to be a more notorious fellow than he actually was, in order to make his subsequent "redemption" all the more impressive) is just one step removed from the willful self-absorption and shameless self-promotion embraced by the "Me Generation" and its culture of narcissism.

"A Million Little Pieces," which became the second-highest-selling book of 2005 (behind only "Harry Potter and the Half-Blood Prince"), clearly did not sell because of its literary merits. Its narrative feels willfully melodramatic and contrived, and is rendered in prose so self-important and mannered as to make the likes of Robert James Waller ("The Bridges of Madison County") and John Gray ("Men Are From Mars, Women Are From Venus") seem like masters of subtlety and literate insight.

The book sold more than two million copies because it was endorsed by Ms. Winfrey, and because it rode the crest of two waves that gained steam in the 1990's: the memoir craze, which reflects our obsession with navel gazing and the first person singular; and the popularity of recovery-movement reminiscences, which grew out of television-talk-show confessions (presided over by Ms. Winfrey, among others) and Alcoholics Anonymous testimonials.

These two phenomena yielded the so-called "memoir of crisis"—a genre that has produced a handful of genuinely moving accounts of people struggling with illness and personal disaster but many more ridiculously exhibitionistic monologues that like to use the word "survivor" (a word once reserved for individuals who had lived through wars or famines or the Holocaust) to describe people coping with weight problems or bad credit.

They also coincided with our culture's enshrinement of subjectivity—"moi" as a modus operandi for processing the world. Cable news is now peopled with commentators who serve up opinion and interpretation instead of news, just as the Internet is awash in bloggers who trade in gossip and speculation instead of fact. For many of these people, it's not about being accurate or fair. It's about being entertaining, snarky or provocative—something that's decidedly easier and less time-consuming to do than old-fashioned investigative reporting or hard-nosed research.

***

Selection 8.11

In this review of a biography, Janet Maslin does a particularly deft job of interweaving her evaluation of a specific book within the broader context of the life that inspired the book. Readers who come to this review with little knowledge of Gabriel García Márquez, or desire to read a biography of him, will learn why he's important. They'll also learn more about the biographer's art than many reviews of biographies offer.

BOOKS OF THE TIMES
Unraveling the Labyrinthine Life of a Magical Realist
By JANET MASLIN

In a January 2006 interview with a Barcelona newspaper, Gabriel García Márquez, whose memory had begun to fail, deflected a question about his past. "You will have to ask my official biographer, Gerald Martin, about that sort of thing," he said, "only I think he's waiting for something to happen to me before he finishes."

This otherwise doom-laden remark brought good news to the newly designated "official biographer." Mr. Martin at that point had devoted 15 years of his own life to chronicling that of Mr. García Márquez, though he spent a total of only a month in that Nobel laureate's company during his extended research. Until that point Mr. Martin had called this project only a "tolerated biography." It has turned out to be much, much more.

This intensive, assured, penetratingly analytical book will be the authoritative English-language study of Mr. García Márquez until Mr. Martin can complete an already 2,000-page, 6,000-footnote version "in a few more years, if life is kind." He compressed that sprawling magnum opus into 545 pages (plus notes and index), a "brief, relatively compact narrative," so it could be published "while

Published: May 28, 2009.

the subject of this work, now a man past 80, is still alive and in a position to read it." Both author and subject have been treated for lymphoma, Mr. Martin says.

That kind of bluntness runs throughout "Gabriel García Márquez: A Life," and it is essential to the book's success. The last thing this literary lion needed was a fawning, accommodating Boswell. Nor did he need a biographer eager to show off his own flair. When writing about Mr. García Márquez, king of the magical realists, Mr. Martin understands that it is best to stick to the facts and skip the fancy footwork.

Could any biographer have been better suited to this gargantuan undertaking? Absolutely not: Mr. Martin is the ideal man for the job. He has already written studies of 20th-century Latin American fiction; translated the work of another Latin American Nobel laureate, Miguel Ángel Asturias; and written about Latin American history. These are essential prerequisites for unraveling the labyrinthine cultural and political aspects of Mr. García Márquez's peripatetic life. So are Mr. Martin's demonstrable patience, wide range of knowledge and keen understanding of his subject's worldwide literary forebears, from Cervantes to Dostoyevsky to Mark Twain.

Mr. Martin confidently calls Mr. García Márquez, Colombia's best-known storyteller and superstar ("Gabo"), the "Mark Twain of his own land: symbol of the country, definer of a national sense of humor and chronicler of the relation between the provincial realm and the center." But he is just as comfortable linking Mr. García Márquez to less likely literary figures (Virginia Woolf), historical figures who loomed large in his imagination (Simón Bolívar) and dictators, of whom Mr. García Márquez has known more than his share.

This book has the sophistication to weigh its subject's affection for Fidel Castro against the changing currents of left-wing governments over 50 years, sharply revealing the personal revisionism that has sustained this novelist's huge popularity no matter what goes on around him. (Not for nothing has he earned "García Marketing" as one of his nicknames.) The biography can slip readily from the exploits of Bolívar to revolutions in Cuba and France. It can discuss "the most famous punch in the history of Latin America," an occasion on which Mr. García Márquez addressed the Peruvian writer Mario Vargas Llosa as "Brother!" and Mr. Vargas Llosa slugged him in reply. Mr. Vargas Llosa's wife seems to have played a role in this confrontation.

Mr. Martin's book also has the heft to deliver penetrating thematic analyses of each García Márquez work, even if literary criticism is not its first concern. "No one writes," "solitude," "autumn," "funeral," "death foretold," "labyrinth," "kidnapping": these are all words used in García Márquez book titles and, as Mr. Martin asserts, words that imply some challenge to power. In addition to parsing each book and its meaning, Mr. Martin must trace the family stories that figure in the fiction, so that childhood years spent with Mr. García Márquez's maternal grandparents can be seen as seminal to the fictitious setting (Macondo) and family (Buendía) found in "One Hundred Years of Solitude."

The complexity of all this is staggering. So is the magnitude of Mr. Martin's accomplishment in grappling with it. Consider: this is a book that includes four different family-tree illustrations, three devoted to Mr. García Márquez's actual relatives (including those by marriage and by illegitimate birth) and one for the Buendías he invented. It travels with its subject from his European days as a hungry (literally) young journalist to his politically formative glimpses behind the Iron Curtain to his celebrity globe-trotting in later years.

From time to time the book hits a brick wall, as when Mr. Martin unearths the painful story of a thwarted love affair in Paris and Mr. García Márquez refuses to talk about it. Dogged biographer that he is, Mr. Martin perseveres, though never in a salacious fashion. He finds the old flame, connects her with events in the García Márquez canon and explores his subject's ideas about sex and love, about private, public and secret lives. How long has this research been going on? Long enough for Mr. Martin to have a firsthand interview with the mother of a subject who is 82.

Given the global love affair with "One Hundred Years of Solitude" and "Love in the Time of Cholera," which have been popular even in countries (like the United States) often reviled by Mr. García Márquez, this biography would be essential reading even if it delivered just the facts. But Mr. Martin is too dedicated for that, though not admiring enough to make excuses for his subject's transgressions. And he zeroes in on the precise achievements that have meant so much in literary history.

How did the early blueprint for a novel about Mr. García Márquez's childhood turn into a masterpiece about his memories of childhood? How did he bring the town of Macondo to the world by weaving the world into the town of Macondo? And how did his magical realism become this magical? Such questions are in Mr. García Márquez's books. The answers are in this one.

Selection 8.12

Maslin demonstrates her range in her review of this thriller, the sort of novel that The Times might previously have ignored as pulp or genre fiction. As the subsequent interview with Maslin suggests, the same affinity for pop culture that she brought to music and movie reviewing distinguishes her book reviews as well. And look at how well her style suits her subject, with the short, straightforward sentences of the Child review contrasting with the tone of her more literary piece on García Márquez.

BOOKS OF THE TIMES | 'ONE SHOT'
Action Hero Travels Light and Often Takes the Bus
By JANET MASLIN

We first met Jack Reacher at a diner in Margrave, Ga., in 1997. He had just walked in heavy rain from the highway to the edge of town. He was reading somebody's left-behind newspaper when police cruisers pulled into the parking lot, lights flashing, guns drawn.

The diner's five other occupants had lived their whole lives in Margrave. Reacher had been there less than half an hour. But the excitement was all about him. In a very big way, it still is.

Those events—just an opening page's worth—kicked off "Killing Floor," the first novel in what is now Lee Child's hot, indomitable nine-book Reacher series. Reacher stopped traffic instantly, and he has only gotten better over time.

By now the character's hardboiled dialogue and existential drifting have transcended the crime story's limits, to the point where they evoke genres from the American western to the French New Wave. This guy could fit in anywhere. That's really saying something, since he's 6 foot 5 and built like an oak.

Smart, too. That's what saves the Reacher books from empty swaggering and turns them into elegant, logically constructed mysteries. However incompatible they may seem, Mr. Child's tough talk and thoughtful plotting make an ingenious combination, turning novels like his new "One Shot" into pure, escapist gold. Not for nothing do reviewers tell readers to disconnect the phone when the latest Reacher knockout comes along.

"One Shot" begins with a sniper attack in a nameless Indiana city; Mr. Child often likes to bait the hook with an opening action scene. The police investigation is a big success, with clues all over the place. Those clues lead to a trained military sniper named James Barr. Once in custody, Barr has two things to say. "They got the wrong guy" is one. "Get Jack Reacher for me" is the other.

It's not as if Reacher can be summoned in a flash. For 14 years he was a military policeman, but he has been wandering since he left the Army. "He had no debts," Mr. Child writes. "No liens. No address. No phone number. No warrants outstanding, no judgments entered. He wasn't a husband. Wasn't a father. He was a ghost."

The ghost is flesh-and-blood enough to be in a Miami hotel room with a Norwegian dancer when he hears a television report about the shooting. Ah, well: he shrugs her off and heads for the Midwest. When Reacher travels, he likes to do it by bus or on foot, carrying not much more than a razor. For $40 he can fully outfit himself with new clothes.

"You're new in town, aren't you?" another woman asks him when he reaches his destination.

Published: June 9, 2005.

"Usually," Reacher answers.

That's the fine, deadpan terseness that Mr. Child delivers so well. It's what makes Reacher a Dirty Harryish movie hero waiting to happen.

On Page 62, Mr. Child throws in a whammy that might be the best twist some lesser mystery had to offer: Reacher hasn't come to help. He saw Barr go on the rampage once before, in Kuwait City in 1991, but the incident was hushed up. "So I went to see him before he left," Reacher says, "and I told him to justify his great good fortune by never stepping out of line again, not ever, the whole rest of his life. I told him if he ever did, I would come find him and make him sorry." Silence from Barr's sister and lawyer. "So here I am," Reacher says.

Nobody wants to be made sorry by Jack Reacher. The guy bullies only those who deserve it, but he sure can pick a fight. (Potential victim: "I want to see something." Reacher: "What about the inside of an ambulance?") More interestingly, he can predict that fight's outcome with scientific accuracy. Reacher knows why there's no such thing as a five-on-one bar brawl. He knows how to interpret the staccato pattern of bullets firing. He knows why drug dealers often live with their mothers.

That hard-won pragmatic wisdom gets a good workout in "One Shot," once Reacher starts taking apart the Barr case piece by piece. With Mr. Child's minimalism even more streamlined than usual, the story introduces ruthless Russian gangsters, an old Reacher flame who is now a brigadier general ("Feminine as hell"), the proprietor of a sharpshooters' range and a television anchorwoman who embodies the glibness of her profession. She is the kind of television star who, while preparing a breaking-news report on the shooting, finds the words sniper, senseless and slaying coming to mind.

Mr. Child lets the story unfold calmly for a while. Then he brings together all these elements with a terrific climactic episode, an elaborately planned raid on an isolated hideout filled with surveillance equipment. "You're going to look like a beetle on a bed sheet out there," Reacher is told. But Mr. Child, with a cleverness about heat sensors that recalls the use of night vision goggles in "The Silence of the Lambs," gives his hero the ingenuity to outmaneuver even the most calculating, well-protected villains.

The military component to these tactics accounts for some of this series's timeliness. Mr. Child's idea of heroism has nihilism around the edges but a fierce, fighting spirit at its core. In marked contrast to the brooding figures who otherwise dominate contemporary detective stories, Reacher is not one for self-doubt. His is a two-fisted decency. But Mr. Child also gives him amazing powers of deduction, a serious conscience and the occasional touch of tenderness. It's a wildly improbable mixture, one that can't be beat.

A Conversation with . . . Janet Maslin

BOOK CRITIC

© The New York Times

The career of Janet Maslin provides the best example of one of this volume's initial precepts: An astute critic can apply his or her critical instincts across the artistic spectrum. After writing about rock for The Boston Phoenix and Rolling Stone, she spent more than two decades at The Times as a film critic before switching her critical beat to books. This is an edited transcript of an e-mail interview.

How does a book critic read differently from an avid reader?
Here, as elsewhere, I can't speak for anyone else. But I myself underline and make coded notations, because I'll need to assemble what I think are key points and quotable passages to write the review. While I'm absorbing material by reading, I'm also sizing it up it as I go along, trying to figure out what's worth pulling out of the whole book for attention. Later, I'll go back over the whole thing and type out those notes before writing a review. It's extremely painstaking and slow—*much* slower than writing a movie review—but it has to be done.

With three book critics on staff at The Times, who decides who reviews what? And how does The Times decide what gets reviewed out of the thousands of titles published?
We work pretty much independently of one another. As chief critic, Michiko Kakutani decides what she wants to do; after that, I work around her. That's quite easy because there are so many books from which to choose. The Times' overall policy is better reflected by the Sunday section and what it chooses to review. I think we daily critics operate on the assumption that if we miss something, it can still be covered by the Sunday section. So we don't worry about being comprehensive.

I look for books that (a) are worth reading and (b) can be written about in an interesting way. Sounds very simple. But sometimes it's not.

You were previously a rock critic and for decades a film critic. Are the critical principles and processes that you employ as a book critic similar? Or is each medium different to write about?
My overall tactics have been the same with all three. That initially made me sound a little odd for a book critic, I think. My emphasis is not on scholarship or overview. It's on assessing the writer's specific work in each new book and

describing it from the standpoint of a more or less regular person. Any subject can lend itself to this treatment. One recent example: "Lords of Finance," a book I found fascinating and terrifically informative even though I knew nothing about the international business issues on which it's centered. But I love it when an author is a good explicator. This guy [Liaquat Ahamed] happens to be a brilliant one, bringing a whole career's worth of experience to bear on financial issues. Long story short: I read to find out about things I didn't necessarily know about beforehand. And to be entertained too.

You review more of what some might call popular or genre fiction than The Times previously covered. Do you make a distinction between that and what some might call literary fiction? Do you apply different critical principles?
Look, I happen to like pulp fiction. I don't think The Times dealt with much of it before I came along. And I'm interested in knowing what mainstream tastes are like; I was when it came to popular movies too. But there's a limit. Long ago I thought it would be fun to read the whole bestseller list and write a feature about that. Now I think that would be a nightmare. Because a lot of what's popular is boring, repetitive and truly without merit.

The popular fiction that I do has to be balanced with more substantive stuff. Reading too much of it would be like eating cotton candy. I look at the overall schedule and make sure I keep switching genres, degree of seriousness, fiction, nonfiction, whatever. I'd do that as a reader and I do that as a critic. Incidentally, I'm able to read and review pretty much the same books I'd be reading anyway. I rarely get around to major books that Michi [Michiko Kakutani] has reviewed. But I don't review anything that I wouldn't read as a civilian.

How do you deal with the issue of plot when reviewing fiction—how much to reveal without some readers feeling that you have spoiled the novel for them?
Giving away too much plot is a cheap trick. It boosts the review, but it spoils the book for everybody else. It's also lazy for a critic to recycle somebody else's story. I like to use direct quotes frequently, but I think that's different. When you read a review, don't you want some notion of what the book sounds like?

Do you direct your reviews equally to the few who might buy and read the book and to the many more who likely won't?
Well, I have lots of enthusiasm for anything I like. I buy books and send them to my friends all the time. But I assume, as I did with movies, that many people will read the review and leave it at that. It's even more true of book reviewing. Sometimes I'll love a book but never find another living soul who's seen it.

How do you envision your readership? Is it different from when you were reviewing films? Is it different at The Times than if you were reviewing books elsewhere?
I just don't. Never have. I write with an eagerness to communicate with the reader but not with a sense of who the reader is. Especially the Times reader;

Times readers now are surely very different from the ones I started out with. Or, as we say at The Times, the ones with whom I started out.

The pronouns are inadvertently revealing: I wind up using *you* fairly often, but I try not to use *I*. You (see?) have to earn the right to impose a first-person presence on your readers. The critics I have most respected and admired, like Vincent Canby, used *I* with probity, wit and discretion. Now, maybe because of the influence of bloggers, it gets thrown around too easily. Not every critic is somebody you (see?) need to know personally. I don't care what the critic's nephew thought of the movie.

How much influence do you think one of your reviews can have in a book's finding a popular readership?
Depends. Sometimes it's mysterious and sometimes it's quantifiable. If I'm crazy about something and write about it early enough, it may actually budge in an upward direction in its online sales ratings. Beyond that, I don't know.

When it came to movies, we could perhaps make a hit out of something obscure. But we could never kill a mass-market stinker if people wanted to see it badly enough. And authors, even more than film stars, can be such brand names that the caliber of their work is beside the point. Nothing I say about John Grisham will prevent even one person from buying a Grisham book at an airport. But if I spot another guy like that in the early stages, I'm happy.

Do you prefer to use your space for positive or negative reviews? If a book by an unknown author isn't very good, are you more likely to write a negative review or just not review it at all?
Look, readers *always* like negative reviews better. Nastiness sells. That's just the way of the world. As a film critic I had hot-and-cold-running opportunities to clobber things, and those are the reviews that got mentioned most often.

But now I don't do that anymore, because in this job it's a waste of everyone's time. I don't want to read a bad book by an unknown writer, let alone write about it. Bad books by very well-known writers aren't often interesting either, because those writers could be writing several cookie-cutter bad books a year. No news there.

And the type of review least likely to hold anyone's interest is the lukewarm review of so-so fiction by the second-tier novelist. Those are the books that have the toughest time getting noticed.

One last thing: Sydney Pollack once told me that he thought using movie stars in a film was shorthand. In "The Way We Were," he didn't have to explain who Barbra Streisand and Robert Redford were; he just put them on the screen and the rest was easy.

I wish it were that way for books, but only occasionally (say, with Philip Roth) is there that kind of instant familiarity. So a book reviewer has some very basic work to do. He or she has got to explain what this is, who wrote it, what it's trying to do and whether it succeeds. Starting from scratch. If you can present all that in an interesting way and hold the reader's attention throughout, you're doing it right.

MAKING CONNECTIONS

1 The reviews of "Beloved" and "One Shot" use very different writing styles and tones. Do the critical principles applied by Michiko Kakutani to Toni Morrision differ from those applied by Janet Maslin to Lee Child? If so, how?

2 Choose one of the pieces on nonfiction and one on fiction from this chapter. List the ways in which the writers' approaches differ. Are there any ways in which they're the same?

3 From Janet Maslin's interview, how does she see reviewing books as similar to reviewing movies and music? Then turn to the movie chapter in this book and look for examples of those differences in action.

4 What are the challenges of selecting a single American novel as the "best" of the last 25 years? What would be on your list of best books, and how would you defend your choice?

5 If critics of fiction don't write too much about plot, what else do they write about? Choose one of the books you thought of in Question 4 and start sketching out what you'd say in a review.

introduction: reportage profiles and trend pieces

EVEN WHEN RELYING ON REPORTING SKILLS for something other than a review or a critical essay, the critic remains a critic, an arbiter of significance. She doesn't disengage her critical faculties just because she's writing about something more than her own opinion. Value judgments begin with the choice of subject: that *this* artist is worth profiling, *this* trend worth exploring. The piece will proceed to show why.

The keys that we have frequently mentioned as highlighting every review—description, analysis, context, interpretation—will be found in the longer reported pieces as well. Yet these pieces present additional challenges. When you're writing a review, it isn't as difficult to sustain a consistency of tone, because it's *your* opinion, *your* argument, *your* voice. A reported piece features at least one other voice and generally many more. The critic who is writing such pieces must pay particular attention to framing and flow, so that the reader has the sense that the article begins and ends where it should, and proceeds from start to finish in a manner that practically seems inevitable.

The challenge in sustaining the reader's attention increases exponentially, the longer the piece and the more components it contains. The reader risks little with an 800-word review; by the time he has skimmed the first three or four paragraphs, he's almost halfway through and figures he might as well finish. With a 7,000-word profile or a 5,000-word trend piece, the reader knows from the outset that he must commit for the long haul, which he won't do unless the piece compels him from the start. Thus, though this advice may seem counterintuitive, it's even more crucial to have a strong hook toward the beginning of a longer feature than a shorter review.

Profiles in particular often include so much critical evaluation (the justification for profiling this particular artist) that some publications let the profile of a musical act serve also as the review of its latest release. Rarely will The Times feature a lengthy Sunday profile of an artist and then review that artist's CD on Monday. The profile has already provided enough critical commentary to serve that function. Profiles might also preview an act that is scheduled to perform in New York, often followed by a concert review (frequently by a different critic).

By contrast, a profile of an actor or an author will almost never substitute for a review. Films and plays are such collaborative ventures that profiles of one principal cannot serve to evaluate the whole (though such profiles generally feature plenty of critical commentary). Since book criticism makes such a distinction between an author's life and her work, a profile that focuses on the life won't substitute for a review that focuses on the work. At The Times, book, film and theater critics rarely write profiles (at least on their own beats), though popular music critics often do.

Trend pieces and enterprise stories are an important part of any critic's beat, allowing the journalist to move beyond the consumer-guide element of a review by stretching critical muscles to show how the artistic parts fit within the cultural whole. They can also serve to preview a performance or an event, to put it in larger context, to underscore its significance as part of a broader phenomenon.

As you're reading the pieces in this chapter, you might want to return to some earlier chapters to compare some of the longer critical essays, see how easily they could have been converted into reported trend pieces and discuss whether they would have benefitted from such reporting.

In the following two chapters, we will analyze reported pieces that are generally longer than the opinion pieces previously read (often so long that only the opening section can be included; you're encouraged to read the entire piece online). And we'll see how the same sort of critical instincts apply to the reported forms of arts and culture journalism as well.

profiles

THE FIRST PART OF THIS BOOK FEATURED PIECES SPE-
CIFIC to arts and culture journalism. The second part includes the arts and
culture version of features that are common in all sorts of journalism. Profiles,
for example, you'll find in sports, business, fashion, dining—in every sort of
journalism that has a "human interest" element. (And what sort of journalism
doesn't? If humans aren't reading us, who is?)

Across the spectrum, the best profiles show the subject coming alive on
the page. These stories don't read like encyclopedia entries or strings of dis-
embodied quotes. They often employ literary technique—description, setting,
dialogue, character development, narrative momentum—to put the reader in
the room with the subject and let this encounter illuminate the person.

What distinguishes the arts profile is the artistic component. Our focus in
a profile of the artist is what that artist has done—and why, and how. Exploring what the artist has done requires the same sorts of considerations that go
into the review. An evaluation tells the reader why this subject is worth writing (and reading) about, with description and analysis of the work typically
supporting the evaluation. Context is the essence of the profile, providing the
depth about the person and the motivation behind the art, the interrelationship
between the life and the work. And all of this needs to be focused in such a
manner that the profile plainly has a hook, one central point it's making about
the person and his or her art.

In this chapter you'll find profiles by two types of writers. The first are
specialists in the profile, with subjects that aren't restricted to an artistic genre.
The opening profiles by Lynn Hirschberg from The New York Times Magazine are prime examples. (They typically run to thousands of words; one
complete profile would fill this chapter.)

She explores various facets of popular culture—and the industries that
support it—with literary flair and psychological depth that help her readers
get to know her subjects perhaps even better than the subjects themselves
sometimes do. The writer of such a lengthy profile might spend days, weeks,
even months with the subject—the sort of access granted The Times and major
media organizations but that poses more of a challenge to writers at smaller
publications. Some of this time is spent just hanging around, seeing the subject in all sorts of different circumstances, letting the person reveal himself or
herself over time.

Profiles by critics tend to have more of a critical, less psychological focus. The profile by Michael Kimmelman shows an artist revealing herself through her insights into the art of others. Michiko Kakutani typically doesn't profile authors from her literary beat, but turns her critical incisiveness toward other subjects; the extended introduction to her profile here of playwright/actor Sam Shepard is almost pure criticism. (She has subsequently reviewed Shepard as an author of prose narratives.) In each of the profiles that follow, analyze the interplay of interview, biographical and critical material, a balance that will shift depending on subject and writer.

In popular music, writing profiles is usually an integral part of the critic's beat, with such pieces providing plenty of critical insight. They frequently substitute for a CD review and/or serve as a concert preview. Consider the paragraphs in Ann Powers's profile of Leonard Cohen that could come straight from a review of his new release.

One note: Journalism typically discourages the "single source" story, but many shorter profiles (in the 1,000 to 1,500-word range) rely only on the subject of the story for interview quotes. Those that use only the subject as a source place even more responsibility on the writer to provide the critical context, the balancing perspective. The journalist who has enough time and space should generally seek to talk to others, because the more people you talk to, the more facets of a profile subject you'll see. The way a person *thinks* he's coming across to the world is not necessarily how the world actually perceives him. In each of the interviews that follow, pay attention to the number of different sources and what perspective each contributes.

Selection 9.1

A profile by Lynn Hirschberg in The New York Times Magazine is something of a journalistic event—at least in arts and culture circles. Typically provocative and revelatory, and always exhaustively long, her profiles not only cast their subjects in fresh light, they often cast fresh light on the industry or profession as a whole. Here she examines a different kind of record label head—one hired not only to "save the company" but also "maybe the record business"—and an uncommonly thoughtful actor. Look at the difference between the two profiles, how the first begins with such compelling scene setting (written in the present tense) while the second begins with the recollection of a memory (written in the past tense). Watch for the way she introduces other voices into the story, with secondary sources speaking early in each piece. In each case, the journalist's style serves both the substance and the subject. And look for the amount of detail, both in scene and action, that places readers right next to the subject, allowing us to see him through the writer's eyes. (As always, the reader is encouraged to finish these stories online.)

The Music Man

By LYNN HIRSCHBERG

Rick Rubin is listening. A song by a new band called the Gossip is playing, and he is concentrating. He appears to be in a trance. His eyes are tightly closed and he is swaying back and forth to the beat, trying at once to hear what is right and wrong about the music. Rubin, who resembles a medium-size bear with a long, gray beard, is curled into the corner of a tufted velvet couch in the library of a house he owns but where he no longer lives. This three-story 1923 Spanish villa steeped in music history—Johnny Cash recorded in the basement studio; Jakob Dylan is recording a solo album there now—is used by Rubin for meetings. And ever since May, when he officially became co-head of Columbia Records, Rubin has been having nearly constant meetings. Beginning in 1984, when he started Def Jam Recordings, until his more recent occupation as a career-transforming, chart-topping, Grammy Award–winning producer for dozens of artists, as diverse as the Dixie Chicks, Slayer, Red Hot Chili Peppers and Neil Diamond, Rubin, who is 44, has never gone to an office of any kind. One of his conditions for taking the job at Sony, which owns Columbia, was that he wouldn't be required to have a desk or a phone in any of the corporate outposts. That wasn't a problem: Columbia didn't want Rubin to punch a clock. It wanted him to save the company. And just maybe the record business.

What that means, most of all, is that the company wants him to listen. It is Columbia's belief that Rubin will hear the answers in the music—that he will find the solution to its ever-increasing woes. The mighty music business is in free fall—it has lost control of radio; retail outlets like Tower Records have shut down; MTV rarely broadcasts music videos; and the once lucrative album market has been overshadowed by downloaded singles, which mainly benefits Apple. "The music business, as a whole, has lost its faith in content," David Geffen, the legendary music mogul, told me recently. "Only 10 years ago, companies wanted to make records, presumably good records, and see if they sold. But panic has set in, and now it's no longer about making music, it's all about how to sell music. And there's no clear answer about how to fix that problem. But I still believe that the top priority at any record company has to be coming up with great music. And for that reason, Sony was very smart to hire Rick."

Though Rubin maintains that his intention is simply to hear music with the fresh ears of a true fan, he has built his reputation on

Published: September 2, 2007. Full text available at: www.nytimes.com/2007/09/02/magazine/ 02rubin.t.html?pagewanted=all.

the simultaneously mystical and entirely decisive way he listens to
a song. As the Gossip, which is fronted by a large, raucous woman
named Beth Ditto, shouts to a stop, Rubin opens his eyes and nods
yes. This is the first new band signed to Columbia that he has been
enthralled by, but he is not yet sure how to organize the Gossip's
future. "Let's hear something else," Rubin says to Kevin Kusatsu,
who would, at any other record company, be called an A & R executive. (Traditionally, A & R executives spot, woo, recruit and oversee
the talent of a record company.) "We don't have any titles at the new
Columbia," Rubin explains, as Kusatsu, the first person Rubin hired,
slips a disc out of its sleeve. "I don't want to create a new hierarchy to
replace the old hierarchy."

Rubin, wearing his usual uniform of loose khaki pants and bil-
lowing white T-shirt, his sunglasses in his pocket, his feet bare, fingers a string of lapis lazuli Buddhist prayer beads, believed to bring
wisdom to the wearer. Since Rubin's beard and hair nearly cover his
face, his voice, which is soft and reassuring, becomes that much more
vivid. He seems to be one with the room, which is lined in floor-to-
ceiling books, most of which are of a spiritual nature, whether about
Buddhism, the Bible or New Age quests for enlightenment. The
library and the house are filled with religious iconography mixed with
mementos from the world of pop. A massive brass Buddha is flanked
by equally enormous speakers; vintage cardboard cutouts of John,
Paul, George and Ringo circa "Help!" are placed around a multi-
armed statue of Vishnu. On a low table, there are crystals and an old
RadioShack cassette recorder that Rubin uses to listen to demo tapes;
a framed photo of Jim Morrison stares at a crystal ball. In Rubin's
world, music and spirituality collide.

***

Selection 9.2

*Again, compare the opening here with that of the previous profile. How does
the approach differ, and why?*

A Higher Calling

By LYNN HIRSCHBERG

When he was 12 years old, Philip Seymour Hoffman saw a
local production of "All My Sons" near his home in Rochester, and
it was, for him, one of those rare, life-altering events where, at an

Published: December 21, 2008. Full text available at: www.nytimes.com/2008/12/21/magazine/
21hoffman-t.html.

impressionable age, you catch a glimpse of another reality, a world that you never imagined possible.

"I literally thought, I can't believe this exists," Hoffman told me on a gray day in London early in the fall. He was sitting in the fifth row of the audience at Trafalgar Studios in the West End, where he was directing "Riflemind" (a play about an '80s rock band that may or may not reunite after 20 years), dressed in long brown cargo shorts, a stretched-out polo shirt and Converse sneakers without socks. His blond hair, still damp from showering, was standing in soft peaks on his head, which gave him the look of a very intense, newly hatched chick. At times, especially when he is in or around or anywhere near a theater, Hoffman, who is 41, can seem like an eager college student—bounding from seat to stage to give direction, writing feverishly in a notebook about a feeling he wants an actor to convey, laughing at an in-joke regarding a prop that keeps disappearing—but when the conversation shifts to a discussion of his acting in movies like "Capote," for which he deservedly won every award that's been invented, or "Doubt," out this month, he seems to turn inward and ages markedly. "The drama nerd comes out in me when I'm in a theater," he explained now, as the actors rehearsed. "When I saw 'All My Sons,' I was changed—permanently changed—by that experience. It was like a miracle to me. But that deep kind of love comes at a price: for me, acting is torturous, and it's torturous because you know it's a beautiful thing. I was young once, and I said, That's beautiful and I want that. Wanting it is easy, but trying to be great—well, that's absolutely torturous."

Hoffman took a gulp of coffee from a large cup that he was holding in a brown paper bag. He turned his attention to the stage, where two actors were rehearsing a sex scene. "Riflemind," which unfolds over a weekend, is a self-conscious study in wounds: long-simmering battles are reignited and secrets are revealed. The play has a predictable middle-aged-angst narrative that is somewhat glamorized by its rock-star milieu: the drugs may be stronger, but the emotions are oddly detached. Hoffman's fascination with "Riflemind"—he directed it in Sydney, Australia, last year and, when we met, had been in London for several weeks preparing this production—can be explained by both his commitment to theater and by the fact that the play is written by Andrew Upton, the husband of Cate Blanchett. Hoffman met Upton and Blanchett when he appeared with her in "The Talented Mr. Ripley." "On that movie, we shot only one or two days a week," Hoffman recalled. "Much of the time, I was in Rome with Cate and Andrew. I have a hard time having fun, but that was heaven. And I must really like Andrew—my girlfriend, who is in New York, is about to have our third child, and I am here." Hoffman paused. "I don't get nervous when I'm directing a play. It's not like acting. If this fails, I wouldn't be as upset by it."

Hoffman jumped out of his seat and ran to the stage. He proceeded to correct the sex scene. He bent the actress back over a couch and metamorphosed into a desperate character, the former manager of the band, driven by the hope of sudden riches and his lust for the guitar player's wife. He played just enough of the scene and, then, he switched back to being Phil, the regular guy in the baggy shorts. It was stunning. "I don't know how he does it," Mike Nichols, who has directed Hoffman on the stage ("The Seagull") and in movies ("Charlie Wilson's War"), told me later. "Again and again, he can truly become someone I've not seen before but can still instantly recognize. Sometimes Phil loses some weight, and he may dye his hair but, really, it's just the same Phil, and yet, he's never the same person from part to part. Last year, he did three films—'The Savages,' 'Charlie Wilson's War' and 'Before the Devil Knows You're Dead'—and in each one he was a distinct and entirely different human. It's that humanity that is so striking—when you watch Phil work, his entire constitution seems to change. He may look like Phil, but there's something different in his eyes. And that means he's reconstituted himself from within, willfully rearranging his molecules to become another human being."

From his first roles in movies like "Scent of a Woman," in which he played a villainous prep-school student, to the lovesick Scotty J. in "Boogie Nights," to the passionate and ornery rock critic Lester Bangs in "Almost Famous," Hoffman has imbued all his characters with a combination of the familiar and the unique. It's not easy; it's the sort of acting that requires enormous range, as well as a kind of stubborn determination and a profound lack of vanity. In the theater, Hoffman finds refuge in being part of a community. Theater presents considerable difficulties—Hoffman said his most challenging role for the stage was as Jamie Tyrone in "Long Day's Journey Into Night" on Broadway ("That nearly killed me"). But when he speaks about his work in films, Hoffman's struggles sound lonelier: his childhood dream was to be on the stage, and the fulfillment of that fantasy seems to mitigate some of the strain Hoffman experiences when he is acting.

"In my mid-20s, an actor told me, 'Acting ain't no puzzle,'" Hoffman said, after returning to his seat. "I thought: 'Ain't no puzzle?!?' You must be bad!" He laughed. "You must be really bad, because it is a puzzle. Creating anything is hard. It's a cliché thing to say, but every time you start a job, you just don't know anything. I mean, I can break something down, but ultimately I don't know anything when I start work on a new movie. You start stabbing out, and you make a mistake, and it's not right, and then you try again and again. The key is you have to commit. And that's hard because you have to find what it is you are committing to."

***

Selection 9.3

This critical profile finds a photographer illuminating her own aesthetic through her responses to the art of others. Michael Kimmelman compresses much of what we might expect to read in a conventional, biographical profile into the third and fourth paragraphs, focusing the rest on the artist's personal tour of the Metropolitan Museum of Art, during which she "tends to talk about her own work when she looks at the works of others." This is less than half of the full piece—which should be read in its entirety and is part of a series, one that inspired a similar series by music critic Ben Ratliff, who has profiled jazz musicians by listening to some of their favorite recordings with them.

At the Met With Cindy Sherman: Portraitist in the Halls of Her Artistic Ancestors
By MICHAEL KIMMELMAN

Cindy Sherman can't remember the last time she visited the Metropolitan Museum of Art. Today she's in the lobby, along with the tourists, fishing around the information desk for a map. What is there to see, she asks? She is open to suggestions. She has heard about a show of works by Nadar, the 19th-century French photographer, but doesn't know much about him. Might as well start there, she says.

On the way she pauses, by chance, at a William Lake Price photograph from 1857, a stagy picture of someone dressed as Don Quixote. "I never look at these sorts of photographs," she admits, then happens to glance at the label. "Theatrical staging has found renewed relevance in the work of such contemporaries as Cindy Sherman," it says. Ms. Sherman smiles, slightly embarrassed.

Of all the American artists who came to prominence in the 1980's, Ms. Sherman may be the most compelling and significant. She is almost certainly the most consistently celebrated: while the skyrocketing careers of many of her 80's contemporaries have fizzled along with the market that fueled them, hers has held steady. She began in 1977, having just settled in New York City after art school in Buffalo, by taking a series of smart and artfully crude black-and-white photographs of herself that imitated B-movie stills and celebrity snapshots from the 1950's and 60's. An undercurrent of sadness, even pain, ran beneath the photographs' surface of irony and camp. That undercurrent turned, rather startlingly, into a torrent of gore and rage: she switched to using a larger format and often lurid colors, and to concocting increasingly horrific and surreal images. Some of them were based on fairy tales, others on fashion spreads and pornography.

Published: May 19, 1995. Full text available at: www.nytimes.com/1995/05/19/arts/at-the-met-with-cindy-sherman-portraitist-in-the-halls-of-her-artistic-ancestors.html.

Until recently, at least, Ms. Sherman starred in her own works, which is why many people may think they know what she looks like. Uncannily, she doesn't resemble any of her own pictures, not even the ones that seem fairly straightforward. She is, at 41, handsome, thin, with cropped brown hair that falls in bangs. She can remind you of Jean Seberg. Considering that she has become, through no effort of her own, a darling of academics and has inspired reams of arcane post-modernist criticism, it's also pleasing to discover how plain-spoken, unpretentious and down-to-earth she is.

Like many artists, Ms. Sherman tends to talk about her own work when she looks at the works of others in the museum. She reacts enthusiastically to what's on view, but art history per se doesn't interest her much. She has an omnivorous appetite for images and sure instincts for adapting them to her own purposes, but she isn't concerned about their past. She once said her goal was an art that was accessible, "not one that you felt you had to read a book about" to understand. Her work is intuitive and improvisational, as well as intel-ligent, and it is prompted as much by the props she has bought at flea markets and through medical-supply catalogues as by the works of art she has seen in museums and reproductions.

"Even when I was doing those history pictures," she says of a touted series of photographs she loosely derived from Old Master paintings, "I was living in Rome but never went to the churches and museums there. I worked out of books, with reproductions. It's an aspect of photography I appreciate, conceptually: the idea that images can be reproduced and seen anytime, anywhere, by anyone."

Around the corner from Price's "Don Quixote," in a gallery of 20th-century photographs, Ms. Sherman spots a 1927 picture by the German photographer Otto Umbehr, who called himself Umbo. It depicts a young woman's uplighted face. "I love any image of a woman from that era: I love to look at the way they did their finger-nail polish or their makeup," says Ms. Sherman, who is forever dis-guising herself in her own photographs. "Also, look at the dust spots and cracks. God forbid I should sell a piece to a museum or collector that has a little crack in the corner. Early on, I was purposely making things that were badly printed and haphazard."

"But now," she says, laughing, "my work's just too expensive for people to want it unless it's perfect."

Next to the Umbo is a photograph by Margaret Bourke-White, a kind of abstraction from 1934, and one by Harold Edgerton that is also seemingly abstract: his famous image of a drop of milk filmed at one hundred-thousandth of a second. "If this sort of early experimen-tal photography were done now," she says, "it obviously wouldn't be so interesting because every student since then has fooled around with emulsion and doing bad prints and out-of-focus prints and all that. But back then there was a sense of discovery."

"I guess for me the interest is also in recognizing my roots," she says. "I'm illiterate in the historical, classic knowledge of photography, the stuff teachers attempted to bore into my head, which I resisted. The way I've always tried to cull information from older art and put it into my work is that I view it all anonymously, on a visceral level. Lately I've been looking at a lot of images from Surrealism and Dada, but I never remember which ones are the Man Rays, say, because I'm just looking for what interests me."

✳✳✳

 STORY**SCAN**

Selection 9.4

Let's take a closer look at how a music critic uses the profile to evaluate the music within the context of the life.

MUSIC
Down From the Mountain, Singing With More Serenity

By ANN POWERS

Here's a Zen question: does spending the better part of five years in a mountaintop abbey, meditating and cooking, cleaning and putting chains on the abbey's truck, change a person? Leonard Cohen, having descended last year from the enclave of Joshu Sasaki Roshi in the hills above Los Angeles, would like to suggest that he is still the same old romantic known for his ways with wine, women and song. Or perhaps not.

Some editors resist opening with a question, but such a riddle provides an intriguing intro to this profile of an artist who has returned from a spiritual retreat.

This context subtly provides necessary information for the reader who hasn't been following Cohen, but doesn't belabor the point for those who know where he's been.

In Zen fashion, the answer to the question is something of a paradox, demanding that the reader continue in order to resolve the central issue: What has changed? What has not?

Published: October 28, 2001.

Why "neatly?" First hint of a positive evaluation.

When a subject is as quotable as Cohen, and has such a distinctive voice, introduce that voice as early as possible.

So it's the subject who is insisting that nothing much really changed, that life goes on.

Yet the interviewer presses him to admit that "six hours of meditation a day" is a somewhat radical change from the ordinary. "Acknowledged" indicates a response to her prodding, rather than a revelation offered independently.

Journalist and subject continue to play cat and mouse—she suggesting a difference in perspective—which the reader is likely to share—from his insistence on "ordinary life."

A great transition between the routine of the spiritual retreat and the routine of recording the music. Necessary, because the music ultimately is where the reader's interest in this musical artist lies.

"It's hard to say, because one is doing only the thing one is doing," he said during a recent interview in Manhattan to promote his 10th studio album, neatly titled "Ten New Songs." "When I finished the last tour, in 1993, I was approaching 60 and my old teacher was approaching 90. So I thought it was appropriate to spend more time with him. I went up there on a kind of open-ended basis, and I stayed for five or six years and came back down, but there was no thematic rupture."

"The songs were written during that period," he continued. "But it is hard to say what the influence of a teacher and a very close friend was. Friends are continually influencing each other in subtle ways."

Mr. Cohen acknowledged that six hours of meditation a day may have made a mark. "Yes, well, anytime you concentrate your life on anything and make some even mild effort at avoiding distraction, the general tone of your being will improve," he said. Yet like many a Zen riddler before him, Mr. Cohen played down any aura of enlightenment. "There's no place where ordinary life doesn't prevail," he said.

In the monastery, he rose before dawn, interacted with a small coterie and prepared many meals. Later, making "Ten New Songs" in his Los Angeles home studio, he did the same. The monks were replaced by his collaborators, Sharon Robinson and Leanne Ungar, and the salmon teriyaki he made for Sasaki Roshi was traded for tuna sandwiches.

The writer who in earlier songs, poems and stories had painted smoky visions of Joan of Arc and countless less metaphorical lovers was now pursuing something more plain. His new compositions reflected a mind bent on clarity. "Ten New Songs" is not about conversion, however, or the cleaning away of old fascinations. It's a musical account of how subtle a change in perspective can be.

The shift is noticeable from the album's first cut, "In My Secret Life." An electronic drumbeat and a teasing lick from the guitarist Bob Metzger lead in to a soulful chorus of women's voices, a Cohen trademark. Then comes his burnished croak, a thorn among the roses, mourning the loss of a drifting paramour. It's all so familiar, but beneath the song's veneer another story emerges.

"I wanted the song to begin like a classic rock 'n' roll song, a rhythm-and-blues song," Mr. Cohen said. "And then it becomes more honest as it moves along." The transition comes when Ms. Robinson, who provided all the women's voices, emerges as a soloist. The brandy sniffer's lament becomes a murmur of the universal spirit. "Hold on, hold on, my brother. My sister, hold on tight," she sings, her multitracked voice directing the lament to where the border between despair and transcendence blurs.

A paragraph of analytical comparison, one that could have fit easily into a review by changing past tense ("was," "reflected") to present tense.

Again, this paragraph of description could come straight from a review—particularly inspired is the "burnished croak, a thorn among the roses." Anyone familiar with Cohen's music will hear it in this paragraph.

A quote in which the artist explains his motivation returns the piece to conventional profile mode, though the rest of the paragraph, again, is critical analysis.

Ending the paragraph, this short quote is almost a throwaway, with what precedes it putting the new music in the context of his career.

A second source? Just barely, in a profile where the critic's perspective more often counters the subject's.

Here's the evaluation, later than it would likely have come in a review, but we already know the writer likes the music. If she didn't, she either wouldn't have written about the artist or she would have registered reservations much earlier.

An even more transcendent evaluation.

A return to the tension between the spiritual and the mundane—or perhaps a recognition of the spiritual within the mundane.

It's appropriate that a woman's voice should emerge as the herald of the divine, since Mr. Cohen's main haunt has always been the intersection of sex and the psyche. Ms. Robinson has worked with Mr. Cohen off and on for two decades and was the co-writer of favorites like "Everybody Knows." On "Ten New Songs" her role is expanded: she is credited as sole producer and pictured with Mr. Cohen on the cover. "The album is really a duet," he said.

Ms. Robinson preferred to call the album a close collaboration. "I think of this work as a continuation of Leonard's previous work," she said. "The changes I see are very natural ones, brought about by experience, continuous effort, introspection and study."

A Zen poem describing great wonders begins: "I came and I returned. It was nothing special." "Ten New Songs" takes a similar attitude. Like all of Mr. Cohen's songs, these celebrate great beauty and mourn tragic loss, but they do so with striking composure. In these songs, Mr. Cohen, the graying hero, is dancing with the one conquest he knows he can't make.

That shadowy object of desire is whatever causes the rare experience of unity, felt through sex, meditation, revelation or art. Ms. Robinson represents the calling forth of this force throughout the album, only to have Mr. Cohen's prosaic baritone return the music to the day to day.

"Boogie Street," for example, begins with another prayerlike passage, quickly overcome by Mr. Cohen's muttered list of everyday concerns. "I'm wanted at the traffic jam," he sings, as Ms. Robinson's lament for heaven's "crown of light" lingers in the background.

Like the previous two paragraphs, this continues in review mode, with the context of a profile offering more space for description and analysis than a review in The Times likely would.

Mr. Cohen quoted his lyric in conversation. " 'You kiss my lips and then it's done, I'm back on Boogie Street,' " he said. Then he elaborated: "We're continually moving from whatever it is that overthrows the notion of the self, back to the burden of the self. But if you're lucky, you come back to Boogie Street with the residue of the other experience. That cools you out."

Again, a brief return to the convention of profile, with the artist explaining his motivation.

Coolness permeates "Ten New Songs"; that's another way it strays from Mr. Cohen's usual after-midnight mood. This deviation is aural, and again its catalyst was Ms. Robinson. She and Ms. Ungar, the album's engineer, worked with Mr. Cohen to use studio software that created a sound that's intimate yet unearthly.

More critical context; after earlier showing how this is an extension of or progression from previous work, here we learn how it's a departure (or "deviation").

"We didn't start out with a particular direction in mind, but about halfway through, the use of sampled instruments and synths became a deliberate choice," Ms. Robinson recalled. "We liked the cohesive, impersonal sound and the way it worked with Leonard's voice."

The second source provides a collaborator's perspective.

The working process from the artist's perspective, one of the revelations the profile offers that a review can't.

Mr. Cohen described the process in more detail. "Sharon would present demos to me," he recalled. "Our intention was to replace these synthesizer sounds with live musicians, but I began to see that her demos were of a very high quality. I began to insist that we keep the demos and change the keys because that's easy to do with the software available now."

More context about process with a short quote as the kicker to the paragraph.

The private nature of this recording process was enhanced by the clean sound sought by Ms. Ungar, who has contributed a similarly introspective ambiance to albums by Laurie Anderson and Joy Askew. Mr. Metzger, the album's only live musician, is Ms. Ungar's husband. "It's a very, very close affair," Mr. Cohen said, chuckling.

Working with only a few friends allowed Mr. Cohen to relax and, as meditation teachers often say, turn his gaze inward.

Purely critical analysis that continues throughout this paragraph. Plainly Powers continues to function primarily as a music critic even when shifting to profile mode.

The sense on many songs is of a personality touching unknown elements of itself. The lyrics combine the earthy details of country music (which Mr. Cohen loves) with an almost biblical oracularity, and they are served by the translucence of synthesized sound. In this way, "Ten New Songs" evokes that hardest to grasp Zen idea: the oneness of mind and body, earth and heaven, now and then.

Within this context, "Ten New Songs" furthers Mr. Cohen's well-seasoned themes. "The Land of Plenty," a surprisingly humble protest song, touches on the sometimes apocalyptic political vision he elucidated on the 1993 album "The Future." "That Don't Make It Junk" shows the humor of earlier glass-raisers like "That's No Way to Say Goodbye." Mr. Cohen's hobby of rewriting psalms gets full play on the stately "Here It Is," while his literary bent shows in the beautiful "Alexandra Leaving," a reworking of a poem by the early 20th-century Greek writer C. P. Cavafy.

Again, context that compares the new music to what has come before.

At the same time, "Ten New Songs" discreetly turns away from the mysticism many seek from Mr. Cohen. Longing remains, but the need to resolve it, or even fully indulge its power, has diminished. For those uninclined to seek Eastern wisdom in Mr. Cohen's music, that sense of serenity can be seen as the wisdom of aging, a singular mind's reflections turned by time toward commonalities. Mr. Cohen himself would probably take this view. He is just as weary of being held up as a saint as he is of being called the ultimate bohemian.

A transitional paragraph that continues in critical mode before setting up the concluding quote.

"Heroism is very high maintenance," he said. "After a while, when tremendous energy is devoted to maintaining this hero as the center figure of the drama, the evidence accumulates that this hero is relentlessly defeated. So at a certain point the modest wisdom arises that it would be best to let this hero die and get on with your life."

Some editors and professors discourage beginning or ending a story with a quote. Great writers know that such rules are made to be broken, and that each story (particularly such a Zen-infused story) must teach us how best to tell it.

Selection 9.5

Though the second part of this expansive profile is more conventionally bio-graphical, this long introductory section is pure criticism, with even the quotes from actor/playwright Sam Shepard focusing on his art rather than his life or himself. As the chief book critic for The Times, Michiko Kakutani brings a sharp critical incisiveness to her profiles (she typically avoids authors, whose work she might review, as subjects). Look at how the critical commentary on the subject's "ongoing process of self-creation and re-invention" proceeds seamlessly into a more conventionally biographical profile. But the structure makes plain what interests the critic most, and the subject seems to concur. "Personality is everything that is false in a human being," says Shepard, a provocative remark in a personality profile.

Myths, Dreams, Realities—Sam Shepard's America
By MICHIKO KAKUTANI

"I drive on the freeway every day,"says a character in Sam Shepard's "True West." "I swallow the smog. I watch the news in color. I shop in Safeway . . . there's no such thing as the West any-more! It's a dead issue!"

For the play's two heroes—Austin, an aspiring screenwriter, intent on making it in Hollywood; and his brother, Lee, a desert rat who makes a living as a petty thief—the West represents two very different places. There is the old west, remembered mainly from the movies now, as a place where Manifest Destiny was an almost palpable notion, a place which promised a way of life that was as free as the land and the sky. And there is the new west, crisscrossed by highways and pockmarked by suburbs—the west that Hollywood tycoons and tract-housing developers built on the mortgaged dreams of the pioneers.

In "True West," which is currently running Off Broadway at the Cherry Lane—a television adaptation will be shown this Tuesday on public television's "American Playhouse"—Mr. Shepard uses these two disparate visions of California not only to delineate the deep, contradictory craving in the American character for both freedom and the security of roots, but also to explore the gap between our nostalgic memories of the past and the bleakness of the present. Mr. Shepard himself says "if I'm at home anywhere, it's in the west—as soon as I cross the Mississippi, I don't feel the same"—but the idea of the West that he cherishes exists only as a memory now in the swiftly receding landscape; its romantic ideals, like the old American Dream, vanished long ago with the frontier.

Published: January 29, 1984. Full text available at: www.nytimes.com/1984/01/29/theater/myths-dreams-realities-sam-shepard-s-america.html.

At 40, Mr. Shepard has won a Pulitzer Prize and emerged as the preeminent playwright of his generation. In an astonishing body of work—some 40 full-length and one-act plays, as well as poetry, short stories and a volume of autobiographical sketches—he has put forth a vision of America that resonates with the power of legend. Surreal images bloom in his work—men turn into lizards; carrots and potatoes grow miraculously in a barren garden; an eagle carries a cat off, screaming into the sky—and strange, almost hallucinatory transactions occur. And yet the work remains firmly grounded in the facts of our own history and popular culture. Whether he is writing about rock-stars, old-time gangsters or the contemporary family, Mr. Shepard's voice remains distinctively American; his humor, dark; his language, at once lyrical and hip.

He has created a fictional world populated by cowboys and gun-slingers, ranchers and desperadoes, but these characters all find that the myths they were raised on somehow no longer apply. Eddie the wrangler-hero of "Fool for Love"—currently playing at the Douglas Fairbanks—finds that he has nothing better to lasso than the bedposts in a squalid motel room. The Hollywood hustlers in "Angel City" look out their window and see not the fertile valleys of the Promised Land, but a smoggy city of used-car lots and shopping centers—a city waiting for apocalypse. And the old-time outlaws, who pay a visit to the present in "The Unseen Hand," discover that there are no more trains to rob, that there is no place for heroics, that it is no longer even possible to tell the good guys from the bad.

What happens when these characters are forced to face up to the disparity between their lives and a heroic, if imaginary past, is almost inevitably violent. Indeed violence—the emotional violence of people shattering each others' dreams with verbal volleys, if not actual physical blows—is a commonplace in Mr. Shepard's insistently male world. "I think there's something about American violence that to me is very touching," he explains. "In full force it's very ugly, but there's also something very moving about it, because it has to do with humiliation. There's some hidden, deeply rooted thing in the Anglo male American that has to do with inferiority, that has to do with not being a man, and always, continually having to act out some idea of manhood that invariably is violent. This sense of failure runs very deep—maybe it has to do with the frontier being systematically taken away, with the guilt of having gotten this country by wiping out a native race of people, with the whole Protestant work ethic. I can't put my finger on it, but it's the source of a lot of intrigue for me."

As the frontier receded, so did the old values and dreams, and in its wake, says Mr. Shepard, it has left a craving for belief. This hunger not only makes people needy for self-definition, but also, as in "Curse of the Starving Class," susceptible to the promises of fake messiahs. "People are starved for the truth," he says, "and when something comes along that even looks like the truth, people will latch on to it because everything's so false. People are starved for a way of life—they're hunting for a way to be or to act toward the world. Take anything—I don't see the punk movement as any different from, say, the evangelist movement. They're both taken on faith—on one hand, faith in costume, and on the other, faith in a symbolic Christ."

Indeed the search for a role, for a way of acting toward the world, remains one of the central preoccupations of Mr. Shepard's characters. Deprived of the past and any sort of familial definition—in play after play, fathers do not even recognize their sons—they try to manufacture new identities. They make up remarkable stories about themselves, but in shedding various costumes, poses and personalities, they often misplace the mysterious thing that makes them who they are.

"Personality is everything that is false in a human being," explains Mr. Shepard. "It's everything that's been added on to him and contrived. It seems to me that the struggle all the time is between this sense of falseness and the other haunting sense of what's true—an essential thing that we're born with and tend to lose track of. This naturally sets up a great contradiction in everybody—between what they represent and what they know to be themselves."

Victims of this contradiction, Mr. Shepard's characters live "in at least two dimensions—one has to do with fantasy, the other with reality." Some of them have the ability to conjure up their fantasy life at will—as a result such mythical heroes as Captain Kidd, Mae West and Jesse James make appearances on stage—while others are content to simply impose their fantasies on family and friends. In some cases, the characters actually undergo bizarre transformations on stage—they become, in a sense, who they think they are.

It is a peculiarly American notion, this sense that, like Gatsby, one can spring from the "Platonic conception of himself," that identity is not something fixed by family or class, that one can grow up to become anything—the President or a movie star. It offers, on one hand, the promise of self-made riches and fame; and on the other, the perils of dislocation and anomie. Mr. Shepard, himself, talks of experiencing "this kind of rootlessness I don't think will ever be resolved," and the facts of his own life suggest an ongoing process of self-creation and re-invention.

An army brat, whose family had migrated during his childhood from Fort Sheridan, Ill., to Utah to Florida to Guam, the playwright spent his high school years in Duarte, a small town east of Los Angeles, where his father had an avocado farm. He was born Samuel Shepard Rogers—a name that "came down through seven generations of men with the same name"—and nicknamed Steve to distinguish him from his father. Years later, he would learn that Steve Rogers had been the original name of Captain America in the comics, but by then, he'd dropped the Rogers and the Steve and reincarnated himself as Sam Shepard.

As a boy, Steve Rogers had played at being a cowboy and a musician and a movie star—for days he practiced Burt Lancaster's grin in

"Vera Cruz," "Sneering. Grinning that grin. Sliding my upper lip up over my teeth"—and the Sam Shepard who later populated his dramatic world with these same mythic figures would also try on those roles in life.

The kid from California, whose exposure to cowboys had been limited to "seeing Leo Carrillo, the Lone Ranger and Hopalong Cassidy in the Rose Parade," eventually went East where, as the singer Patti Smith recalled, he became "a man playing cowboys"; he traded in his "beat" outfit of the 50's—a turtleneck, peacoat and dark pants—for a flannel shirt, straw Resistol hat and jeans. And while he'd never achieve the celebrity of his idols—Johnny Ace, Jimmie Rodgers and Keith Richards—he would also become an accomplished musician, joining the Holy Modal Rounders, a rock band, in the late 60's.

The movie stardom has come more recently: after several "rural parts" in "Days of Heaven," "Resurrection," "Raggedy Man" and "Frances," Mr. Shepard last year played the test pilot Chuck Yeager in "The Right Stuff"—a role which not only conferred on him a kind of matinee idol status, but which also coalesced, in a single image, the archetypes of Western hero and space-age pioneer. Suddenly, he was up there on the screen playing one of those "pilots with fur-collared leather jackets" he'd dreamed about as a kid, and being acclaimed as the heir to Gary Cooper—strong, centered and coolly sexy.

∗

Selection 9.6

Who is Jerry Seinfeld the person? Who cares? It isn't until the eleventh para-graph that this profile includes any biographical detail beyond Seinfeld's smash television series (just beginning its third season at the time) and what it reflects of his views on comedy. The result is a revelatory glimpse into the comedic val-ues behind a show about "nothing." Though The Reader initially had a review of "Seinfeld" slated for inclusion, this profile made a review superfluous.

TELEVISION
How Does Seinfeld Define Comedy? Reluctantly
By GLENN COLLINS

Jerry Seinfeld was free-associating in his serene, off-center way about his decidedly off-center sitcom, the one that NBC has cleverly titled "Seinfeld." "Some of the writers who want to work on the show, they have a hard time getting a grip on what funny is," he was saying in his calm cadences. "They give us all these sitcom ideas. I tell them we don't want sitcom ideas. I tell them what we don't want to do, but it's hard to explain what we do want."

Published: September 29, 1991.

He was pacing his improbably clean apartment on Central Park West in Manhattan on a recent afternoon, trying once again for a precise calibration of the idiosyncrasies of human experience, just as he has done on thousands of comedy stages for the last 15 years. "But then," Mr. Seinfeld said, "we'll come up with an idea about—well, what if you heard that Robert Stack lived in the building across the street—and you set out trying to find out if that were true? Or then we'll have another odd idea about going out on a date with a Vietnamese girl who owns a pig. Now that, that's a *great* idea."

Then how does he define comedy? "Reluctantly," he said, laughing. "Rather than define the comedy on our show by what we don't do, I can tell you what we *do* like." He paused, then said, deadpan: "Robert Stack. Vietnamese. Girls. Pigs."

Such is the clear and persistent comedic vision that informs the 9:30 P.M. Wednesday showcase for Mr. Seinfeld's cable-ready cool. Since its first run in the spring of 1990, the show has attracted a steadily growing following. "Seinfeld," which finished in the top 10 at the end of its tryout last spring, smoked its competition on this season's opening night, Sept. 18, with a convincing 15.1 rating and a 25 share in the Nielsens. (Share is the percentage of television sets that are tuned to the program; each rating point equals 921,000 homes.)

Now, after two seasons as something of an hors d'oeuvre on the NBC programmers' appetizer plate, "Seinfeld" faces its first full season as a main course of the fall comedy lineup, with its own presold audience. The show's respectability is all the more remarkable for its blatant betrayal of the Conventional Canons of the Sitcom. "Seinfeld" is, arguably, the most idiosyncratic comedy on network television. So far, the comedian's efforts have been applauded not only by audiences and NBC, but also by critics.

The epicenter of the show's punch is Mr. Seinfeld's keenly observed, carefully timed, contemplative humor about life's minutiae, people's foibles and mankind's quotidian moments of angst. The 37-year-old Mr. Seinfeld, a zen meditator for two decades who is as contemplative off stage as on, is brimming with insight on the subject he cares most about. A Seinfeldian self-analysis is revealing about the state of comedy as well as the state of Jerry Seinfeld.

"One of the great things about comedy," he said, "is its very enigmatic quality. One of the things I love about it is that it's so impenetrable, inscrutable, impervious to technology or mastery."

"That's what's so offensive about the average sitcom," he continued. "A sitcom idea, well, you know exactly where it's going to go. But we wanted to do a show where, well, you don't *care* where it goes. At all. As long as it doesn't go where you think it's going to go. Most sitcoms set up the situation and plug in one-liners. We try—I emphasize, try—to make the situation itself funny."

In his weekly venture into eponymity, Jerry Seinfeld the stand-up comedian stars as a stand-up comedian named Jerry Seinfeld; in each show he demonstrates how the mundane events in his off-stage life inspire material for his on-stage act. Like the real Seinfeld, his video clone is single and hangs out with a repertory company of single characters. Jason Alexander, who won a Tony Award for his role in "Jerome Robbins's Broadway," plays George, Mr. Seinfeld's friend and manager. Julia Louis-Dreyfus plays Elaine, a pal and former girlfriend, and Michael Richards plays Jerry's nutso neighbor, Kramer.

"Seinfeld" is set in New York—in fact, it's so Noo-Yawky that it has featured the exterior of the quintessential Greek coffee shop, Tom's Restaurant on 112th Street and Broadway. Though it is taped in Los Angeles, much of its energy still comes from Mr. Seinfeld's New York experience.

"I hope the show illustrates the discipline I learned through the years in my stand-up act," Mr. Seinfeld said. Starting in 1976, he became a nightly toiler in the laugh game at Catch a Rising Star, the Improv and the Comic Strip. "There was no work anywhere else," he said. "So we saw everyone, every night. We did a lot of hanging out—from, say, 9 to 1 or 2 A.M. at the clubs, and then in the coffee shop till 3 or 4."

Said Mr. Seinfeld's sister, Carolyn Liebling: "Jerry says he always knew he was going to be a comedian. But he never told the family—he just started going to Catch every night."

Said Mr. Seinfeld: "I took no more than a day off. Four years of pretty much working for free, picking up $30 and $50 gigs to support yourself. I think it takes five years just to learn how to express yourself, to know what to say."

After four years of working in New York, "I had 25 minutes of material," Mr. Seinfeld said, "so I went to Los Angeles." His first big break came a year later, on the "Tonight" show. "I remember the date, May 7, 1981," Mr. Seinfeld said. "Every comedian knows that date—their own, I mean. So, here I had five years of going out every night and developing my act, and I was going to take all the chips I'd developed and put them into the center of the table on one five-minute bit."

He scored un succes de Johnny. "Suddenly I was lifted from the pack, in L.A." Since then he has been on the show 25 times.

On stage and television, Mr. Seinfeld is an amiable, collegiate presence whose PG-rated, neat-as-a-pin comedy is wry, gently sarcastic and graced with cross-generational appeal. The public Seinfeld is a truth-teller in his own reflective way. Deadpan, skeptical—but not a know-it-all. When prodded to define his on-stage character, he said, "It's hard to say what I am. I know what I'm not." After an endless pause, he continued: "I'm an overly thoughtful, overly observant guy. I'm not a wiseguy, but I guess I have an attitude."

"Martin Mull said that my whole act is about monomania. I suppose that's right. Little explorations: my comedy is in the cracks. I talk about the fascination of moments in between the ones that people talk about."

On stage, these moments include Mr. Seinfeld's disquisition on dry cleaning ("What the hell is dry cleaning fluid? It's not a fluid if it's dry"), his supermarket routine ("Very important, the rubber divider stick—I don't want other people's items fraternizing with my items") and the Seinfeldian take on scuba diving ("A great activity, where your main goal is to not die").

And, of course, there is Mr. Seinfeld's signature breakfast cereal routine ("Milk-estimation skills—so important. What do you do when you get to the bottom of the bowl and you still have milk left? Well, I say, put in more cereal!")

The first idea for the television show was hatched in the spring of 1988 "at the Westway Diner at Ninth and 44th Street with Larry David, over the usual late-night comedy coffee," he said, referring to the co-creator of the show who is now its executive producer. NBC and Castle Rock Entertainment had asked if Mr. Seinfeld wanted to do a special; the comedian asked his friend and fellow stand-up gypsy, Mr. David, if he had any ideas.

"It would be funny to demonstrate the relationship between the material and the life," said Mr. Seinfeld. "The show is still pretty much what we conceived on that night."

Said Mr. David, a comic who first met Mr. Seinfeld in 1976 and who is the model for the character George on "Seinfeld": "I've never watched a lot of sitcoms, nor has Jerry. We're not following any kind of formula—no rules or anything—it's just our sensibility. Luckily so far they're letting us get away with it."

Mr. Seinfeld does not fully understand the roots of his own comic impulse. He was born in Brooklyn and grew up on Long Island in Massapequa. ("It's an old Indian name that means 'by the mall,'" said Mr. Seinfeld.) His late father, Kalman, who ran a commercial sign business, "was naturally funny, had a very good sense of humor," said Mr. Seinfeld's mother, Betty, who now lives in Florida. "He just wanted to make people laugh."

Growing up, Mr. Seinfeld was "the wiseguy type—you know, the snide comment in the back of the room," he said. He graduated from Queens College as a communications major in 1976, "and the night I graduated, I started going to the clubs." That July he gave his first performance in front of a paying audience on a tiny showcase stage in a fondly remembered, now-defunct restaurant on West 44th Street, the Golden Lion Pub.

A few nights later, Mr. Seinfeld recalls, "Jackie Mason was in the audience. After the show he came up to me and said, 'It makes me sick, you're going to be such a big hit.' His words carried me for the next four years."

Mr. Mason, who is always ready to theorize about comedy, recalls that Mr. Seinfeld was "a natural." "I saw this kid, he was so personable," Mr. Mason continued. "He was secure and calm. He had a great natural comedy style—an ingratiating quality. His humor was founded on basic truths and universal subjects."

These days, when Mr. Seinfeld isn't in Los Angeles or on the road, he lives in his ultrasleek apartment in Manhattan with its spectacular Central Park views, decorated in an all-grays-and-blacks look that he called "clean tech, which is high tech without the attitude."

The comedian, a lean, high-fiber-powered 5-foot-11, may not have been designated as "The Sexiest Man Alive" in People magazine this year, but he is enthusiastically engaged in the single life portrayed on his show. He joked about this last month at the Emmy Awards, for which he was co-host, pondering whether to date Miss U.S.A. or Miss Universe, who were both on the program. "I didn't know whether to go for the entire nation or the galaxy," he said.

As a stand-up comedian, Mr. Seinfeld has been criticized for "not dredging up the deep pain," as he put it, "you know, for not revealing myself. But anyone who's seen what I do knows I *am* revealing how my mind works. All right, so I talk about cereal, and not existentialism or drug addiction. I work with the material that is natural to me."

He says he loves stand-up because "it's my lifeline to what I do and how I relate to people, and what's funny," he said. Before "Seinfeld" he used to do more than 300 club and concert dates a year. These days, "I'll go out to work in a few clubs every few nights," he said.

Why continue the stand-up life? "The stage experience is very pure," he answered. "It's very empirical. An authentic moment in your life. You hope that you'll do some routine that can pull out of yourself something that would be especially fine."

He spoke very slowly: "You have to know how *far* you can get. Something that hasn't been done. And there is no one else who can do it—because no one else can do you."

The director Mike Nichols is the subject of a retrospective. Tony Cenicola/The New York Times

Selection 9.7

In contrast to most of this chapter's profiles, the title here indicates that the story will reveal the man responsible for the work—that is, will make the "Master of Invisibility" visible. In doing so, the journalist who had previously served long and well as the editor of The New York Times Book Review relies far more on outside sources than is typical of arts profiles, allowing those who have worked for Mike Nichols to offer the sort of appreciative insight that wouldn't be characteristic of the subject in speaking about himself.

FILM
Mike Nichols, Master of Invisibility
By CHARLES McGRATH

Mike Nichols, the subject of a two-week retrospective starting Tuesday at the Museum of Modern Art, is not an obvious choice for a place as artsy and highbrow as the MoMA film department. MoMA retrospectives tend to be awarded to brooding European auteurs— Bernardo Bertolucci and Milos Forman were the last two—and not to commercial Hollywood directors who include on their résumé pop hits like "Working Girl," "The Birdcage" and, just recently, "Charlie Wilson's War."

[As the Times later corrected: The Bernardo Bertolucci retrospective is scheduled to take place next year; it has not already been presented.]

Except for a puzzling string of duds in the mid-'70s, almost all of Mr. Nichols's movies have made money, and a few, like "The Graduate" and "Carnal Knowledge," have been recognized as cultural landmarks. But because of their commercial shimmer, their way of eliciting exceptional performances by top-of-the-line stars, it's sometimes hard to say what makes a Nichols movie a Nichols movie. They seem like vehicles for actors, not the director, whose stamp is in leaving almost no trace of himself.

"If you want to be a legend, God help you, it's so easy," Mr. Nichols said the other day over coffee in his Times Square office. "You just do one thing. You can be the master of suspense, say. But if you want to be as invisible as is practical, then it's fun to do a lot of different things."

If his movies have a common denominator, it's probably their intelligence and, though Mr. Nichols doesn't think of himself as a writer, their writerly attention to detail. They're almost invariably based on good scripts, from which he extracts extra layers of nuance. The organizer of the retrospective, Rajendra Roy, the chief curator of film at MoMA, said: "Here is a guy who is in some ways quintessentially

Published: April 12, 2009.

Hollywood, and yet you can see in his movies a consistent through-line. He's an example of how popular cinema can be vision based."

Nora Ephron, who wrote the script for Mr. Nichols's movie "Heartburn" and co-wrote his film "Silkwood," said recently: "It's supposed to be a given that Mike doesn't have the visual style of, say, a Scorsese. But that isn't fair. Mike doesn't use the camera in a flamboyant way, but he has a style just the way a writer who's crystal clear has a style. He has an almost invisible fluidity."

She added: "One of the main things about Mike's movies is that, with a few exceptions, they're all really smart movies about smart people. They're about something. And he's funny. You're certainly not going to lose a joke. And if there's one hidden, he'll find it."

Mr. Nichols is now 77 but hardly slowing down. Among the possible projects on his plate are movies based on scripts by David Mamet and Tony Kushner and a theatrical revival of a Harold Pinter play. He is beginning to think about simplifying and de-accessioning, though.

He's unloading his horses, for example. He used to own 150 but is now down to 6, and they're "on the way out," he promised. He also doesn't listen much anymore to his classical record collection.

"As a young man I got to a bad stage where I knew every recording of every piece," he said. "But I spoiled it. I was a pseudo-expert without any real knowledge."

"Until about a week ago I thought 'Vesti la giubba' meant 'clothe the Jew,' " he added, referring to the famous aria in which Pagliacci sings about putting on his clown costume. "So I came to love silence, because it's so rare, and it's now my favorite aural condition."

[As The Times later corrected: The character Canio sings the aria, not Pagliacci. "Pagliacci" is the name of the opera in which the aria appears.]

Still boyish looking, Mr. Nichols retains an impish grin and the deadpan, quicksilver wit that for a while made him and Elaine May the most innovative comedians in the United States. Paragraphs spill out of him as if outlined: the three reasons for this, the four most important examples of that. And Mr. Nichols's greatest improvisation is still himself. He wakes up every morning in his Fifth Avenue apartment, collects himself and, wearing a wig and paste-on eyebrows, plays a character called Mike Nichols.

He was born Michael Igor Peschkowsky, the son of a White Russian doctor who emigrated to Berlin after the Russian revolution, and he arrived in New York in 1939, at the age of 7, permanently hairless (a reaction to whooping cough vaccine) and with almost no English. All he could say was: "I do not speak English" and "Please, do not kiss me." He enrolled at the Dalton School, where an early classmate was Buck Henry, and set about cultivating what he calls his "immigrant's ear."

"Semiconsciously I was thinking all the time: 'How do they do it? Let me listen,' " he recalled, and added: "I'll tell you the most extreme example of immigrant's ear in all of Western civilization.

My grandfather, Gustav Landauer, was quite a well-known writer in Germany. He was also very political, and he was part of the two-week provisional Weimar government after the kaiser fell. When the government fell, he was taken to the police station and beaten to death. His best friend, who was also in the government, escaped, made his way to Sante Fe, changed his name to B. Traven and wrote 'The Treasure of the Sierra Madre.' That's the ur-immigrant story."

Mr. Nichols's story is scarcely less dramatic. His father died when he was 12, plunging the family into genteel poverty. Lonely and self-conscious about his looks, he found solace in the movies and theater, thanks in part to the generosity of Sol Hurok, who had been one of his father's patients.

He attended the University of Chicago, floundered a bit, and then was heaped with undreamed-of success, first with Ms. May, whom he met in college (along with Susan Sontag and Ed Asner) and next as a theater director. His string of Broadway hits (including "The Odd Couple" and "Spamalot") may be even more remarkable than his movie record, and Mr. Nichols is one of very few in the performing arts to score the grand slam of major American entertainment awards: he has a Grammy, an Oscar, four Emmys and eight Tonys. He is a shrewd dealmaker, and he has been rewarded like a foundling prince, so that along the way there were countless girlfriends, multiple wives (Diane Sawyer, to whom he has been married since 1988, is his fourth), paintings, cars, a stable.

The only thing he doesn't have enough of anymore is time. He used to love to develop a play out of town, then close it down and put it aside for a few months. "Everything gets simpler on the shelf," he said. He also recalled, with amazement, how long he was allowed to work on "The Graduate," which he directed when he was in his mid-30s.

"We prepared that film for about a year," he said. "They gave us a little bit of money—about three million bucks—and we rented some space out at Paramount and went to our bungalows every day. I remember one day the art director came and said that when Mrs. Robinson got undressed maybe we should see the marks from the straps of her bathing suit. That was a day's work—time just spent soaking yourself in a subject."

He and Buck Henry, the screenwriter, spent three or four weeks working just on the famous montage sequence in "The Graduate," he said, and he added: "It's painful and hard to remember now how long and how carefully we worked. I really do think it's important to sit with a text for as long as you can afford to, reading and talking and doing what I call 'naming things,' which is just explaining what happens in every scene. Now you have to do it all in your head, and you have to do it pretty damn fast, because nobody's going to pay you to do prep. You're going to have to do it on your own time. It can be done, of course, but it's just much harder—unless you're Buñuel, and I think about him pretty much every day. You have to look for a way to free yourself, and he had the best conceivable way: he just jumped to the surreal."

Ms. Ephron compared Mr. Nichols's way of preparing to psychoanalysis. "You sit there for days and days," she said, "and he keeps asking questions. What is this scene in the movie about? What does it remind you of? You free associate. And eventually you figure it out."

Mr. Nichols is a great believer in the single big idea, the controlling metaphor or idea that defines a picture—the notion that Benjamin in "The Graduate," for example, is on a conveyor belt, just like his suitcase. But he is also like a psychoanalyst in that he trusts a lot in the unconscious. The point of all the preparation, he said, is to get to the point where you're surprised. And, he added, "You want to keep doing it until you get to the thing nobody could have planned."

The famous ending of "The Graduate," for example, came about because as it came time to film the scene where Dustin Hoffman and Katharine Ross get on the bus, Mr. Nichols found himself growing unaccountably irritable. "I told Dustin and Katharine, 'Look, we've got traffic blocked for 20 blocks, we've got a police escort, we can't do this over and over. Get on the bus and laugh, God damn it.' I remember thinking, What the hell is wrong with me? I've gone nuts. The next day I looked at what we'd shot and went, 'Oh my God, here's the end of the movie: they're terrified.' My unconscious did that. I learned it as it happened."

During the filming of "Angels in America" for HBO, he recalled, he was amazed by Meryl Streep. "I said to her, 'How did you ever think of making Ethel Rosenberg funny?' And she said, 'Oh, you never know what you're going to do until you do it.' That's it. That sentence says it all, and it's what happens when you're in the very highest realms of this stuff. The director can't make it happen. It's about all being in the same place and being moved by the way each of your imaginations kindles everyone else."

Ms. Streep said: "What makes Mike so great is one of the hardest things for people temperamentally drawn to directing. People who direct tend to want to be in control, and Mike's gift is knowing when to take his hands off and just let it happen. A lot of directors are still dealing with the text when you're on the set. Mike has done all that beforehand, so when you get on the set you feel it's a secure world where all the architecture is in place. You can jump as hard as you want and the floor won't give way."

Mr. Nichols said he had to keep reminding himself how new his profession was. "Movie acting was invented less than 100 years ago—movie acting with sound," he explained. "You know how Harold Bloom says that Shakespeare invented us? It's a fascinating idea, and you can go quite far with it. You could say that it's in talking movies that inner life begins to appear. You can see things happen to the faces of people that were neither planned nor rehearsed. This is what Garbo was such a master of: actual thoughts that had not occurred before that particular take. And you can see this taking tremendous leaps with Brando and Clift and then with Streep."

He added: "The greatest thrill is that moment when a thousand people are sitting in the dark, looking at the same scene, and they are all apprehending something that has not been spoken. That's the thrill of it, the miracle—that's what holds us to movies forever. It's what we wish we could do in real life. We all see something and understand it together, and nobody has to say a word. There's a good reason that the very best sound an audience can make—in both the theater and the movies—is no sound at all, just absolute silence."

Selection 9.8

It's fairly easy to grab readers with a profile of someone they're already interested in; the bigger challenge is pulling them into the story of a subject whose name they don't know. In contrast with the longer pieces in this section, fledgling critics might more often find themselves writing shorter, single-source profiles (such as this one by a veteran Times reporter).

Yale Senior, a Vietnam Memorial and a Few Ironies
By B. DRUMMOND AYRES JR.

"I don't even know how to draft yet," said Maya Ying Lin with a laugh, enjoying one of the many ironies in her first place finish in the national competition to design a memorial to veterans of the Vietnam war.

She held up the winning entry. It was a soft pastel, a landscape of subtle greens, with a simple, black, V-shaped wall tucked gently into the side of a slight rise.

Miss Lin, a slight first-generation American of Chinese parentage, had come up with what seemed more a work of modern art than a concept for a $7 million monument to be situated on the mall near the Lincoln Memorial.

Nevertheless, a few weeks ago the Vietnam Veterans Memorial Fund found her concept the best of the 1,421 contest entries submitted and awarded her the $20,000 contest prize. She arrived in Washington a week or so ago, found a walk-up apartment in Georgetown to share with some friends, and now is working on the final design.

Not Trained Architect
When the contest officials made their decision earlier this spring, they did not know that Miss Lin was not a trained architect. They discovered that she was, instead, a 21-year-old senior at Yale University, about to graduate with a bachelor's degree in architecture, but with several years of graduate work and several years of apprenticeship still ahead before she could put "architect" after her name.

Published: June 29, 1981.

The officials found, too, that the Vietnam war was not one of the big issues in her life. She was too young for that.

And, finally, they learned that when she submitted her memorial concept for a classwork grade at Yale, she was awarded a "B."

"The classroom job was a little sloppy," she explained. Then, a smile creasing her face, she added, "My professor entered the war memorial contest, too."

Of course, none of that was important to the contest officials; it was only subsequently ironic. What they were looking for was a design that honored the 57,692 dead of the Vietnam war without making a political or military statement about the war's controversial nature.

They rejected concepts that were heroic, concepts that were partisan, even a concept that was, basically, a helicopter pad. Then, strolling about the giant government aircraft hangar in which the 1,421 designs were displayed, they came upon Miss Lin's pastel and were captured.

"It is uniquely horizontal, entering the earth rather than piercing the sky," the contest officials said in their statement of acceptance, alluding to the nature of most monuments in this city.

"This is," they continued, "very much a memorial of our own times, one that could not have been achieved in another time or place."

Many of the nation's architecture critics agree. The Lin design has been highly praised.

As for Miss Lin, she is taking it all in stride, pleased and enjoying herself, but far from overcome by sudden fame. "I liked my idea," she said, self-assured despite her youth and inexperience. "That's why I entered the contest."

Miss Lin did not go to college with an architecture career in mind. "I didn't really know what I wanted to be," she said. "I just knew I wanted to be in some profession since I'd grown up as a 'faculty brat.'"

Miss Lin's father and mother are both professors at Ohio University in Athens, where she was born. Her father, Henry Huan Lin, is dean of fine arts and her mother, Julia Chang Lin, teaches English and Oriental literature. Both left China shortly after World War II, Mrs. Lin to attend Smith College on a scholarship, Mr. Lin to escape possible imprisonment by the conquering Chinese Communist forces.

"My father's family was fairly prominent," Miss Lin said, adding with a chuckle, "I think way back there were some relatives who were architects. Some day, I'd like to visit China."

Miss Lin's parents did not meet until after they arrived in the United States. Besides Miss Lin, they have a son, Tan, a 24-year-old poet who recently graduated from Columbia University and resides in New York.

Took Many Courses

Since she was unsure about choosing a career when she arrived at Yale, Miss Lin initially signed up for a wide array of courses, including a number in photography. "It's something I really enjoy," she said, "along with cooking and making my own clothes which, incidentally, I find I like better than anything I can buy." So how did she come to settle, in the end, upon architecture as a major?

"One day," she recalled, "I was just staring up at the ceiling, at all the lines and painting on it and the like, and, suddenly, I decided I was going to be an architect. Just like that."

While a number of architecture courses were required in her major, she was also required to balance her curriculum with liberal arts and other general courses. "An undergraduate architecture major just scratches the surface of being an architect," she said. She plans to spend her $20,000 in prize money to continue her studies at Yale after working here on the memorial plan.

While in Europe several summers ago, Miss Lin found herself fascinated by the elaborate monuments and memorials in many city cemeteries. Then, last year, someone suggested to the architecture department at Yale that her class take a seminar in funerary architecture.

"I thought it was a great idea," she recalled. "I guess, like a lot of people, I've always been intrigued with death and man's relation to it."

To Draw Passers-By

As one of the projects in the architecture course, Miss Lin was required to design a memorial to World War III. She came up with a brooding mound, shot through with dark, circuitous passages and tunnels, a "journey to an awareness of death, one meant to terrify," as she puts it.

While her class was still studying funerary architecture, word arrived that Congress had authorized use of a two-acre site a few hundred yards northeast of the Lincoln Memorial for a Vietnam war memorial. It was to be built with public donations. The design would be chosen in a national competition, much as designs were chosen for the United States Capitol and the Washington Monument.

At the urging of their professor, Andy Burr, Miss Lin and her classmates decided to enter the competition. In the end, however, only she and professor actually submitted entries.

Miss Lin says she made her memorial V-shaped and burrowed it slightly into the ground, up to about 10 feet at the apex, to draw passers-by. "The V-shape doesn't have anything to do with 'Vietnam' or 'victory' or 'veterans,' " she explained. "I hate war, all war. But Vietnam was something I only remember as a child. There's no particular great issue about it for me."

Once drawn into the memorial, the visitor will be confronted, left and right, by polished black walls of granite, each 200 feet long. On the walls, in chronological order, will be the names of the 57,692 Americans who died in Vietnam.

The memorial is scheduled to be dedicated on Veterans Day 1982.

MAKING**CONNECTIONS**

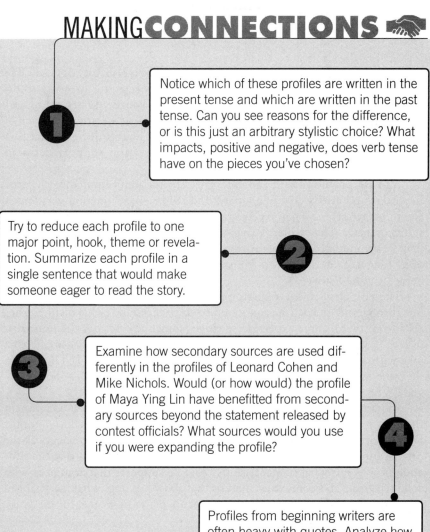

1 Notice which of these profiles are written in the present tense and which are written in the past tense. Can you see reasons for the difference, or is this just an arbitrary stylistic choice? What impacts, positive and negative, does verb tense have on the pieces you've chosen?

2 Try to reduce each profile to one major point, hook, theme or revelation. Summarize each profile in a single sentence that would make someone eager to read the story.

3 Examine how secondary sources are used differently in the profiles of Leonard Cohen and Mike Nichols. Would (or how would) the profile of Maya Ying Lin have benefitted from secondary sources beyond the statement released by contest officials? What sources would you use if you were expanding the profile?

4 Profiles from beginning writers are often heavy with quotes. Analyze how one of these profiles reveals personality through descriptive detail. What can the writer tell the reader that the quotes can't?

trend and enterprise pieces

THIS LAST CHAPTER IS SOMETHING OF A CATCH-ALL, incorporating stories that require the arts reporter or critic to do some research and to interview more than one source. Many trend and enterprise stories in particular reflect the journalist's critical acumen—they simply wouldn't exist if the arts journalist hadn't decided that this was a significant trend or development, an assertion supported by an argument.

As with profiles, trend and enterprise stories aren't limited to the arts. Reporters and critics covering an arts and culture beat function very much like other reporters: They receive tips. They cultivate sources (and sources cultivate them). They collect string—the journalistic adage for saving strands they've accumulated on other stories until that ball of string becomes a story of its own (e.g., quotes saved from interviews for various profiles finding a home in a trend story).

The basic elements of trend stories in the arts pages are the same ones you'll find throughout journalism: some contextual background (what distinguishes now from then), some expert perspective (somebody besides the journalist to say, "Yes, this *is* a trend), some anecdotal examples (in journalism, here's a joke with a ring of truth: Two is a coincidence; three is a trend). Ultimately, the trend must have some significance, an answer to the questions "So what?" and "Who cares?"

But arts features, like all arts stories, typically have a critical component that distinguishes them from straight reportage. Thus, when media columnist David Carr reports that live performance has supplanted recordings as the driving force in a musician's career, he is making the argument that the situation now is not what it was recently. And he supports that argument with solid reporting and contextual analysis that show not only what has changed but why it has, evaluating how the changes are better or worse (for the artist, for the consumer, for the industry).

When Margo Jefferson, a Pulitzer Prize–winning critic (and former op-ed columnist) for The Times, reports on the decline in African-American theater in Los Angeles, showing the bicoastal reach of The Times' cultural coverage, she is not merely detailing a trend, she is arguing that it matters, and why it matters.

Even a comparatively straightforward news story such as music industry reporter Jeff Leeds's piece on Radiohead's revolutionary marketing of music straight to consumers, for whatever the listener wishes to pay, has a strong element of critical context. This isn't simply a story about Radiohead; it's about a music industry in upheaval, and what the example of one very popular band might mean for the marketing of popular music in general. As a beat reporter rather than a critic, Leeds doesn't provide an evaluative component, but offers more contextual analysis than you'll find in straight reporting.

One difference between The Times and most of the nation's other news outlets is that The Times has sufficient resources to have both critics who focus on various forms of arts and culture—music, books, films, television, etc.—and reporters whose beat is the music, publishing, movie or television industry. For journalists employed elsewhere, if your beat is popular music, you might well be responsible for news stories and business analysis as well as reviews and profiles.

Quality arts reporting from The Times could fill an entire volume of its own. What's important to remember is that critics who work for a news organization remain reporters as well, yet they don't suspend their critical faculties or analytical responsibilities when reporting a story. Critics are always critics; reporters are always reporters. Journalists who cover an entire arts and culture beat function as both, drawing from the professional resources of each role as the assignment demands.

Selection 10.1

Because The Times is richer in cultural resources than any other newspaper (or site) in the country, it can divide beats among critics and reporters. Motoko Rich writes trend stories, news stories and profiles on the books beat, but not reviews. Still, this piece of arts journalism on the state of literary journalism definitely has a point of view—just see who gets the last word. But she allows a full range of perspectives, showing that this is not an issue with two sides, but many sides. And look how she humanizes her story. Even if you think you're writing about ideas, issues or trends, remember the first principle of feature writing: People want to read about people.

Are Book Reviewers Out of Print?
By MOTOKO RICH

Last year Dan Wickett, a former quality-control manager for a car-parts maker, wrote 95 book reviews on his blog, Emerging Writers Network (emergingwriters.typepad.com/), singlehandedly compiling almost half as many reviews as appeared in all of the book pages of The Atlanta Journal-Constitution.

Published: May 2, 2007.

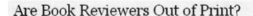

Are Book Reviewers Out of Print?

By MOTOKO RICH
Published: May 2, 2007

Correction Appended

Last year Dan Wickett, a former quality-control manager for a car-parts maker, wrote 95 book reviews on his blog, Emerging Writers Network (emergingwriters.typepad.com/), singlehandedly compiling almost half as many reviews as appeared in all of the book pages of The Atlanta Journal-Constitution.

🔍 Enlarge This Image

The Los Angeles Times recently merged its book review into a new section combining the review with the Sunday opinion pages.

Readers' Opinions

Forum: Book News and Reviews

Mr. Wickett has now quit the automotive industry and started a nonprofit organization that supports literary journals and writers-in-residence programs, giving him more time to devote to his literary blog. The Atlanta Journal-Constitution, meanwhile, has recently eliminated the job of its book editor, leading many fans to worry that book coverage will soon be provided mostly by wire services and reprints from national papers.

The decision in Atlanta — in which book reviews will now be overseen by one editor responsible for virtually all arts coverage — comes after a string of changes at book reviews across the country. The Los Angeles Times recently merged its once stand-alone book review into a new section combining the review with the paper's Sunday opinion pages, effectively cutting the number of pages devoted to books to 10 from 12. Last

The New York Times

Mr. Wickett has now quit the automotive industry and started a nonprofit organization that supports literary journals and writers-in-residence programs, giving him more time to devote to his literary blog. The Atlanta Journal-Constitution, meanwhile, has recently eliminated the job of its book editor, leading many fans to worry that book coverage will soon be provided mostly by wire services and reprints from national papers.

The decision in Atlanta—in which book reviews will now be overseen by one editor responsible for virtually all arts coverage—comes after a string of changes at book reviews across the country. The Los Angeles Times recently merged its once stand-alone book review into a new section combining the review with the paper's

Sunday opinion pages, effectively cutting the number of pages devoted
to books to 10 from 12. Last year The San Francisco Chronicle's book
review went from six pages to four. All across the country, newspapers
are cutting book sections or running more reprints of reviews from
wire services or larger papers.

   To some authors and critics, these moves amount to yet one
more nail in the coffin of literary culture. But some publishers and
literary bloggers—not surprisingly—see it as an inevitable transition toward a new, more democratic literary landscape where anyone
can comment on books. In recent years, dozens of sites, including Bookslut.com, The Elegant Variation (marksarvas.blogs.com/
elegvar/), maudnewton.com, Beatrice.com and the Syntax of Things
(syntaxofthings.typepad.com), have been offering a mix of book news,
debates, interviews and reviews, often on subjects not generally covered by newspaper book sections.

   For those who are used to the old way, it's a tough evolution.
"Like anything new, it's difficult for authors and agents to understand
when we say, 'I'm sorry, you're not going to be in The New York Times
or The Chicago Tribune, but you are going to be at curledup.com,' "
said Trish Todd, editor-in-chief of Touchstone Fireside, an imprint of
Simon & Schuster. "But we think that's the wave of the future."

   Obviously, the changes at newspaper book reviews reflect the
broader challenges faced by newspapers in general, as advertisement
revenues decline, and readers decamp to the Internet. But some writers (and readers) question whether economics should be the only driving factor. Newspapers like The Atlanta Journal-Constitution could
run book reviews "as a public service, and the fact of the matter is that
they are unwilling to," said Richard Ford, the Pulitzer Prize–winning
novelist.

   "I think the reviewing function as it is thoroughly taken up by
newspapers is vital," he continued, "in the same way that literature
itself is vital."

   Mr. Ford is one of more than 120 writers who have signed
a petition to save the job of Teresa Weaver, The Atlanta Journal-
Constitution's book editor. The petition, sponsored by the National
Book Critics Circle, comes as part of the organization's effort to save
imperiled book coverage generally. "We will continue to use freelancers, established news services and our staff to provide stories about
books of interest to our readers and the local literary community,"
said Mary Dugenske, a spokeswoman for the newspaper, in an e-mail
message.

   Coming as it does at a time when newspaper book reviews are
endangered, many writers, publishers and critics worry that the spread
of literary blogs will be seen as compensation for more traditional
coverage. "We have a lot of opinions in our world," said John Freeman, president of the National Book Critics Circle. "What we need is

more mediation and reflection, which is why newspapers and literary journals are so important."

Edward Champion, who writes about books on his blog, Return of the Reluctant (edrants.com), said that literary blogs responded to the "often stodgy and pretentious tone" of traditional reviews.

The brute fact is that while authors and publishers may want long and considered responses to their work, sometimes what they most need is attention. Last year, when Random House published "This Is Not Chick Lit," a story collection with contributions from authors like Jennifer Egan and Curtis Sittenfeld, it generated a lot of online chatter as various bloggers debated whether the book was pretentious or a welcome correction to an oversubscribed genre. "All the slow but steady online exposure helped build a grass-roots thing," said Julia Cheiffetz, the book's editor at Random House, who noted that "This Is Not Chick Lit" is now in its sixth printing with 45,000 copies in print.

But while online buzz can help some books, newspapers can pique the interest of a general reader, said Oscar Villalon, books editor at The San Francisco Chronicle. Blogs, he said, are "not mass media." The Chronicle, for example, he said, has a circulation of nearly 500,000, a number not many blogs can achieve.

On the other hand, committed readers who take the time to find a literary blog may be more likely than a casual reader of the Sunday newspaper to buy a book. "I know that everyone who comes to my site is interested in books," said Mark Sarvas, editor of The Elegant Variation, a literary blog that publishes lengthy reviews.

And newspaper book reviews, which are often accused of hewing too closely to "safe choices," could learn something from the more freewheeling approach of some of the book blogs, said David L. Ulin, who edits the book review at The Los Angeles Times.

"One of the troubles with mainstream print criticism is that people can be too polite," Mr. Ulin said. "I feel like an aspect of the gloves-off nature of blogs is something that we could all learn from, not in an irresponsible way, but in a wear-your-likes-and-dislikes-on-your-sleeves kind of way."

Maud Newton, who has been writing a literary blog since 2002, said she has the freedom to follow obsessions like, say, Mark Twain in a way that a newspaper book review could not, unless there was a current book on the subject. But she would never consider what she does a replacement for more traditional book reviews.

"I find it kind of naïve and misguided to be a triumphalist blogger," Ms. Newton said. "But I also find it kind of silly when people in the print media bash blogs as a general category, because I think the people are doing very, very different things."

One thing that regional newspapers in particular can do is highlight local authors. "While I'm all for the literary bloggers, and I think the more people that write about books the better, they're not necessarily as regionally focused as knowledgeable, experienced long-term editors in the South or Midwest or anywhere where the most important writers come from," said Sam Tanenhaus, the editor of The New York Times Book Review.

Many local authors view the decision at The Atlanta Journal-Constitution as a betrayal of important local coverage.

"With the removal of its cultural critics, Atlanta is surrendering again," wrote Melissa Fay Greene, author of "Praying for Sheetrock" in an e-mail message. "We all lose, you know, not just Atlantans, with the disappearance from the scene of a literate intelligence."

Of course literary bloggers argue that they do provide a multiplicity of voices. But some authors distrust those voices. Mr. Ford, who has never looked at a literary blog, said he wanted the judgment and filter that he believed a newspaper book editor could provide. "Newspapers, by having institutional backing, have a responsible relationship not only to their publisher but to their readership," Mr. Ford said, "in a way that some guy sitting in his basement in Terre Haute maybe doesn't."

Selection 10.2

Like Motoko Rich with the publishing industry, former Times reporter Jeff Leeds covered the music industry but did not review music. This is the closest piece in this section to a straight news story, yet its speculation about the implications for the music industry (particularly in the last paragraph) makes this a story about more than a new Radiohead release. Look at the range of sources he interviews in his reporting. Are all necessary perspectives represented? The reference to a hit by the Clash in the lead engages the interest in rock fans without confusing those unfamiliar with the lyric.

Radiohead to Let Fans Decide
What to Pay for Its New Album
By JEFF LEEDS

LOS ANGELES, Oct. 1—Should they stay or should they go now?

It is the question of the moment in music circles, where a short but growing list of recording stars that includes Prince, Madonna, Nine Inch Nails and—as of Sunday night—Radiohead have indicated their willingness to depart from the conventions of music sales and the control of the four multinational corporations that dominate the industry.

Published: October 2, 2007.

In the latest instance the members of Radiohead, the respected British rock act, said that the band would sell its new album, at least initially, exclusively as a digital download and allow fans to decide how much to pay for it, if anything. In a statement yesterday, the band said it had begun taking orders for the album, "In Rainbows," which will be available beginning Oct. 10.

The band also said it expected a conventional CD release of the album early next year, though Radiohead, which fulfilled its contract with the music giant EMI Group with the delivery of the 2003 album "Hail to the Thief," has yet to settle on specifics. An array of labels of various sizes are said to be on the hunt for the rights to distribute the album, though the value of such a deal for a record company could be reduced if the band elects to keep the digital sales entirely to itself, leaving only sales of the old-fashioned plastic CD.

For now, the band said it would also sell an expansive (and expensive) physical version of the album—including two vinyl LPs and an expanded CD package with extra new songs and photographs—through its Web site, radiohead.com, for 40 pounds (about $82).

The biggest buzz, though, came from the band's digital pricing plan, which represents a break from the industry standard established by Apple's iTunes service, the leading digital-music retailer, which generally sells individual songs for 99 cents apiece, and complete albums for $10 to $12. Though the band had been an early adopter of online marketing, it didn't sell its recordings on iTunes, a stance that arose from its desire to sell its albums in their entirety.

In Radiohead's plan, fans will choose their own price for the digital version of the 10-song "In Rainbows," which it said would be sold as a download without copy restriction software, known as digital-rights management. In effect, the band is asking fans to establish a monetary value for music, even when widespread piracy means that it would be available free.

Early reaction suggested that listeners would pay, but less than they would for a CD in stores. The blog Idolator.com carried a poll in which the plurality of voters—almost 40 percent—said they would pay from $2.05 to $10.12.

Radiohead is making a subtle dig at the iTunes pricing model, a move that drew plaudits from some record executives, who have pressed Apple to offer a mix of prices. Radiohead is introducing "variable pricing to the extreme," said one executive, who requested anonymity because he had not been authorized to speak about the band's plans.

"It'll be interesting to see what Radiohead's uber-fans actually pay," said Josh Deutsch, chairman of the upstart Downtown Records label. "It's pretty hard to beat free." Mr. Deutsch said it was difficult to draw conclusions from the decision: "Having said that, it does suggest that the record companies don't have the same amount of control they once had over distribution."

Whether Radiohead's move will lead to a shift for the industry is far from clear. In taking over more of its own sales, the band risks losing what connection it has with the mass market and turning into a niche operation. Indeed, not all artists choose to depart the major-label structure when the opportunity arises—Bruce Springsteen, for one, decided to renew his relationship with Sony Music's Columbia label when his contract was near expiration.

Selection 10.3

The prolific, culturally eclectic David Carr serves as the media columnist in the Monday business section of The Times, but he has also blogged (on Web site video as well as in print) during Oscar season, writes profiles for the arts section and pieces for The New York Times Magazine and often indulges his interest in popular music. This business column from the Bonnaroo music festival suggests that he attended as a fan as well as a journalist: He plainly aligns himself with artists forging a new direction rather than an industry in decline and moves deftly between the specifics of the festival he attended and an analysis of the larger industry issues. Again, examine the range of the reporting and the critical context within which it is set.

THE MEDIA EQUATION
Live Music Thrives as CDs Fade
By DAVID CARR

A little over a week ago, Patterson Hood, a guitarist and singer in the Drive-By Truckers, stood in front of a sleepy but amped noon crowd at Bonnaroo, the music festival in Manchester, Tenn., explaining profanely that it was time to, um, wake up. As he kicked into "The Righteous Path," a song from the group's new-ish record "Brighter Than Creation's Dark," it was if the space in front of him was filled with sunburned bobble-heads, each bouncing in unison to every word: "Trying to hold steady on the righteous path, 80 miles an hour with a worn-out map."

Like much of Bonnaroo, the set was a display of the fealty between band and audience so thunderous that you barely hear the sound of a dying business.

Yes, the traditional music industry is in the tank—record sales are off another 10 percent this year and the Virgin Megastore in Times Square is closing, according to a Reuters report, joining a host of other

Published: June 23, 2008.

record stores. That would seem to be bad news all around for music fans—70,000 of whom showed up in this remote place to watch 158 bands play—and for Mr. Hood and his band.

Not so, he says.

"The collapse of the record business has been good for us, if anything. It's leveled the playing field in a way where we can keep slugging it out and finding our fans," he said while toweling himself off after the set.

With their epic Southern rock sounds whose influences range from William Faulkner to Lynyrd Skynyrd and the kind of musicians who don't live for a photo shoot, the Drive-By Truckers were never going to be record industry darlings. As it is, they have found a sustainable, blue-collar business model of rock stardom in which selling concert tickets and T-shirts have replaced selling CDs.

"Thank God they can't download those," said Mr. Hood, the son of the famed Muscle Shoals Sound Studio bassist David Hood. "They follow us from city to city, see the shows, get drunk and buy shirts."

After investing early and continuously in the Web, the Drive-By Truckers have a MySpace page with 37,000 friends, offering four songs from "Brighter Than Creation's Dark" with almost 800,000 downloads alongside a touring schedule that would put James Brown in his prime to shame. This week, they will be in five cities and two countries (Canada, remember?).

Before file sharing tipped over the music business, bands used to tour in support of a record. Now they tour to get the dough to make a record. Cheap recording technology, along with all manner of electronic distribution, means that bands don't need to sign with a giant recording label to get their music out there.

It has been going on a while. Ani DiFranco, the singer/songwriter, saw the future back in 1991 and skipped signing with a label, making her own records instead. "She would tour, endlessly, in her Volkswagen bug, and have two envelopes, one for the gig money and one for the record money," said Scot Fisher, the manager and president of Righteous Babe Records, the label they created.

There are still pop acts that drop a record from on high with the help of a big label and see touring as a nuisance, but Bonnaroo in particular is a place where bands and fans have a much closer relationship, with direct sales of merchandise and recorded product. It can make for intimate ties: a woman in a cowboy hat who was carpeted with tattoos was asked the name of a particular song. "I don't know what the name is, but I know who it's about," she said, with a wink.

In a sure sign of détente between the old and new faces of the business, Metallica, which very publicly went after file-sharers with corrosive rhetoric and aggressive legal tactics, showed up at Bonnaroo.

Back in the day, Metallica had good facts—downloaders were stealing their work—and a bad argument, one that could not stand up to a shift in paradigm where many fans walk around with their entire music collection in a shirt pocket. "We support live music," the band's singer and guitarist, James Hetfield, told the cheering hordes.

Established bands like Metallica and Pearl Jam, which also played Bonnaroo, may have taken some hits on overall sales. But the lower (iTunes) and nonexistent (file-sharing) profit margins on recorded product are a little easier to take, because ticket prices have doubled in the last 10 years, according to Gary Bongiovanni, editor in chief of Pollstar, a trade magazine that covers the live music industry.

For some bands, like the jam band Umphrey's McGee, some music sales are a direct offshoot of the shows. The band reserves five tickets at every show for people who want to tape it and also records every set with room mikes and the sound board. Three-disc sets are burned on the spot and sold for $20. (Other bands have taken to popping the evening's performance onto a thumb drive and selling that to departing fans.)

"If we can break even on a recording, then the rest of the business will take care of itself," said Joel Cummins, the keyboard player in the band. "I think that the Internet gives us a way of getting connected with our fans. We get to make the kind of music we like—it's definitely a little more complicated than just three chords and the truth—and use a long-tail business model to find and play for people who want to see what we can do live."

The buy-share-trade dynamic was visible all over Bonnaroo, whether it was food, space in the tent or other substances. To one crusty old attendee, it felt a bit like the Yippie camp-in at Spokane that he stumbled onto back in 1974. (Speaking of which, when did tie-dye come back, and how can we make it go away again?)

But for musicians, the network is all part of the business. Selling out, once the death knell for bands seeking credibility, has now become an end in itself.

"This is by far our best record, if you ask me, so the tickets for shows are doing really well," said Mr. Hood, sounding very much like an old label hand. "But then, the gas prices are killing us."

Selection 10.4

Here is the most explicit example within this section of a critical point of view within a reported piece, as the Pulitzer Prize–winning critic and columnist obviously considers it a crucial matter of cultural significance far beyond Los Angeles (since plenty of theater companies in other cities face similar challenges) to find answers to the questions in the headline (which she didn't write) and the lead (which she did). If the "distress" she expresses in the first person weren't enough, the last paragraph leaves no doubt where her sympathies lie.

Will Theater in Los Angeles Fade to White?

By MARGO JEFFERSON

How does a majority theater support minority playwrights?

You probably stumbled over the phrase "majority theater." It is awkward, but no more awkward than "minority playwrights"; it's just unfamiliar. Majority groups don't need such ID tags. They're considered the norm.

In traditional mainstream theater, that "majority" consists of playwrights, producers and directors who are largely white, male, middle class and free of physical disabilities. So let's rephrase the question: how do mainstream theaters make space for all those minorities, those "others" whose lives are rarely shown on their stages?

Recently, this familiar question has aggressively reared its head in Los Angeles. Michael Ritchie, the new artistic director of the powerful Center Theater Group, announced that starting in July, four programs devoted to minority play development would be eliminated: Other Voices (for the disabled), the Latino Theater Initiative, the Asian Theater Workshop and the Blacksmyths Theater Lab. These labs were founded in the 1980's and 90's by Mr. Ritchie's predecessor, Gordon Davidson, and their goal was to commission and develop new works.

The Center Theater Group is made up of the 750-seat Mark Taper Forum, the 2,000-seat Ahmanson Theater and the Kirk Douglas, a new 300-seat theater devoted to new plays in Culver City. In explaining his decision, Mr. Ritchie said the programs were not effective in getting plays onstage, generating only dead-end readings and workshops. Those are "a luxury we can no longer afford," he said. "We have to focus on production and focus less on play development."

Of course no one claims there is only one blueprint for nurturing talent, and Mr. Ritchie insists that he is committed to developing works by minorities. Still, the announcement had a grim symbolic resonance, especially coming shortly after Los Angeles elected its first Latino mayor in more than a century. For the moment, something tangible was being replaced by something hypothetical.

The issue has resonance far beyond the West Coast. What is the role of powerful theaters like the Center Theater Group, or Lincoln Center and the Public Theater in New York, or the Arena Stage in Washington, in developing other voices?

The Cuban-American playwright Eduardo Machado, who got his first big break at the Mark Taper in the early 1990's, says the big nonprofits are not doing enough. Mr. Machado now heads Intar in New York, the only company in the United States devoted to works

Published: August 7, 2005.

in English by Latino writers. Like all small companies, Intar must fight for every arts council dollar it gets. "If none of the minority theaters get city money, isn't it the responsibility of the bigger companies to represent the entire population?" Mr. Machado asked. "They're public institutions, not private enterprises."

After all, if minorities are still marginal in the theater, it's a different story outside the stage door. The majority of Angelenos are not white. And though the majority of Angelenos are women (as are the majority of Americans), inside the theater, women are just one more underrepresented group.

When Ellen Stewart founded the La MaMa Experimental Theater in New York City more than 40 years ago, she wanted to create a truly international center for artists. She calls it a theatrical pot in which no culture melts down. "You put work in and you take work out," she said. "You give others your choices; you get their choices. You infuse each other."

This vision is rarely found in the United States. Chay Yew, the playwright and director who ran the Taper's Asian Theater Workshop and is now out of his job, is right to ask: "Is the theater still doing an effective job of reflecting and representing the world we live in, or is it merely reflecting a select few? If so, we deserve the dwindling, aging audiences."

In Mr. Davidson's time, the Taper mounted six productions a year and the Ahmanson was mainly devoted to touring shows. The theater has grown and its policies have changed. This time, the board wanted an artistic director who could mount 20 or so productions a year. For the 2005–2006 season, six are planned for the Taper, seven for the Ahmanson, and nine for the Kirk Douglas.

The Williamstown Theater Festival in Massachusetts, where Mr. Ritchie was stage manager for years and then artistic director from 1996 through 2004, has long been famous for elegant, crowd-pleasing productions that feature celebrated playwrights (Chekhov, Shaw, Coward, Miller), and star well-known-to-famous actors (Blythe Danner, Gwyneth Paltrow, Sam Waterston, Jesse L. Martin and Kate Burton, Mr. Ritchie's wife). His tenure there has been described as profitable and successful.

The Center Theater Group's offerings this season make Mr. Ritchie's commercial focus very clear. The lineup is tasteful, respectable and very conventional. The Taper season includes works by David Mamet, Alfred Uhry and Chekhov (a "Cherry Orchard" that will star Annette Bening).

The Ahmanson will import brand-name hitmakers like Robert Wilson, Matthew Bourne and Dame Edna. The Web site tells potential ticket buyers that "We are in final negotiations with major British talent" for a production of "The Importance of Being Earnest."

Mr. Ritchie proudly cites two new musicals that he hopes the organization will send to Broadway. One, still in development, involves the music of Kander and Ebb; the other, "The Drowsy Chaperone," is an homage to 1920's Broadway musicals. Clearly this is the "everything old is new again" principle.

The Mark Taper Forum's two world premieres will explore the range of the history play. Robert Schenkkan, best known for the sprawling, romantic "Kentucky Cycle," will be represented by "Lewis and Clark Reach the Euphrates." And Culture Clash, a dynamic trio of Latino writer-actors, will present "Power and Water," a tough-minded look at Los Angeles history. This work, Mr. Ritchie said, represents part of his streamlined new model for play development: "I came to them and told them: you have a slot. I will guarantee you a production. Now let's develop a piece."

The other minority voices will be heard in the small Kirk Douglas. Nilo Cruz, the Pulitzer Prize–winning Cuban-American playwright, is adapting "A Very Old Man With Enormous Wings," a story by Gabriel García Márquez, for young audiences. Another program will be devoted to a group of solo artists. Given the disproportionate number of women and minorities in solo performance, variety should be no problem.

Still, so far, no female playwrights appear on the roster of 22 plays this season, although "The Drowsy Chaperone" does have a female lyricist. Otherwise, as the former head of the Blacksmyths lab, Brian Freeman, observed: "It's jaw-dropping, the sheer number of plays by white men."

Mr. Ritchie insists the doors are still wide open to minority writers. "The difference is, it's one door," he said.

In an ideal world there should be just one door. In the real world, though, that door usually isn't wide enough for minorities or women to pass through until labs and workshops devoted to their work become part of an institution.

The Center Theater Group's minority labs had problems; work too rarely made it to the main stage. And Mr. Ritchie's view of what he called the "slow, meandering process" of play development was shared by some lab veterans. Readings and workshops that lead nowhere can feel like slow torture if the theater's artistic director ignores them.

But Mr. Ritchie didn't have to ignore them. The labs used to hold a yearly festival of readings called "New Plays for Now"; it was supposed to provide the Taper and other interested Los Angeles theaters with plays they could develop.

"Last spring we flagged the plays we thought were most likely for production," Mr. Freeman said. "Michael did not attend a single one. When questioned about it, he said he doesn't believe in readings."

On that point Mr. Ritchie agreed, saying: "I generally don't attend readings. My strength is getting plays from the page to the stage." To which Mr. Freeman responded: "What does that say to actors, directors, audiences? It's about not being in the conversation."

So who is Mr. Ritchie including in the conversation about what gets produced? I find it distressing that Luis Alfaro, who had run the Latino Playwrights Initiative before being made director of new play development, lost his job. And I find it distressing that there is only one minority woman on Mr. Ritchie's artistic staff. No one should have to bear that burden, artistically or practically.

When I asked Mr. Ritchie who else on his staff would be on the lookout for interesting new work by nontraditional writers, he assured me, "Oh, virtually everybody."

More specifically, he promises joint productions with small Los Angeles companies that cultivate new writers, directors and actors. This season, for example, he will join forces with the Robey Theater, a black company, and the Greenway Arts Alliance to produce Thomas Gibbons's "Permanent Collection" at the Kirk Douglas. Mr. Ritchie proudly said: "The idea for us is not to take ownership of the production, but to give those companies greater exposure. The intent is that it's more to their benefit than to ours to do those productions."

Hopefully, such money and exposure will benefit the playwrights and the companies. But this plan is hardly daring. The Robey produced "Permanent Collection," which has had more than 20 productions around the country, last year. And Mr. Gibbons is white.

At this point, I'm sure, some readers are thinking, "Talent is not an equal opportunity employer." It certainly isn't. Most of the plays produced by traditional mainstream theaters are written by white men; many of these plays are terrible. Quality isn't the barrier. Access is. Experience is. Exposure is.

Loy Arcenas is a Filipino-American set designer who has worked for some of the best theaters in the country. He is directing now, at the Ma-Yi Theater in New York, which presents plays by Asian-American writers. "You don't just become a good writer or terrific writer," he said. "You need to be helped. Nurtured. You have to have the ability to fail. The only way you can do that is to be put in the same league as everybody else."

Directors, producers, even audiences need to be nurtured too. Our cultural realities are changing rapidly. How does art map those changes? How do we learn to see the world differently and stretch our imaginations in unexpected ways?

Asked about his theater's place in the city of Los Angeles, where whites now make up only about 30 percent of the population, Mr. Ritchie answered: "Los Angeles is probably the most diverse and vibrant city in America right now. It's to our well-being to be as diverse and vibrant as possible."

Let us hope he lives up to the far more eloquent words of Joseph Papp. Papp's Public Theater helped create a long, still singular tradition of artistic excellence through diversity. Thirty years ago, he wrote: "What fills me with everlasting hope is the diversity of the people who make up this impossible cosmopolis. . . . New York's energy has always come from the bottom of the heap, the minorities . . . the Irish after the potato famine, Italians, Jews, Puerto Ricans. . . . And long before any of them, the blacks. As Shakespeare wisely said, 'the city is the people.' I say amen to that."

Selection 10.5

The headline on this next piece (which the reporter doesn't write; the copy editor does) suggests a paradoxical value judgment, that there's a danger when the "reality" of TV gets too real. Again, the last word proves revelatory, invoking a "delicate balance" rather than coming down hard on either side.

When Reality TV Gets Too Real
By JEREMY W. PETERS

On a recent episode of "Intervention," A&E's documentary series about addiction, no one was stopping Pam, an alcoholic, from driving.

As she made her way to the front door—stopping first at the refrigerator to take a swig of vodka for the road—viewers could hear a producer for the show speak up.

"You have had a lot to drink," the voice from off camera said. "Do you want one of us to drive?"

Pam was indignant. "No, I can drive. I can drive," she mumbled.

She then got into her car, managed a three-point turn out of the parking lot and drove off. The camera crew followed, filming her as she tried to keep her turquoise Pontiac Sunfire between the lines.

Perhaps more than any other program on television now, "Intervention" highlights the sticky situations that reality-show producers can find themselves in as they document unpredictable and unstable subjects or situations. In recent years, producers and networks have increasingly pushed the boundaries of television voyeurism in search of another ratings hit.

At times, this has proved problematic for television networks. There have been several lawsuits related to shows like "Big Brother" and more recently, CBS found itself facing accusations that it had created dangerous working conditions for children in its reality program

---

Published: October 8, 2007.

"Kid Nation," in which children aged 8 to 15 toiled in the New Mexico desert to build a working society on their own.

In the case of reality-TV documentary shows like "Intervention" and the various incarnations of "The Real World" and "Road Rules" on MTV, producers can be witnesses to crimes, raising the question of when they are obligated to step out from behind the camera and intervene.

Sometimes the crimes they film are relatively minor, like underage drinking or fisticuffs. But in other cases, like on "Intervention" and VH1's "Breaking Bonaduce," in which the star, the former child actor Danny Bonaduce, got behind the wheel after he had been drinking and bragged how a car crash would make great television, the program's subjects can put themselves and innocent bystanders at great risk.

And legally, producers are treated like witnesses: they bear no responsibility to intervene.

"The law in the United States doesn't require you to step in and save people," said David Sternbach, counsel for litigation and intellectual property matters for A&E Television Networks. "And it doesn't require you to stop a crime that's in the works."

Often, of course, they have good business reasons not to: people on the edge make for good television. "Intervention" is one of A&E's top shows. This year it has drawn up to two million viewers on its best nights. The premiere of "Kid Nation" attracted 9.1 million viewers but slipped the next week to 7.6 million.

The first season of "Breaking Bonaduce" helped VH1 increase its prime-time ratings in 2005, though they faded in the second season. And a wide following for "Cops," Fox's police ride-along reality show, has kept it on the air since 1989.

A&E said "Intervention," has never been sued. And legal experts said that making a case against it or other documentary programs like it would be difficult because the subjects were being filmed in their own homes, engaging in activities that they would be pursuing regardless of whether a camera crew was there.

"This is their life with me or without me," said Sam Mettler, "Intervention's" creator and executive producer. The program takes other steps, like requiring potential subjects to undergo psychological evaluations and keeping a family member of the addict on call 24 hours a day during filming, to avoid being negligent.

To make a case for negligence, legal experts said, the accusing party would need to prove that the reality program created a situation that put its subjects in jeopardy. A "Big Brother" cast member sued CBS, for example, in 2002 after another cast member with a criminal record held a knife to her throat. CBS settled the case for an undisclosed amount.

When the sister of a woman who appeared on ABC's "Extreme Makeover" committed suicide in 2004, the contestant sued the network for wrongful death and other charges. The contestant, who was competing to win free plastic surgery but lost, claimed that her sister had felt so guilty about mocking her appearance on the program that she killed herself. ABC settled the case for an undisclosed amount last year.

But if a subject on a show like "Intervention" or Fox's "Cops" series were to injure someone while engaging in illegal activity, a case for negligence would be more difficult to make because producers are merely observing.

"Television producers are not policemen," said Michael J. O'Connor, whose firm White O'Connor Curry in Los Angeles, Calif., has represented reality shows like "Survivor" and "America's Next Top Model." He added: "On a moral level, you get to the point where stepping in seems like it would be something you'd want to do. But from a legal standpoint, third parties causing injuries to other third parties is not something a television program is really responsible for."

Being absolved of legal responsibility for his documentary subjects, however, does not make shooting the program any easier.

"I've had children of alcoholic parents there watching their mother in a drunken stupor, watching their mother pass out, watching their mother throw up," Mr. Mettler said. "Those innocent children as casualties of their mother's addiction was just emotionally heart-wrenching. The trauma of that is horrible, just horrible."

"Intervention," which ends each episode with an actual intervention, has arrangements with substance-abuse rehabilitation centers across the country that provide free in-patient treatment for addicts on the program.

"Morally and ethically, none of us can feel good watching someone hurt themselves or hurt someone else. And I'm not going to stand by and have someone who is drunk get behind the wheel of a car and kill someone," Mr. Mettler said.

Mr. Mettler himself has had to step out from behind the camera on a number of episodes to prevent someone from driving drunk. In one case, he followed a crack addict named Tim through a swamp. Tim had crawled into a drainage pipe and threatened suicide, so Mr. Mettler had to talk him out.

And in another episode, Mr. Mettler's field producers called paramedics after an alcoholic they were filming overdosed on the sedative trazodone. Laney, a wealthy divorced woman who drank half a gallon of rum a day and traveled long distances in limousines because she did not like putting her cat on commercial jets, swallowed the pills while the cameras were off. She told producers what she had done after they saw her chugging a bottle of juice to wash the pills down.

"Our first position is that this is a documentary series, we are there capturing real people in their real lives," said Robert Sharenow, A&E's senior vice president for nonfiction and alternative programming. "If there was an immediate danger, that was sort of our line. If the person was putting themselves or anyone else in immediate danger, then we'd cross the line."

He added: "It's a very, very delicate balance."

Selection 10.6

Part of what defines this as an "enterprise story" is that it simply wouldn't appear without the enterprise of the reporter. While it has a bit of a news peg in its opening invocation of Patricia Bosworth's biography of Diane Arbus, its exploration of the common equation of creative genius and madness (or at least "inner turmoil") is an issue as timeless as art, thoughtfully explored at the sort of length that a Sunday piece permits. And the journalist signals his own attitude toward this "awful cliche" early on, before casting his net expansively wide in his critical inquiry (with one paragraph comparing Abstract Expressionist painting and the Doors' Jim Morrison). Are there are any essential perspectives missing from the interviews?

How Inner Torment Feeds the Creative Spirit

By SAMUEL G. FREEDMAN

During Diane Arbus's funeral, the photographer Richard Avedon turned to a friend and whispered, "Oh, I wish I could be an artist like Diane." The friend, Frederick Eberstadt, answered, "Oh, no, you don't." Their brief exchange—as recounted in Patricia Bosworth's biography of Arbus—raises the charged questions surrounding the tormented, even self-destructive, creative artist. Chief among them is where reality ends and mythology begins.

Arbus personified the artist whose inner turmoil—depression, dislocation and a taste for risk bordering on a death wish—fueled her creations, those moving and disturbing photographs of drag queens and hermaphrodites, celebrities and Siamese twins. But Arbus was also a woman defeated by depressions so debilitating she often could not work and, ultimately, chose not to live. Finally, Arbus represented an artist who gained more fame, who was indeed romanticized, more for living on the edge than for the artistry she brought back from that emotional frontier.

It is no wonder, then, that Arbus—that the entire issue of the "mad artist," as the awful cliche has it—should both attract and repel, as it has for literally thousands of years. Aristotle spoke of "divine madness," Renaissance scholar Marsilio Ficino of the "Saturnine temperament." The playwright August Strindberg declared that few

Published: November 17, 1985.

people were "lucky enough to be capable of madness," and the poet John Berryman opined, "The artist is extremely lucky who is presented with the worst possible ordeal which will not nearly kill him."

For both creators and scientists, the subject is an extraordinarily loaded one—even more so now, when popular culture so glorifies violent and bizarre behavior. The American artistic landscape is littered with the corpses of the brilliant, from painter Mark Rothko to poet Anne Sexton to musician Charlie Parker, and one must wonder if they died in part because sycophants with safer lives so celebrated their excesses. For contemporary artists like the jazz musician Jackie McLean and the writer Raymond Carver true creativity began only after conquering their respective addictions to heroin and alcohol. To them, and many other creators, the image of the self-destructive artist not only invites futility or death but denies the value of disciplined craft.

There is no question that many creative artists, perhaps the vast majority, are centered and sane.

There may be just as many self-destructive bakers as painters, but psychiatrists and biographers do not analyze their cakes. It is the tormented artist and not the untroubled one—the Vincent van Gogh, not the Peter Paul Rubens—who provides the stuff of tabloid notoriety and romantic embellishment.

But if that image is inflated, neither is it groundless. For many artists, creation is a constant act of balancing the dark side that allows introspection with the brighter one that turns raw material into finished product. One result of the process, "The Iceman Cometh" by Eugene O'Neill, is now playing at the Lunt-Fontanne. The play, set in a saloon ironically called Harry Hope's, closely parallels O'Neill's years of uncontrollable drinking in dives like Jimmy-the-Priest's and the Hell Hole. It is impossible to imagine O'Neill having written the play without becoming the virtual ascetic he did; yet it is equally impossible to imagine him writing as rendingly about self-destruction and self-delusion without having lived both.

O'Neill's life and work raise some of the most frightening—and central—questions about creativity. Can the forces that make you creative also kill you? Can you live with control and yet create free of restraint? Can you live enough of the dark side to tell the tale without becoming a casualty? The equilibrium is precarious. As the playwright Arthur Miller wrote of Strindberg: "Strindberg not only suffered what by most definitions would be madness, but managed it like a conductor managing an orchestra. It makes his suffering no less real and painful to say that it was always being turned over and over by the bloody fingers of his mind."

In Sam Shepard's work that tension is frequently embodied by pairs of brothers—Lee and Austin in the play "True West," Travis and Walt in the film "Paris, Texas." These characters represent the polarity in the playwright himself. "Somewhere there's a myth about the wolf and the sheep," Mr. Shepard said, "and man carries both inside him. And the process of keeping alive is trying to have these two cohabit, trying to carry on a balance between these two parts, because one's always trying to devour the other. And the one that wants to devour— the wolf—is the animalistic one, the one that operates on impulse and is pretty insane.

"There's definitely a struggle going on, and it's answered in different ways. Some people do it with drinking or drugs. The difficulty is trying to accept that this is the condition you're living with, the condition of these two parts banging up against each other, and the constant threat of being overthrown by one."

Like Mr. Shepard, the film director Martin Scorsese has consistently made art that derives from, and in turn reflects, his own turbulence. The emotional palette of Mr. Scorsese's surrogates ranges from the paranoia of Paul Hackett in his current "After Hours" to the volcanic violence of Travis Bickle in "Taxi Driver." Perhaps the most clearly autobiographical statement is Jimmy Doyle, the saxophonist portrayed by Robert DeNiro in "New York, New York." Doyle is a singular musician and an impassioned lover; he also is a brutal predator, jealous of his wife's success as a singer, quick to damage those nearest him.

"Jimmy Doyle was very much a picture of myself and DeNiro at that time," Mr. Scorsese said. "We recognized that contrariness and difficulty, and we improvised on it. Because out of that does come the work, does come the art. The trick is, how much does it get to you? 'New York, New York' was not a complete success because the 'wolf' took over. 'Raging Bull' was a better mix of visceral stuff and form.

"There's a creative urge that gets inside you, like 'Alien.' For me, it's a constant battle of deciding when not to explode, when to use that emotion to feed you creatively. There's a constant fear, because you're pushing something to the edge. And at the same time, there's a fear you might become too civil, too sane."

A study of 47 prominent contemporary British artists by Dr. Kay Jamison, a professor of psychiatry at the University of California at Los Angeles, suggests there is a clinical model for the tug-of-war Mr. Shepard, Mr. Scorsese and so many other artists have described. Dr. Jamison found that more than half of the British artists had been diagnosed as manic-depressive, compared to six percent of the general population. A study of writers by Professor Nancy Andreasan of the University of Iowa showed that 67 percent suffered from an emotional disorder, while only 13 percent of the control group did. Their findings by no means represent the definitive answer to whether creativity and madness are connected, but they at least indicate that it is more than an empty cliche.

The question, then, is whether manic-depression and other emotional disorders serve the creative process, or actually impede it. "Most people who are manic-depressive are more reflective, introspective, can deal with more existential issues when they're depressed," Dr. Jamison said. "And if you think of a classic kind of manic wit, like Lenny Bruce, there's a rapidity of association and an ability to reach instantly back into the mind. It's clear that if you give hypomania [the medical term for the manic state] to an already creative person you give them a big advantage." As if to underscore the point, Dr. Jamison helped produce a Los Angeles concert last May entitled "Moods and Music." It featured compositions by Handel, Schumann, Wolf, Berlioz and Mahler—all of whom, she maintained, were manic-depressive.

Dr. Barry M. Panter, an associate professor of psychiatry at the University of Southern California and the director of an annual conference on "Creativity and Madness," cites a similar chemistry between emotion and creativity. "The material artists use for their art," Dr. Panter said, "comes from the primitive levels of their inner lives—aggression, sexual fantasy, polymorphous sexuality. What we know about the development of personality is that we all go through these stages and have these primitive drives within us. As we mature and are 'civilized,' we suppress them. But the artist stays in touch with and struggles to understand them. And to remain so in touch with that primitive self is to be on the fine line between sanity and madness."

Yet it remains largely an individual matter how an artist handles such powerful forces, or fails to. For a playwright like Athol Fugard, an alcoholic who stopped drinking in 1983, one of the hardest parts of abstinence was giving up the liberating effect of liquor. Anyone who saw " 'Master Harold' . . . and the boys," a self-lacerating memory play, can well imagine how an alcohol-fed melancholy helped Mr. Fugard touch the old wounds that underlie the work. "When I was writing a play," Mr. Fugard recalls of his old process, "I would start drinking after sunset and then fairly steadily into the night. And that last carafe of wine at night—that spell of wildness—was when I would set up the ideas that I'd work on soberly the next day."

By the time Mr. Fugard began work on the follow-up play to "'Master Harold,' " "The Road to Mecca," he had stopped drinking. The prospect of writing without alcohol was terrifying. " 'Mecca' was hard for me because I didn't have that moment of madness at night," he said. "I had to ask myself, could I still get into my dark side? Could I still put my dark side forward without the aid of a drug? And, obviously, alcohol was a powerful drug for that. Nothing I could do could replace it. I've found other things—running, biking, Buddhist mantras. And maybe my art now will be more about light than dark."

Few artists as a group so depended on tapping their subconscious urges, and indulging their conscious desires, as the Abstract Expressionist painters, the cluster of New York artists who flourished in the 1940's and 1950's. The results were groundbreaking work and tragic ends—suicides for Mark Rothko and Arshile Gorky, violent deaths for Franz Kline and Jackson Pollock. Pollock, the mercurial, hard-drinking

"Wyoming cowboy" who died in an auto accident, in particular inspired the kind of posthumous cult one associates with rock stars like Jim Morrison, the victim of a drug overdose at the age of 26.

Robert Motherwell, one of the major Abstract Expressionists still painting, has often spoken of the psychological nature of his work; he has described his process as free association—itself a term drawn from psychoanalysis—and "a state of anxiety that is obliquely recorded in the inner tension of the finished product."

"One of my best friends is a psychiatrist," Mr. Motherwell said in a recent interview, "and last summer I asked him, if he had to define psychoanalysis in a single sentence, how would he put it? And he said, 'Chris Hardman put it best—psychoanalysis is the study of self-deception.' And it may be that the deep necessity of art is the examination of self-deception. It's not that the creative act and the critical act are simultaneous. It's more like you blurt something out and then analyze it. After each brushstroke, you're analyzing it. Is this stroke an authentic expression or not? Most painting in the European tradition was painting the mask. Modern art rejected all that. Our subject matter was the person behind the mask. And we all know genuine analysis like that is shattering to go through. There's a terrible price to be paid for the constant analysis, constant doubt."

No other art form, perhaps, resembles Absract Expressionism as closely as modern jazz. Both depended on improvisation. Both drew heavily on the psychology of the creator. Both were innovations that had to fight for legitimacy in the cultural world. Just as such outer forces fed the inner fires of the painters, so they did for jazz musicians nearly a generation later; and that barely contained rage expressed itself in the raw and rending sounds of avant-garde jazz.

"The music became a way to be both beautiful and angry at the same time," said Jackie McLean, a saxophonist whose 40-year career spans the innovations of bop, modal and free jazz. "It wasn't a choice to be angry. The anger was caused by the suffering. The angriest music you heard was in the '60s, when they shot down Kennedy, King, Malcolm X, Medgar Evers. It was a decade of death, and what can a musician do but reflect the times he's in. We're mirrors. Some of the saxophonists you heard—Ayler, Coltrane, Marion Brown—sounded like a ghetto child being beaten. It's not something a musician wants. It's not conscious. It just is. I didn't realize why I played the way I did in the '60s until much later. And when I listened back to those records, at times it felt like it was someone else playing."

There is one more parallel between modern jazz and Abstract Expressionism. Both became fixed in the public mind—correctly or not—with the stereotype of the dissolute artist. Some of the most brilliant jazz musicians, from Buddy Bolden to Bud Powell, literally went mad. The hero of the bebop era was Charlie (Bird) Parker, a ferociously inventive saxophonist and a heroin addict from his late teens until his death at 35. The jazz wisdom once held, "To play like Bird, you got to be like Bird." Mr. McLean, one of his foremost disciples, remembers just how pervasive—and destructive—the advice was.

"There were young musicians who weren't addicted who tried to look like they were—eyes half-closed, striking that slouched pose—because all of the people we admired had fallen prey," Mr. McLean said. The irony is that Parker himself argued against such admiration. The writer A. B. Spellman, in "Black Music: Four Lives," tells of Parker demanding that Mr. McLean kick him in the rear end on a Greenwich Village street as a kind of public censure. "Parker told me early on to try to follow the example of people like Horace Silver, the guys who had it all together," Mr. McLean recalled. "But it was already too late, because I was hopelessly addicted. And five years after Parker told me that, I had my first arrest."

Mr. McLean ultimately served several years on Rikers Island on narcotics charges and lost his cabaret card, which was tantamount in jazz to losing the right to work. Mr. McLean has long since cured his heroin addiction and he now teaches music at the University of Hartford. His relatively serene life has not noticeably cooled his creative fires, and, asked if his hard times taught him anything, he says only, "Survival."

The writer Raymond Carver is another artist who actively disputes the image of the self-destructive creator. He speaks as someone who initially used the myth to excuse his own drinking. What Parker was to Mr. McLean, Hemingway was to Mr. Carver. "I tried to look around the arts for anyone who drank more than I did, and took solace in that," Mr. Carver said. "I'd read that Richard Burton was drinking a fifth a day while doing a play or that Fitzgerald and Hemingway and Faulkner and everyone was drinking hard and the work was significant, the work still is significant. You kidded yourself. You rationalized your drinking."

In time, Mr. Carver says, he required no such rationale. Addiction itself supplanted reason, and he lost several years to alcoholism in the mid-1970's. "It was a completely destructive activity," he said. "Nothing good came out of it for me. Any artist who is alcoholic is an artist despite the alcohol, not because of it. I never wrote so much as a line that was worth a nickel when I was under the influence of alcohol. When I was in the height of my drinking—the all-night sessions, the blackouts, the hangovers—I did no writing."

Yet Mr. Carver's short stories gather their power in part because they bear witness. Some stories, like "Where I'm Calling From," depict alcoholics. More commonly, drinking is the major recreation of Mr. Carver's blue-collar characters, a diversion from, or balm for, unfulfilled lives. If none of the characters are yet alcoholics, almost any may become one. What, then, would Mr. Carver write about, without the binges and mornings-after in his past?

"I've been asked that question many times," he said, "and I just don't know the answer. Before I started drinking, I burned to write, and I might've written more if I hadn't wasted those years. But, of course, I would not have written stories about drinking. It's the only life I had, so I can't say I wish I hadn't lived it. Material comes to writers in different ways, and the drinking I was involved in suggested things to me, though only in retrospect. In a way, I have come back to testify. But I could just as easily have gone down the toilet, if I'd turned right instead of turning left."

MAKING**CONNECTIONS**

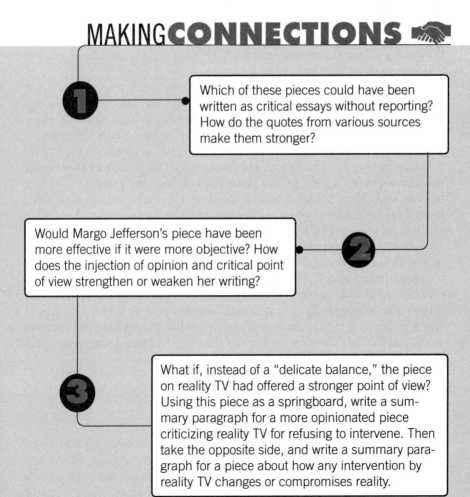

1. Which of these pieces could have been written as critical essays without reporting? How do the quotes from various sources make them stronger?

2. Would Margo Jefferson's piece have been more effective if it were more objective? How does the injection of opinion and critical point of view strengthen or weaken her writing?

3. What if, instead of a "delicate balance," the piece on reality TV had offered a stronger point of view? Using this piece as a springboard, write a summary paragraph for a more opinionated piece criticizing reality TV for refusing to intervene. Then take the opposite side, and write a summary paragraph for a piece about how any intervention by reality TV changes or compromises reality.

how publication in The New York Times changed my career

I CAN'T CONCLUDE THIS VOLUME without relating how publication in The Times transformed the career of one journalist. I became the popular music critic for the Chicago Sun-Times in 1981, after doing similar work for the alternative-weekly Chicago Reader for five years. Whatever the quality of my stories and reviews, they went largely unnoticed beyond Chicago, in those days before the Internet.

Sitting across from me in the Sun-Times features department was Brent Staples, who had also been at the University of Chicago and the Reader when I was, though we hadn't known each other. When Brent was hired as an editor by The New York Times Book Review, I started receiving calls from him.

He gave me a few assignments before moving on (he continues to serve on the editorial board of The Times), and they changed my life. Every time one of my reviews would appear in The Times I would hear from magazine editors in New York, eager to kick around some ideas. None of them had previously known my byline or work from Chicago, but The Times validated me. One of those reviews, to bring this volume full circle, was on a biography of Bob Dylan by Robert Shelton, whose early celebration of a little-known folksinger in The Times had proven so prophetic.

And those pieces for Rolling Stone, as well as the pieces for The Times that had led to them, generated plenty of other work in top newspapers and other national magazines. The best way of convincing an editor that you're worth publishing is to show him or her that other editors have deemed you worth publishing. The more prestigious the clip, the more doors it can open. Here's the clip that opened more doors than any for me.

STORY**SCAN**

The review that follows had a particular impact. In those days, The Times Book Review didn't necessarily start reviews on the front page, so this one on Page 3 (and a jump) was the section's longest review, accompanied by more photos than the section usually devotes to a book. Even though I gave a mixed review to a book generated by Rolling Stone, something about the piece attracted the interest of Anthony DeCurtis, one of the magazine's top writers and then editor of its reviews section. I started writing regularly for Rolling Stone—first album reviews for Anthony, but soon live reviews and profiles for other editors as well.

Three-Chord Music in a Three-Piece Suit

By DON McLEESE

We never did outgrow it, this hopped-up musical hybrid, this raucous noise that ultimately made all of popular culture march to its beat. When rock first began to shake, rattle and roll its way across the American consciousness, we children of the 1950's were told that it was at best a freakish fad—the musical equivalent of the Hula-Hoop or Davy Crockett's coonskin cap. At worst, it was the sound of the civilized social fabric unraveling. By the end of that decade, there were signs that this rude, frenzied musical aberration had spent its energy.

When the Beatles gave rock-and-roll a much-needed jolt, the moptops were generally regarded as a sociological phenomenon of a particularly silly season. We would soon leave this awkward age behind, we were assured. We would outgrow rock and adolescence together, and if we listened to music at all it would be good music, adult music. Guy Lombardo. Jerry Vale. Broadway show tunes. We would reflect on that loud, crazy music of old and laugh at the follies of youth.

Rather than losing its baby boom constituency, rock has matured along with its audience. For better or worse, rock is now pushing 40, and is showing the usual signs of middle age. The music of teen-age rebellion has become increasingly conservative and

The first person plural "we" immediately invites identification between writer and reader. The adjectives—"hopped-up," "raucous," "frenzied"—have a bull-in-a-china-shop energy that befits the subject matter (the bull) and the publication (the china shop). "Shake, rattle and roll" works for the many who will get the song-title reference without confusing the few who don't know it. But all that alliteration would make some editors squirm.

dismissive, as was the original (adult) cultural consensus

Too much "we"? As an editor, I might now question the repetition, but it reinforces the identification, while the rest of the paragraph highlights the difference in perception between then and now.

Transitional, and the change in tone shows it; word choice is more subdued, "mature."

Published: December 28, 1986. Book reviewed: Rock of Ages: The Rolling Stone History of Rock & Roll. By Ed Ward, Geoffrey Stokes and Ken Tucker.

Compare the energy of the first part with the complacency of the second.

The boy journalist sure loves his alliteration.

Three grafs before the first mention of the book, and even this graf is cultural context rather than anything about the book itself. As we saw in the book chapter, nonfiction reviewers frequently concern themselves with the subject that inspired the book as well as the specific book.

Widening the cultural net to suggest implications beyond popular music.

commercially risk-free. Whereas rock-and-roll had a hungry sound— the populist squall of cultural outsiders battering down the doors—the corporate rock of the 80's is fat, flabby, self-satisfied. Music that once represented a vital alternative to slickness and glitz has succumbed to show business as usual. What was once a cultural revolution has become just another consumer commodity.

"Rock of Ages" arrives at a time when rock has become particularly interested in its past. Within the last two years, an industry previously known for its notoriously short attention span has established a rock-and-roll hall of fame, and record companies have been reissuing and documenting their former glories with uncommon care (a responsibility that previously fell to European and Japanese labels, while American companies treated their own vaults like yesterday's papers). The success of Bruce Springsteen and similar artists has spearheaded a return to roots-oriented American musical values. Tina Turner and James Brown have established themselves as hot new stars with fans who are young enough to be their grandchildren.

Whereas rock once represented a cultural vanguard, it has become a reflection of the country's conservative yearnings. Time travel to a more innocent past has become a recurring theme in the movies; the popularity of President Reagan (before the arms deal with Iran became news) similarly suggested the possibility of a return to earlier, simple times. Rock radio continues to reject most new music in favor of familiar "Big Chill" fare, forcing contemporary artists to rerecord older hits in their bid for airplay.

Can this music that once celebrated the urgency and immediacy of the moment race onward by looking backward? The positive view is that rock is once again recharging and replenishing itself by returning to its earliest, best impulses. The cynical view is that rock is a spent force, filling a void in popular entertainment until something more vital comes along, continually recycling itself because it has nothing new to offer. In the latter view, much of what has passed for rock since its mid-60's peak of creativity isn't rock at all.

Transitional question, a paragraph-opening technique that some writers are tempted to overuse.

Not surprisingly, "Rock of Ages" reflects the former, more optimistic view. The book was commissioned by Rolling Stone, which has seen itself follow a pattern of development similar to that of the music it covers. Whereas the biweekly magazine began in the 60's as the voice of the counterculture, it has since become a leading organ of hip upward mobility. The publisher, Jann S. Wenner, has marketed rock-and-roll the way Hugh Hefner has marketed female flesh—as an accessory to the good life. With a vested interest in rock as product, Mr. Wenner writes in the introduction that "the adaptability of rock and roll in an era of blinding changes in the way we live is nothing short of a miracle" and that "rock and roll has a marvelous capacity for regeneration and renewal." Since the Rolling Stone imprint takes precedence over the credits accorded the book's three authors, one assumes that Mr. Wenner had the last word as well.

Finally, after six grafs of what impatient readers might dismiss as throat clearing, we get to the book itself. If I'd been following the dictates I've subsequently formulated, both that first mention and an evaluation would be higher up.

A more provocative assertion than anything that has come before and one that sets the stage for the argument at the crux of the review.

Rock is music that elicits a strong, immediate response—love it or hate it—and the best writing on rock not only captures the music's passionate, provocative spirit, it shares it. Through its use of three writers to cover three separate stages in rock's history, "Rock of Ages" opts for something closer to a textbook treatment. Ed Ward, Geoffrey Stokes and Ken Tucker are all respected journalists; Mr. Ward and Mr. Tucker have written almost exclusively about rock and popular music, while Mr. Stokes has ranged wider over the pop culture spectrum. With "Rock of Ages," each demonstrates a deep affection and affinity for the subject. Even so, the need for their separate sensibilities to be sub-sumed within a coherent whole results in an unsuitable objectivity—at odds with the personal involvement that the music demands. If Gibbon could track the entire decline and fall of the Roman Empire, isn't there one writer with the scope and skill to trace the development of three-chord rock-and-roll?

Mr. Ward, the author of "Michael Bloomfield: The Rise and Fall of an American Guitar Hero," covers the cultural upheaval of the 50's and takes the long view in setting the stage. He starts with the development of American popular music during the Civil War and shows how a combina-tion of factors—sociological, techno-logical, economic—eventually led to a cross-fertilization of musical styles and an increase in leisure-time entertain-ment. With the baby boom and the boom of prosperity after World War II, teen-age America had the clout to demand a popular culture all its own. If rock-and-roll wasn't inevitable, it was far from the inexplicable nightmare that some considered it at the time.

Times style on second reference, which sounds even stuffier when writing about rock.

Here is the essence of the argument, in these two highlighted passages: A collaboration can't produce the personal response of the best rock writing.

Ha ha. I write to amuse myself, even if no one else thinks it's funny.

A purely descriptive graf that ends with a summary of the author's analysis.

As Mr. Ward's fascinating account makes plain, the physical appeal of popular music has long been held in disdain by cultural elitists. Well before rock-and-roll was derided as "jungle music," early ragtime jazz was considered "beneath contempt for people of quality." The delta bluesman Robert Johnson, now widely celebrated as a great American original, was called an "embarrassment" during his own era. Once jazz gained a certain respectability, the hot rhythms and showmanship of the saxophonist Louis Jordan were looked upon as "crude by jazz fans." The more music elicits basic responses and arouses basic desires, the more it is feared. The blacker the music sounds, the less fit it is for civilized ears. If it feels good, it must be bad.

evaluative

Again, a primarily descriptive graf that ends with the reviewer amusing himself.

The book comes closest to a definition of rock-and-roll when Mr. Ward writes that by 1954 "the groundwork had been laid for a teen-oriented, rhythm-and-blues-based music with country elements." Country artists from Bob Wills to Hank Williams had been absorbing black influences into their own music, while Southern rhythm-and-blues retained a country flavor. There was musical miscegenation at a time when segregation was the common rule, and the spontaneous combustion of rock-and-roll brought the whole thing to a boil. Elvis Presley recorded a blues song on one side of his first single, a bluegrass song on the flip side, and ignited a cultural explosion. Popular music would never be the same again, and neither would the sons and daughters of America.

"The American Heritage Dictionary" cited this as a usage example for "miscegenation," another example of the clout of The Times that I inflict on my students. Stop him before he alliterates again!

More fevered language that befits the subject matter.

Although Mr. Ward writes with insight and enthusiasm about Chuck Berry, Jerry Lee Lewis, Little Richard and others whose 50's music has left

praise . . .

. . . tempered by criticism throughout the rest of the graf

A transitional graf that, like the next, concerns the subject in general rather than the book in particular.

This is the reviewer's analysis, not necessarily the book's, reinforcing the sense that the response to music—and to books about it—proceeds from a personal perspective.

a lasting cultural imprint, his account of the decade's latter years attempts to cram too much into too little space. Every year has its own chapter, and every chapter is filled with snippets about practically every record that made its mark on the Billboard charts. While Mr. Ward does his best to turn this disjointed detail into narrative flow, what results too often is history that is merely chronological rather than analytical.

Before "Rock of Ages" changes decades, Mr. Ward writes: "As America sailed into a new decade, rock and roll, the music of hooligans and streetcorner singers, the music of hillbillies who'd listened to too many R&B records, the music of misfits and oddballs, was dead. . . . [It] had passed into the mainstream, fast becoming the province of established corporate interests rather than the renegade visionaries of the past."

As it turned out, rock-and-roll wasn't dead. It was only hibernating, waiting for the alarm from Liverpool. The audience that had grown too old for the prefab Frankies and Bobbys of the early 60's wasn't ready to embrace Frank Sinatra. After the folk boomlet filled the interval, the Beatles restored rock-and-roll excitement through music that recaptured the raw energy of the 50's while planting the seeds for rock's musical maturation. Before long, rock wasn't kids' music any longer. It belonged to everyone.

The resurgence of the 60's seemed to save rock-and-roll, but the cost ultimately might have been more than the gain. As rock became adult, it lost the brashness of youth. As it strove toward art, it sacrificed its reckless spirit. When the Beatles recorded "Sgt. Pepper," the music that once fed on interaction with its audience began sealing itself off in the studio. As rock became a bigger business, it retreated from the populism of old. By the late 60's, the music that had once been more of an equal opportunity employer had become a strong bastion of white male supremacy.

As described by Geoffrey Stokes, a staff writer for The Village Voice, the 60's were a time of radical change and rapid transition, musically and otherwise. Although "the process was hardly linear," Mr. Stokes shows how practically every new development affected everything around it: the Beatles influenced Bob Dylan, Bob Dylan influenced the Beatles, the psychedelia of San Francisco turned all ears westward, the Monterey Pop Festival led to Woodstock and Altamont. Ideas filled the air, and all things were possible.

When Ken Tucker takes over the story in the 70's, rock has grown too big, too fast and in too many different directions. The music that was once the lifeblood of its constituency was reaching a whole lot more listeners and affecting them a whole lot less. Marginal artists were selling millions of records, and faceless bands were filling huge stadiums. The urgency and spontaneity of earlier times had given way to rigid, larger-than-life gestures. Punk rock made a loud, mid-decade assault on the music's shield of self-importance, winning some battles but ultimately losing the war.

Mr. Tucker, a popular music critic for The Philadelphia Inquirer, is the most critically provocative of the three, but he overdoses on cross-cultural critical shorthand. He hits the mark when he describes Ian Anderson of Jethro Tull as "a first-rate Fagin who wrote like a third-rate Dickens,"

back to the book

Descriptive rather than evaluative, as the review gives Stokes and the '60s comparatively short shrift, seeming to rush through in a manner similar to which it criticized Ward.

transition

Is this Tucker's perspective or the reviewer's? The reviewer knows—it's his own—but it's hard for readers to tell.

praise . . .

. . . tempered by criticism

. . . tempered by criticism

but stretches toward incomprehensibility when he refers to Norman Greenbaum as "the Tom Robbins of 1970" or James Taylor's "Sylvia Plath-in-a-denim-shirt sensibility." Covering the years that should have been easiest to research, Mr. Tucker's

more serious flaws than the previous examples

section waiting for Godot additionally suffers from occasional inaccuracies (MTV broadcasts 24 hours a day, not 12) and omissions (no mention of Stevie Wonder's ground-breaking "Music of My Mind" album within a detailed account of his 70's development).

Mr. Tucker's brief survey of the 80's describes this as "a time of synthesis, regeneration, and rebirth," with performers learning from the 70's "how to be professional with-

Again, is this the author's or the reviewer's perspective? Plainly this review aspires to cultural criticism that extends well beyond an evaluation of the book, as we've discussed in the book chapter on reviewing nonfiction.

out turning into hacks." Compared with the revolutionary potential that rock-and-roll flashed in the 50's, such contemporary accomplishments seem depressingly modest. Although Bruce Springsteen, Elvis Costello, U2, Run-D.M.C. and others are making popular music marked by craft and passion, most of the music that shares the urgency and iconoclasm that once defined rock's spirit is now relegated to the commercially irrelevant fringes.

The organization of "Rock of Ages" reinforces a sense of loss. The 50's end with rock's becoming safe, corporate, professional. The 60's end with Paul McCartney's filing suit to

Good kicker or cultural grandstanding? Maybe the English major just wants to show he went to grad school. Meanwhile, almost a quarter-century later, did hip-hop fulfill that mission or are we still waiting?

dissolve the Beatles. The 70's end with the murder of John Lennon. These days, waiting for someone to reignite that rock-and-roll explosion—as Elvis did in 1954, as the Beatles did in 1963—has become something like waiting for Godot.

For a number of reasons beyond ego, I use my own work in courses as springboards for discussion. First, it allows me to share how I got the assignment and to underscore the importance of building relationships with editors. I always tell my students to get to know their classmates, because you can never tell who might be an editor with assignments somewhere down the road.

New editors tend to bring new writers into the fold. Sometimes they take writers with them when moving to a new publication; sometimes writers try to cultivate relationships with whatever editors have taken their place. (Sometimes both.) It isn't that editors give assignments to friends who don't deserve them, but that there are far more writers capable of doing this work and eager to do it than there are paid assignments. Connections help you get your foot in the door; after that, it's up to you.

Second, since I stress in class that each piece of writing involves dozens to hundreds of decisions, many of them intuitive or unconscious, I know better with my own work how and why those decisions were made. And since those pieces were often written decades before I started teaching, I can explain, and let students suggest, how I might improve on what I had written then, when I was flying by the seat of my journalistic pants. In the process, we can also discuss how, where and why the piece was edited (in this case, it ran pretty much as written). When I'm spending a semester passing judgment on students, they revel in the opportunity to switch roles.

Today, the experience of the fledgling critic will likely differ from mine, for the Internet has changed so much about journalism in general, and arts journalism in particular. With cyber-communities now based on mutual interest rather than geography, it's now far easier to put your work in a place where others might see it, wherever you happen to live. It's easier for the quality of your work to provide its own validation—a validation reinforced by the number of readers it attracts (easier to measure online than it ever was in print). The downside, as Jon Pareles suggests in this book, is that it's tougher to make a career as a professional critic, when so many bloggers and others are out there spouting opinions for free.

Yet The Times still carries an imprint more significant than that of any other news publication. When I submitted my tenure dossier at the University of Iowa, I made sure to feature prominently the best of those pieces from The Times. Because as our journalism department would know as well as anyone, there are newspapers—and then there is The New York Times.

Maybe my career could have taken the course it took without The New York Times. But of the thousands of pieces I've written, the half-dozen or so that I wrote for The Times led to more good things than all the others. Maybe even to this book.